VOICES
OF THE
BULGE

VOICES
OF THE
BULGE

UNTOLD STORIES FROM VETERANS
OF THE BATTLE OF THE BULGE

MICHAEL COLLINS *and* MARTIN KING

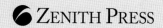
ZENITH PRESS

To the veterans featured in this volume
and to their comrades who did not make it home
to have their voices heard.

First published in 2011 by Zenith Press, an imprint of MBI Publishing Company, 400 1st Avenue North, Suite 300, Minneapolis, MN 55401 USA.

Copyright © 2011 by Michael Collins and Martin King

Unless otherwise noted, all images courtesy U.S. Army.

Maps: Philip Schwartzberg, Meridian Mapping

Zenith Press titles are also available at discounts in bulk quantity for industrial or sales-promotional use. For details write to Special Sales Manager at MBI Publishing Company, 400 First Avenue North, Suite 300, Minneapolis, MN 55401 USA.

To find out more about our books, join us online at www.zenithpress.com.
Designer: Diana Boger
Front cover image: *Imperial War Museum (EA50557)*
Back cover image: Time to eat for American GIs. *National Archives*
Frontis image: Soldiers of the 2nd Armored Division take a break during their advance across the snow-covered fields of the low countries. © *Mary Evans/The Image Works*

LIBRARY OF CONGRESS CATALOGING-IN-PUBLICATION DATA
Collins, Michael, 1984-
     Voices of the Bulge : untold stories from veterans of the Battle of the Bulge / Michael Collins and Martin King.
              p. cm.
     Includes bibliographical references.
     ISBN-13: 978-0-7603-4033-2 (hbk. w/jkt)
     ISBN-10: 0-7603-4033-1 (hbk. w/jkt)
     1. Ardennes, Battle of the, 1944-1945. 2. Ardennes, Battle of the, 1944–1945—Personal narratives, American. 3. Veterans—United States—Biography. 4. United States. Army—Biography.
5. Veterans—Germany—Biography. I. King, Martin, 1959- II. Title.
     D756.5.A7C657 2011
     940.54'219348—dc22
                    2010044524

Printed in China

CONTENTS

Maps

PROLOGUE

THE BATTLE OF THE BULGE was the largest land battle in United States military history. It began on December 16 at 0530. Green troops of the 106th Golden Lion Division were rudely awakened from their winter sojourn by the menacing rumble of Tiger and Panther tanks on the move. Just over the German/Belgian border, out in an area known as the Schnee Eifel, three German armies had assembled almost under the noses of the Allies. The Allies were completely taken by surprise by this attack.

Imagine being a young American out there in 1944. It's the worst winter since records began with temperatures often falling below negative 28 degrees Celsius. Your main priorities are keeping warm and keeping your belly full. You're a long way from home, and although you do not know it, you are in imminent danger of being killed or captured, or both. Some of those young guys from the United States had not even seen real snow, let alone fought in it. Suddenly you are awoken from your restless sleep by the sound of explosions and "Screaming Meemies," Nebelwerfers spitting out shells in your general direction. Hell really is unleashed as soldiers from the German army throw everything they have at you. How absolutely terrifying that must have been. Now put yourself in the place of a young German soldier on the offensive. Confident, motivated, and ready for action, but that confidence would take a severe battering within a few short days. Then there were the civilians living in peaceful old communities that had existed and thrived for centuries in the Ardennes. They had reluctantly endured four years of occupation, but in September 1944, they had found themselves liberated from the yoke of Nazi tyranny by advancing Allied forces. For them, life was getting back on track—until December 1944. Some of the civilians found their lives irrevocably changed by the sequence of events that unfolded in the Ardennes during that bitter and vicious encounter.

These are the true stories of the survivors of that terrible battle in their own words.

Preface

Martin King: I know the Ardennes, and I know about the infamous Battle of the Bulge. It's a very tranquil place now, but back in the winter of December 1944–1945, it was anything but. I live in a small village near Antwerp, and I have spent more than twenty years looking around those hallowed fields and forests. Meticulously inspecting foxholes, bomb craters, bullet holes in masonry, and other evidence of the massive battle that occurred there in the winter of '44–'45. Evidence is vital to a battlefield historian, and thankfully there's still plenty of it to be found down in the Ardennes, and the good thing is that one does not have to look too hard to find it. During my time researching the battle, I'd read virtually everything ever written about it; moreover, I'd met many veterans who'd actually been there at the time, and to a man, they fascinated me.

I met Michael Collins in person back in July 2006 when he visited Belgium with his family. After his visit to the Ardennes, we exchanged a few e-mails about the Battle of the Bulge, and some time later we came up with the idea of writing about it. We did not want to contradict and analyze the existing accounts of the battle, or be accused of attempting to write the definitive account of it. Our mission had a higher purpose: to collate as much factual information as possible and write the story from the ground up, based as much as possible on the recollections of the last surviving veterans of that battle. Therefore, we decided to loosely divide each chapter into four sections. First, there's the historical timeline, i.e., what was going on during that particular day in the battle. Second, there are the veterans' recollections, what they saw and experienced on that day. Third, we've included stories about our personal heroes, and fourth, we talk about the bigger picture, what the people there did not know at the time.

Michael Collins: My journey to the Ardennes began with the discharge papers of my grandfather, Pfc. John A. Collins Jr. I always knew that my grandfather had fought in Patton's Third Army during World War II, but that was it. I also knew he had liberated a few souvenirs from his adversaries at the time, including a Nazi banner, a Luger pistol, and the metal insignia of a German officer's cap. On his discharge papers, I found the name of his unit, 90th Cavalry Reconnaissance Squadron (Mechanized), Troop F. After finding out what unit he fought in and reading a few books about the Bulge, my parents and I decided in late 2005 that it was time to go over to the Ardennes to see where my grandfather had fought. Since I was going abroad to Cork, Ireland, in July 2006, late June was the time we chose to go. We booked a tour through a tour company, and we saw that Martin King was going to be our tour guide.

When we arrived in Bastogne and saw the town, my parents and I had no idea what to expect, it looked just like any other small European town, except for the Sherman tank turrets at every entrance point and another Sherman tank in the town square. I knew this place was special. When Martin began to take us around the Ardennes region, I saw things I would never have dreamed of seeing, including the foxholes of the 101st Airborne outside of Foy, a King Tiger tank, and one of the best World War II museums in Diekirch, Luxembourg.

The trip was a resounding success and spawned my mission to find out who the veterans were who fought not only in my grandfather's unit but in other unknown units as well. I have traveled across the United States to the 10th Armored Division Western Association Reunion in Phoenix, Arizona, and also just up the road from me to talk to these great men who, like most veterans, do not regard what they did as "anything special." As the greatest generation slowly fades away, the stories they leave will preserve their memory and history not only for the world but, most importantly, for their families and friends, who in many cases had previously no idea about what these men accomplished all those years ago.

Martin King: There are those who write about it and those who talk about it, and then there are the often very emotional testimonies of those who were there when it all happened. Those who heard the menacing, deep rumble of tanks pummeling the freezing cobble-stones into gravel beneath the snow on those centuries-old roads in southern Belgium. Those who witnessed the horror and devastation of Hitler's last serious offensive in the west do not speak of it easily, but when they do, the least we can do is give them our full and undivided attention. Listen and learn. The generation that experienced World War II firsthand is fading fast, and the ones who are left are not going to be around for too long, so this is quite possibly our last chance to hear them speak.

That idea is what inspired us to start writing. In 2004, I left my position as a lecturer in European history and English at the university in Antwerp to concentrate on other more pressing matters. After years of educating students on the causes and effects of armed conflict throughout history, I thought it was time to get down to something a little more substantial. I'd long been fascinated by the Battle of the Bulge, and I'd spent many a happy hour driving and walking around the area where it occurred, so I thought it was time to write about some of the people who endured that terrible winter, and to write about them while the opportunity was still available.

Tanks support men of an armored division moving up to attack the enemy position in Bastogne, Belgium, while two soldiers attempt to dig a foxhole in the snow-covered ground. © *Topham/ The Image Works*

Two columns of soldiers from the 1st Division march through the snow toward Murringen, Belgium, January 31, 1945. *Lightroom Photos/U.S. Army/TopFoto/Jon Mitchell/Redux*

It was around that time that I had the chance to serve as guide to Marvin S. Walker,* a veteran of the Battle of the Bulge who served with the 106th Infantry Division, 423rd Regiment. He had been wounded and captured at the start of the battle. The 422nd and 423rd Infantry Regiments were encircled and cut off from the remainder of the division by a junction of enemy forces in the vicinity of Schönberg. The division suffered 641 killed and 1,200 wounded. Over 7,000 soldiers were captured and sent to various POW camps throughout Germany.

Marvin was a lively, amiable gentleman who insisted that the chauffeur of our SUV play Patsy Cline's greatest hits on his car stereo throughout the whole tour. This almost drove me to distraction, but I gritted my teeth and endured it. Like most veterans, Marvin was reluctant to say a great deal about his experiences, but as the days passed, I began to learn more about what he'd been through back in 1944.

I took him to the place where he was wounded and then to the parochial hall in Schönberg that served as a temporary hospital before

* Real name withheld by request.

The 7th Armored Division advances cautiously through the snow along a road toward St. Vith in Belgium, February 9, 1945. *National Archives*

the wounded prisoners were sent to POW camps in Germany. The hall was situated behind a small café, and I was astonished to discover that the family who owned it during the war was still living there. The landlord welcomed us warmly and showed us to the empty hall behind his establishment.

Marvin just stood there and looked around silently. After a while he said, "Well, ain't that something. It's the same stone floor they had back then." I could clearly see that here and there were slightly darker patches on the light gray stone. I turned to the landlord and asked him if my suspicions were correct.

"Yes, they were bloodstains," he said.

Just then an old man appeared at the entrance to the hall and shouted "Hello!" at the top of his voice.

"This is my father Hans," said the landlord. "He ran the café during the war, he's eighty-seven years old now, but still as sharp as a razor."

The old man walked up to Marvin and looked him square in the face. Our little party fell silent while these two men eyed each other. "Do you remember me?" asked Marvin tentatively. I translated from English to German.

The old man shook his head and shrugged his shoulders, then dug his hand deep into his right trouser pocket and took out a small crumpled paper bag that he handed to Marvin. Marvin graciously took it and placed the contents on the table beside him. There was a bullet case from an M1 Garand, a brass button, and a faded Golden Lion arm patch from the 106th.

Then suddenly there was a flash of recognition in Marvin's eyes. He looked at the old man and said, "I gave you that patch." The old man studiously put his head to one side and looked hard at Marvin. Then after a few seconds he nodded his head vigorously before giving Marvin an affectionate bear hug.

You would have to be made of reinforced concrete not to be affected by that little scene. A reverential silence descended on our little party. Was it really possible that these two men from different countries, speaking different languages, had met briefly during those tumultuous days back in World War II?

Dr. Richard W. Peterson, PhD, formerly a Weapons Company Sergeant with I Company, 423rd Infantry Regiment, 106th Infantry Division, who was captured the same day as Marvin and held prisoner at Stalag 9-A, Ziegenhain, Germany, prepared the following. In a touching ceremony at the 1995 German-American meeting, he presented each of the German and American veterans a beautifully rendered certificate (each in his own language) in memory of "All Men Who Fought for Their Country":

> Combat veterans hold a secret about life so deep within them that not even they comprehend the power of its mystery.
>
> This great secret cannot be understood by anyone who was never there.
>
> They do not know the secret exists.
>
> So they cannot comprehend the strength it gives to those who do.
>
> We are a part of a charmed circle that we keep tightly closed praying that no more will ever enter.

That's one of the most poignant things I have ever read about veterans. It is that secret, and the power of that mystery, that keeps us hooked.

ACKNOWLEDGMENTS

From Michael: Thanks to my co-author, Martin, for believing in me through the triumphs and difficulties of writing this book; to my family and friends for their love and support; to my parents for dealing with trips around the world doing research; and to my brothers, Chris for his editorial and webmaster skills, and John, who lent an open ear to my frustrations and achievements. A special thanks to 10th Armored Division historians Klaus Fiendler and Howard Liddic. Thanks to Craig Charlton, the 10th Armored Western Association webmaster, for providing the roster list that began my search. Thank you to Warren Watson, webmaster for the Old Hickory 30th Infantry Division website, for providing vital information and support. Gratitude also to Bruce Bird, founder and curator of the Museum of Black World War II History, for his help with information on the Wereth massacre; to John McAuliffe, president of the Veterans of the Battle of the Bulge Central Massachusetts chapter, for helping me with contacting veterans in Massachusetts; to Terry Armstrong for providing photographs and documents about his father, Mason Armstrong; to John Vallely, U.S. military history professor and librarian at Siena College, for his support, advice, and humor during the writing process; to Dr. Bruce Eelman, associate professor at Siena College, for his support and advice; and to Susan Musiak, history teacher at St. Mary High School, for teaching me why history is important and inspiring me to become a historian. Thanks to Richard Kane for his support and help during the publishing process and to our agent, Roger Williams, at the Publish or Perish Agency, Inc., Incorporating New England Publishing Associates. Last but not least, thanks to those who appeared in our book and who shared their stories, no matter what facet of the war they were involved in. They are truly the greatest generation.

From Martin: Many thanks to Freya for all her wonderful dedication and support through the years. Thanks also to Dr. Carlton Joyce for his encouragement and valued assistance; to Professor Roland H. Gaul of the National Military Museum of Die Kirsch, Luxembourg; to the staff at the Historical Center in Bastogne; and to Gerda Coppens, Yves Legreve, Tibaut Coppens, and Miel Leon at Latchdrom for filming the veterans and providing the photo stills. Many thanks to Adjutant Eric "Rony" Lemoine, Michel, Didier, Sebastian, and Sandra at the "Nuts" basement, Heintz Barracks Bastogne for their self-less devotion to duty and loyal friendship; to Andrea Theissen at the tourist office Sankt Vith; to Michel Vanderschaeghe and Marie-Hélène Malmendier at the library in Stavelot for giving us access to their photographs and archives; to Cmdr. Jeffrey Barta of the U.S. Navy and Gen. Graham Hollander, (retired) British Army; and to Ludwig Fischer for his help researching and locating the German veterans featured in this volume. Many heartfelt thanks to *all* the veterans who contributed to this volume. Thanks to Richard Kane at Zenith Press for his grateful and patient assistance and to our agent, Roger S. Williams, at the Publish or Perish Agency, Inc., Incorporating New England Publishing Associates.

During the writing and the publication of this book, several of the veterans featured passed away. May their stories live on forever: Ralph Ciani, James Hanney, Robert Kennedy, and Albert Tarbell.

CHAPTER ONE

The Center of a Storm

16 DECEMBER 1944

I T'S FAIR TO SAY that Col. Count Claus Schenk von Stauffenberg probably provided some of the impetus behind Hitler's plans to mount a counteroffensive in the west. Hitler's relations with his generals had never been particularly amiable, but after the failed attempt on his life at the Wolfsschanze (Wolf's Lair) near Rastenberg, they were understandably at an all-time low. The whole system of command control that worked so well at the outbreak of World War II had started to disintegrate. In fact, it had been going downhill since the Battle of Stalingrad. It was while recovering from the abortive attempt on his life orchestrated by von Stauffenberg on July 20, 1944, that Hitler began to ruminate on the possibility of striking back at the Allies who had waded ashore just forty-five days earlier. *Der Fuehrer* had escaped the assassination attempt with minor injuries and been ordered to bed by his physicians, and although Hitler made the first announcement of the projected counteroffensive in the Ardennes during the meeting on September 16, the idea had been festering in his mind for some weeks prior to that date. August was a nightmare for German forces in the west. Shattered by the weight of Allied guns and armor, hunted and hounded along the roads by the unopposed Allied air forces, captured and killed in droves, there was no doubt that the German forces in France had been routed and were now regarded by many Western commanders as a spent force.

In September, the British and Americans could mount a daily bomber attack of over five thousand planes, but the German will to resist and the means of resistance, so far as then could be measured, remained quite sufficient for a continuation of the war. Patton himself said, "There are still six million Germans that can pick up a rifle." He, for one, knew that the war was far from over.

For the second time in a century, Germany found itself fighting and maintaining a war on two fronts. The strategic and operational problem posed by this was almost as old as Germany itself and had been often analyzed, with solutions previously proposed by the great German military thinkers Helmuth von Moltke, Alfred von Schlieffen (who masterminded the invasion of Belgium in 1914), and Erich Ludendorff. Moltke and Schlieffen, traveling by the theoretical route, had arrived at the conclusion that Germany lacked the strength to conduct successful offensive operations simultaneously in the east and west. The Reich's famous tank commander, Heinz Guderian, the man who could choreograph tank movements with the precision of a ballet, sincerely believed that the war would be settled in the east, whereas OKW (Oberkommando der Wehrmacht—the high command of the Third Reich armed forces), with its chiefs Wilhelm Keitel and Alfred Jodl, saw the Western Front as the paramount theater of operations. Whatever the opinions of his generals were, there is no doubt that Hitler personally lacked many of the qualities he needed to organize and control military affairs with consistent success. That said, Hitler's operational decisions, especially early in the war, were often as good as, or better than, those of his generals. He was, after all, one of the two men who first thought up the campaign plan that the German army used against France with such stunning success in 1940.

Nevertheless, Hitler took the practice of personal command much too far. No military leader could hope to understand the realities of the situation on the ground from hundreds of miles away, and yet he came to believe that he could control all but the smallest units at the front. Hitler started the war using the highly effective system of "command control." Operation *Eben Emael* and ensuing invasions both to the east and the west proved that the system worked. The whole premise of command control was being able to delegate, to have sufficient faith in the competence of your generals to be able to perform their allocated tasks, but by the end of 1942, it began to disintegrate. For example, during the Battle of Stalingrad, Hitler actually had a street map of the city spread out before him so that he could follow the fighting, block by block. After the plot to assassinate him failed, Hitler became even more paranoid and unpredictable. The problem was complex; so were Hitler's mental processes. Hitler was a leader who never found himself distracted or restrained by the facts and who, by nature, clung to an almost mystic confidence in his own strategic ability. He thought that defeat could be postponed and perhaps even avoided by some decisive stroke. To this configuration of circumstances must be added Hitler's implicit faith that the course of conflict might be reversed by his military stroke of genius.

Hitler made the first announcement of the projected counteroffensive in the Ardennes during the meeting of 16 September 1944. It's a well-recorded fact that during the meeting he asked Herman Goering precisely how many aircraft he could get into the air to support this offensive. "Three thousand, mein Fuehrer," replied Goering, to which Hitler retorted with a somewhat sardonic smile, "I think that two thousand will be enough." Is it remotely possible that both of them knew that both of these numbers were unfeasible at that time? There is no simple or single explanation for Hitler's choice of the Western Front as the scene of the great German counterstroke, but nevertheless he had already cast the die.

It was obvious that Hitler was going to do his best to protect the Ruhr area of western Germany because this was the heart of German military production, a fact the Allies knew all too well. Even after the disastrous 1944 Soviet summer offensive, Hitler clung to the belief that the Ruhr factories were far more important to Germany than the loss of territory in the east. Then, too, in the summer and early autumn of 1944, Allied air attacks against the Ruhr had failed to deliver any succession of knockout blows. The very real vulnerability of this area was not yet apparent to Hitler, despite the fact that the hallowed "Siegfried Line" had been breached in the Hürtgen Forest.

Notwithstanding the somber and often despairing reports prepared by western commander Walther Model and his successor, Gerd von Rundstedt, during late August and early September, Hitler and his intimate staff in the East Prussian headquarters continued to give thought to a decisive attack in the west. Sometime around September 6, Jodl gave the Fuehrer an evaluation of the situation inherited by Rundstedt. The task at hand was to withdraw as many troops from the line as possible, refit, and re-form units. As a first step the SS Panzer divisions in the west were ordered out of the line and turned over to a new army headquarters, that of the Sixth Panzer Army. On the scale required, this work could not be completed before the first day of November. Since he was probably listening to a clearer phrasing of his own oblique concept, Hitler agreed to the withdrawal, on the condition that the battlefront be kept as far to the west as possible. The reason, expressed apparently for the first time, was that the Allied air effort needed to be kept at a distance from the Rhine bridges or the consequences might be disastrous. Did Hitler fear that fighter-bombers operating from fields in France or Belgium might leave the Rhine crossing complex stricken and incapable of supporting the line of communications to the armies then on the left bank of the Rhine? Or did he foresee that the Rhine bridges would be systematically hammered in an effort to strangle the German bid for the initiative when the day for the counteroffensive came?

Why did Hitler choose the Ardennes as the location for the proposed counteroffensive? To answer this question simply, the Ardennes would be the scene of a great winter battle because the Fuehrer had placed his finger on a map and made a pronouncement. There was also a historical precedent to this decision, since the German army had used this route before, in 1870 at the beginning of the Franco-Prussian War, in 1914 as part of the von Schlieffen plan, and again in 1940. Nevertheless, it's safe to say that these considerations were not paramount in Hitler's mind at that particular time. It is possible, however, that Hitler had discussed the operational concept of a counteroffensive through the Ardennes with Jodl before the September 16 edict. The relationship between these two men has bearing on the entire "prehistory" of the Ardennes campaign.

Clear evidence indicates that Jodl and a few of his subordinates from the Wehrmacht operations staff did examine the Ardennes concept very closely in the period from September 25, when Hitler gave the first order to start detailed planning, to October 11, when Jodl submitted the initial operations plan. Other less certain evidence indicates that those present in the conference on September 16 were taken by surprise when Hitler made his initial announcement. Jodl definitely ascribes the selection of the Ardennes to Hitler and Hitler alone, but at the time Jodl expressed this view he was about to be tried before an international tribunal on the charge of preparing aggressive war. Even so, the "argument from silence"—the fact that there is no evidence of other discussion about the Ardennes as the point of concentration prior to Hitler's statement on September 16—has some validity.

The most impressive argument for ascribing sole authorship of the Ardennes idea to Hitler is found in the simple fact that every major military decision in the German High Command for months past had been made by the Fuehrer, and that these Hitler decisions were made in detail, never in principle alone.

The major reasons for Hitler's selection of the Ardennes were as follows:

- Hitler ruled out the Alsace-Lorraine area because of the Third Army/Patton's armor and the Meuse River.
- The enemy front in the Ardennes sector was very thinly manned. A normal division front in 1944 was about five miles, but some divisions in that particular area, such as the 106th, found themselves guarding up to twenty-five miles.
- A blow here would force a breach between the British and the Americans and lead to political as well as military disharmony between the Allies. Furthermore, an entrance along this breach would isolate the British 21st Army Group and allow for the encirclement and destruction of the British and Canadians before American leadership (particularly the political leadership) could react.
- The distance from the jump-off line to a solid strategic objective (Antwerp) was not too great and could be covered quickly, even in bad weather. The only serious natural obstacle was the river Meuse that runs from north to south through the Ardennes.

Walther Model was the only general who openly criticized Hitler's plan to attack the Allies in the west. Hitler was convinced the war could still be decided in the Reich's favor by fighting in that direction. For many months, he and his closest advisors had worked to reorganize and re-equip the beaten divisions streaming back to Germany on both fronts. A massive surprise counterattack—deceptively code-named "Wacht am Rhein" (Watch on the Rhine)—against the weakly held Ardennes sector of the American front was prepared.

- Ground for maneuver in the Ardennes area was limited and would therefore require the use of relatively few divisions.
- The terrain to the east of the breakthrough sector selected was very heavily wooded and offered good cover against Allied air observation and attack during the build-up for the assault.
- An attack to regain the initiative in this particular area would erase the enemy ground threat to the Ruhr.

These were all the reasons Hitler needed. Meanwhile Gen. George Patton waited with his Third Army in the Alsace on the assumption that this was where the German army would strike back. Patton, who had often professed that he knew his military history, obviously had

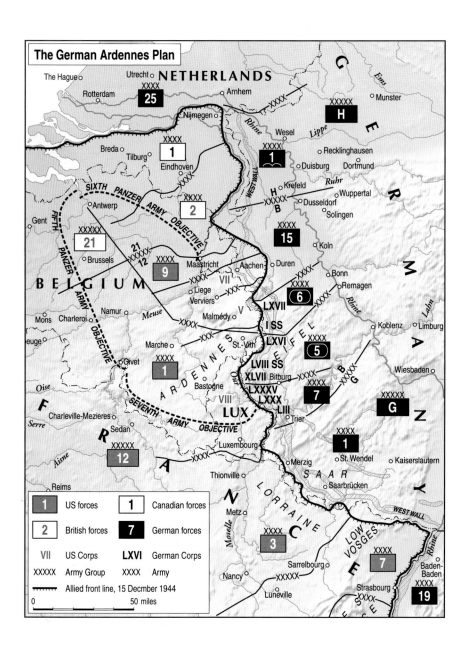

The German Ardennes Plan

The Hague○   Utrecht○   **NETHERLANDS**
Rotterdam○   ○Arnhem   ○Munster
XXXX 25

○Recklinghausen
Nijmegen○   Wesel○   **XXXXX H**
Breda○   ○Duisburg Dortmund○
Tilburg○   **XXXX 1**
Eindhoven○   ○Krefeld   Ruhr   ○Wuppertal
         XXXX 2   ○Düsseldorf
SIXTH PANZER ARMY OBJECTIVE   H ○Solingen
○Antwerp   **XXXXX B**
Gent○   **XXXXX 21**   **XXXX 15**
○Brussels   21 XXXXX 12   ○Köln
FIFTH PANZER ARMY OBJECTIVE   **XXXX 9**   Maastricht○   ○Aachen ○Duren
BELGIUM   Liège○   VII   ○Bonn
Mons○ Charleroi○ Namur○ Meuse Verviers○ V LXVII ○Remagen
○euge   Malmédy○   I SS   **XXXX 6**
Marche○   ○St.-Vith LXVI   ○Koblenz ○Limburg
XXXX 1   LVIII SS   **XXXX 5**
ARDENNES   XLVII Bitburg○   ○Wiesbaden
○Givet   Bastogne   LXXXV   **XXXX 7**   B G
SEVENTH ARMY OBJECTIVE   VIII   LXXX   **XXXXX G**
○Charleville-Mezieres   **LUX**   LIII ○Trier
Serre   ○Sedan   Luxembourg○   **XXXX 1**
XXXXX 12   ○St. Wendel ○Kaiserslautern
Aisne○   ○Merzig
○Reims   Thionville○   **SAAR** Saarbrücken○
○Metz   **LORRAINE**   **WEST WALL**
Moselle   **XXXX 3**   LOW VOSGES
Nancy○ Sarrebourg○   **XXXX 7**   Baden-Baden○
       Luneville○   Strasbourg○   **XXXX 19**

1	US forces	**1**	Canadian forces
2	British forces	**7**	German forces
VII	US Corps	**LXVI**	German Corps
XXXXX	Army Group	XXXX	Army

▬▬▬▬ Allied front line, 15 Decmber 1944

0 ━━━━━━ 50 miles

not studied contemporary history quite closely enough. If he had done so, he would have recognized that the German army had used the route through the Ardennes before, on no less than three occasions (as detailed previously). Never before had there been such polarity of opinions about one general's ability. To put it simply, the armored divisions venerated Patton while the infantry vilified him. Nevertheless, he was to play an integral role during Hitler's attack in the west.

One of the critical problems facing Gen. Dwight D. Eisenhower on the eve of the Battle of the Bulge was a severe shortage of infantrymen. By December 15, Gen. Omar Bradley reported that his army group lacked 17,000 riflemen because of casualties caused by prolonged combat and almost constant exposure to one of the severest winters Europe had ever known. Although Eisenhower ordered the reclassification as infantrymen of as many support personnel as possible, the shortfall continued to grow. The Ardennes-Alsace Campaign only worsened matters, while the Selective Service System in the United States could not close the increasing manpower gap. In response to this, Eisenhower made a momentous decision. Previously, most African-American soldiers in the European theater had been assigned to service units. Now these troops were permitted to volunteer for duty as combat infantrymen, with the understanding that after the necessary training, they would be committed to frontline service. Eventually, some 2,200 were organized into fifty-three platoons and assigned to all-white rifle companies in the two U.S. Army groups. The exigencies of combat had temporarily forced the Army to discard its policy of segregating white and black soldiers. Further on in this volume there are other references to the "invisible" African-American soldiers who fought just as bravely as their white counterparts on the Bulge. The German army was not going to regard them as equals, though.

During the first morning of the Battle of the Bulge, the northern shoulder area of the Bulge, which extended into Germany, contained parts of both the British and American armies.

Robert Kennedy was a member of XIX Corps, which was positioned in the northern area of the Bulge, just outside of Aachen, Germany. Aachen was the first German town to be attacked by the Allied army.

The son of a devoutly pacifist mother, Dwight D. Eisenhower was appointed Supreme Commander of the Allied Expeditionary Forces in December 1943. By mid-December, Eisenhower's forty-eight divisions were distributed along a six-hundred-mile front that stretched from the North Sea to Switzerland.

Kennedy was a German translator/ interrogator, and later he joined the 65th Division.

Robert Kennedy: I was there the first morning that we got the surprise attack. We got up and were near Aachen, just outside the town in a suburban area. The front was just down a little ways. We heard all this firing and wondered what it was, and it was German firing. They were firing over our heads back at the replacement depots, and they had a lot of heavy artillery. Then we found out that the Germans had passed us over and made a turn and presented a front to the south. We were strung out east and west, and back behind us were the British, who were facing the German front. In fact, before we came out of the sack, we heard the firing, and I recall a lot of firing. It was miserably cold morning, and the streets were terrible with ice.

There was nothing much we could do because we did not know what was going on, and they did not advance toward us, just toward the frontlines.

◆ ◆ ◆

WHEN THE BULGE BROKE, the soldiers of the XIX Corps were just outside of Aachen, and even though they did not deal with the first wave of the German attack, they were still part of the Bulge. With the British positioned behind them, the responsibility of the XIX Corps was to make sure the German army did not try to swing northward to get to the Meuse River via Aachen, Germany. The first artillery volleys by the German army were audible to these Allied soldiers, demonstrating how large the offensive really was. As John Hillard Dunn, Company H, 423rd Regiment, 106th Division wrote: "The vortex of a tornado is a vacuum. And that is where we were—in the center of a storm of armor and artillery roaring into the Ardennes." The eerie silence that pervaded those rolling hills out on the frozen Schnee Eifel was broken at 0530 on the morning of December 16, 1944. Nazi *Nebelwerfers* (Screaming Meemies), artillery pieces, and tanks unleashed their hellish fury on the unsuspecting U.S. troops of the 106th "Golden Lion" Division strung out there. Within minutes, the pastoral calm of the Schnee Eifel had been transformed into a raging inferno of apocalyptic proportions as flying metal pierced the arctic air accompanied by the menacing, deep, throaty rumble of advancing Nazi Tiger and Panther tanks, some of the latter equipped with the latest that German military technology had to offer, including "night vision." The green troops of the 106th Division had only arrived in Europe on the December 6. What was it really like to be on the receiving end of that full-scale attack? Two regiments, the 422nd and 423rd, with the 589th and 590th Field Artillery Battalions, were completely cut off and surrounded by the sheer weight and power of the concentrated German hammer blows. The 424th Regiment was driven back. The 106th Reconnaissance Troop, 331st Medical Battalion, and 81st Engineer Combat Battalion suffered heavy casualties. But, despite the vulnerable twenty-seven-mile front that the division had to defend, despite inadequate reserves, supplies, and air support, the valiant men of the Golden Lion Division inscribed their story in blood and courage, and it ranks with the Alamo, Château-Thierry, Pearl Harbor, and Bataan. Field Marshal Sir Bernard L. Montgomery said of them, "The American soldiers of the . . . 106th Infantry Division stuck it out and put up a fine performance. By jove, they stuck it out, those chaps."

At St. Vith, first objective of the German thrust, the 106th held on grimly at a time when every hour of resistance was vital to the Allied cause. The 106th fought with incredible tenacity against superior forces, with pulverizing artillery battering them from all sides; it was men against tanks, guts against steel. Their heroism gained precious time for other units to regroup and strike back. In one of the bloodiest battles of

German and American Pre-battle Dispositions

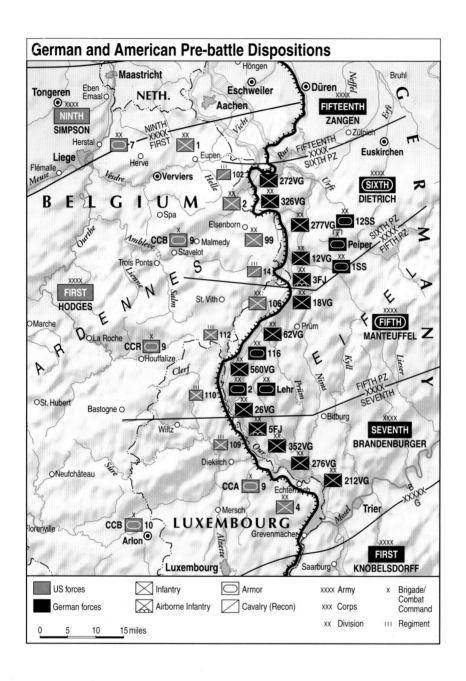

US forces — German forces

Infantry — Airborne Infantry — Armor — Cavalry (Recon)

xxxx Army — xxx Corps — xx Division — ||| Regiment — x Brigade/Combat Command

0 5 10 15 miles

the war, the 106th showed the Germans and the world how American soldiers could fight—and die. When the terrific German onslaught was launched, the 106th had only been on the continent for ten days. The men had made a three-day road march from Limesy, France, to St. Vith, Belgium, in rain, cold, and snow. In the five days they had been on the line, there had been little rest.

St. Vith had been a quiet German-speaking market town at a cross-roads in the "High Fens" area of Belgium next to the German border. Until 1919, it had been geographically in Germany, but the Treaty of Versailles put an end to that. The little road center of St. Vith had seen war before. It was through St. Vith that the Nazi Panzers had rolled to Sedan in 1940; German infantry marched through it in 1914. But it had never been a battleground before that fateful day in December 1944, when it became the epicenter of the German attacks. Its only claim to fame before that was that it was the birthplace of Saint Vitus, later to become associated with a nervous condition called Saint Vitus dance, and there were plenty of frayed and shattered nerves on that freezing December day. Despite the extreme adversity of these conditions, however, soldiers were expected to fight and defend their positions when simply surviving took maximum effort.

Assigned to VIII Corps, the 106th took up positions in a slightly bulging arc along a forest-crowned ridge of the Schnee Eifel approximately twelve miles east of St. Vith.

The 14th Cavalry Group, attached to the 106th, held the northern flank. Next, in the easternmost part of the curve, the 422nd held the line. To the 422nd's right, swinging slightly to the southwest, was the 423rd, and almost directly south was the 424th. Beyond the 424th, on the division's southern flank, was the 28th Infantry Division. The 28th Division had seen its numbers seriously depleted by the badly organized and orchestrated Battle of the Hürtgen Forest in the Aachen-Düren-Monschau triangle a few miles north of St. Vith. St. Vith was headquarters for the 106th, and the rear echelon was in Vielsalm, about twelve miles due west.

During the night of December 15, frontline units of the 106th noticed increased activity in the German positions. The 28th Division

The 106th Infantry Division consisted of three regiments: the 424th, 423rd, and 422nd. The division front was seriously overstretched, covering twenty-five miles and reaching eight miles into Germany. The troops had only been on the line for five days when, after some fierce fighting, two of the regiments were captured. The division's 422nd and 423rd Infantry Regiments were encircled and cut off. They surrendered to the Germans on December 19, 1944, in the largest surrender of U.S. Army personnel during World War II. Nevertheless, they fought with incredible courage and severely disrupted the German army timetable.

farther south in Luxembourg also reported frenzied activity by the German army along the east bank of the river Saar. The main problem was that despite the many warnings about a build-up of German forces, leaders at Allied headquarters remained dismissive. The intelligence was delivered but frequently dissipated and dismissed as it filtered up through the ranks. The men at the top just were not listening. Why was there such a colossal failure to communicate this highly important intelligence to headquarters?

During the re-conquest of France, the extensive network of the French resistance had provided valuable intelligence about German dispositions. Now that Allied forces had reached the German border, this source had evaporated. In France, orders had been relayed within the German army using radio messages ciphered by the Enigma machine, and these could be picked up and decrypted by ULTRA. In Germany, such orders were typically transmitted using telephone and teleprinter.

All commanders operated under a special radio silence order, which was vehemently imposed on all matters concerning the upcoming offensive. The Enigma code breakers at Bletchley Park forwarded information concerning this, but the intelligence had been either ignored or dismissed. Furthermore, German army radio silence proved to be very effective because by December 15, three units of the German army had managed to surreptitiously maneuver themselves into position on the Schnee Eifel almost under the noses of the Allies.

At 0540 on the morning of December 16, the enemy began to lay down a thunderous artillery barrage. At first the fire was directed mainly against the northern flank sector. Slowly, the barrage crept southward, smashing strong points along the whole division front. As the onslaught began, GIs caught unaware burrowed frantically into their foxholes and fortifications to escape. Then they waited tensely for the German army to attack. The morning darkness was illuminated by bursts from medium and heavy field pieces, plus railway artillery, which had been shoved secretly into position.

At 0700 the barrage lifted in the forward areas, although St. Vith remained under fire. Now came the inevitable attack. Wave upon wave of *volksgrenadiers*, spearheaded by Panzer units, smashed against the U.S. Army's lines in a desperate attempt to force a decisive, early breakthrough. They were halted in their tracks as the beleaguered 106th Division tenaciously returned fire. A second attack was thrown against the division. Again, the 106th held. Nazis threw in fresh troops to replace their losses, but there were no replacements for the 106th.

Throughout the day, the attacks increased in fury. Hundreds of well-prepared Germans rushed straight toward the American lines, only to be mowed down or driven back. The deadly, vigilant fire of the stubborn defenders exacted a dreadful toll on the German army. Finally, under pressure of overwhelming numbers, the 14th Cavalry was forced to withdraw on the north flank, giving the Germans their first toehold in the division front. Enemy tanks and infantry in increasing numbers then hacked at the slowly widening gap in an effort to surround the 422nd. In the meantime, a second tank-led assault, supported by infantry and other Panzers, hammered relentlessly at the 423rd and 424th.

Early the next morning, a wedge was driven between the two regiments. This southern German column then swung north to join the one that had broken through in the 14th's sector. Two regiments from the 106th Golden Lion Division, the 422nd and 423rd, were surrounded. The third regiment, the 424th, pulled back to St. Vith.

The Nazis were heading for St. Vith in force. In the ranks of the defenders of St. Vith there was frenzied activity as cooks and clerks, truck drivers and mechanics shouldered weapons and took to the foxholes. Hopelessly outnumbered and facing heavier firepower, they dug in for a last ditch defense of this vital junction. Even though they were almost completely surrounded, the 422nd and 423rd fought on relentlessly. Ammunition and food ran low. Frantic appeals were radioed to headquarters to have supplies flown in, but the soupy fog that covered the frozen countryside made air transport impossible. The two encircled regiments regrouped early on December 18 for a counterattack aimed at breaking out of the steel trap. This bold thrust was blocked by the sheer weight of German numbers. The valiant stand of the two fighting regiments inside the German lines proved to be a serious obstacle to Nazi plans. It forced the Germans to throw additional reserves into the drive to eliminate the surrounded Americans, enabled the remaining units and their reinforcements to prepare the heroic defense of St. Vith, delayed the attack schedule, and prevented the early stages of the Battle of the Bulge from exploding into a complete German victory.

Low on ammunition, food gone, ranks depleted by three days and nights of ceaseless fighting, the 422nd and 423rd battled on from their frozen foxholes and old Siegfried Line bunkers. They fought the increasing horde of Panzers with bazookas, rifles, and machine guns. One of their last desperate radio messages was, "Can you get some ammunition through?" Then, no more was heard from in the two encircled regiments except what news was brought back by small groups and individuals who escaped the trap. Many were known to have been killed. Many were missing. Many turned up later in German prison camps.

A veteran of that terrible encounter, John Hillard Dunn, Company H, 423rd Regiment, 106th Division, recalls those first terrifying days and nights in the direct path of a massive German offensive.

John Hillard Dunn: As I remember it, I was trying to sleep in the ruins of a German farmhouse. It was December, cold and snowing. Squirming about in my sleeping bag, I felt reassured by the three-foot thickness of the wall against which I rested my shivering spine. Sometime in the night, buzz bombs began their cement-mixer noise overhead. I thought that there were more than there had been the night before, and I felt sorry for the quartermaster corps back in Antwerp, which I imagined to be on the receiving end. Later I learned the bombs were dropping on our division headquarters in St. Vith, Belgium, a matter of eighteen miles to our rear. Those buzz bombs were the heralds of a German offensive—the last great Nazi push. For this was the night of December 15, 1944, and von Rundstedt's historic "Bulge" was about to begin.

Our division—the 106th—was newly arrived in the line. We had relieved the 2nd Division on December 12, moving into what, a 2nd Division veteran told me with a perfectly straight face, was a "rest area." Actually, it was a salient; a dagger plunged into the West Wall along the Belgium–Germany frontier near the Luxembourg corner.

We were an odds-and-ends division green as the pine forests that surrounded us; somebody in our 81mm mortar platoon wanted to know, "Why the hell is it thundering in December?" Our laughter was hollow when somebody informed him that those were big guns, and German guns at that.

I never did any fighting with my mortar squad; perhaps it was just as well, as I had never even seen a mortar fired before I went into combat. Not that I was unusual. Half of our platoon hadn't, including at least two corporals whose Form 20s said they were gunners. My first duty as a combat MP convinced me that this was no goldbrick job. I had a chance to scan the detailed maps and for the first time got an idea of our salient. Lafe, a Southern lad, took a long look and said, "Damned if we ain't got Germans on both sides of us."

That remark was underlined for me when I was assigned to traffic duty at a road intersection. This was December 13. The 2nd Division man who had been there greeted me: "Welcome to our Purple Heart Corner." He then explained briefly, "The Heinie artillery has this intersection zeroed in. It ain't under direct observation, but they drop 'em in here every once in a while."

He wasn't kidding. For two days I ducked artillery shells at the intersection. Then came the night of December 15 and the farmhouse with the thick walls. The increase in buzz bombs was not the only significant omen; if we had been veterans, we might have realized that the Germans were getting very bold, that they had too many patrols running around. Already by that afternoon the enemy was playing all kinds of hell with our communications. By nightfall, even our regiment could sense his presence.

I was shaken out of my sack and the shelter of thick walls around midnight to relieve Outpost No. 8. The man remarked, "Somebody's getting trigger-happy around here."

Someone was. A bullet whistled through the dark night over the lonely shed in which I took my post. I could have sworn it came from Outpost No. 7. So I asked into our open-circuit phone, "No. 7, what the hell are you shooting at?"

"I ain't shooting at nuttin. It must be No. 6 on my left."

"Blow it out your ass," No. 6 barked.

"It's probably Headquarters Company huntin' pigs," No. 9 butted in.

The real explanation came later from a captured German: "We were told that we had a green American division," he said. "We were sent in to disrupt communications and to confuse. So we fired at buildings or anything we could spot in the dark."

The cold and weird night, punctuated by small arms fire, wore on. The dawn of Saturday the 16th came, and from my post I could hear a deep thunder. But the rain that followed was steel.

Yet nobody realized on the morning of the 16th that the Germans had begun a monster offensive. Not that we didn't try to guess at what they were doing. In spite of the initial terror, the men around me argued as strongly about German tactics as they had recently debated the American League pennant race. We thought that Fritz was merely taking advantage of our inexperience to run a sortie and in a few hours would return to his comfortable pillboxes and dugouts that overlooked ours from the main ridge of the Schnee Eiffel.

But then they told us we couldn't move our fifty prisoners back to division, and we wondered why.

The vortex of a tornado is a vacuum. And that is where we were—in the center of a storm of armor and artillery roaring into the Ardennes. Already we were bypassed by the onrushing German tanks, and I for one certainly didn't know it, nor would I have believed it had anyone told me.

Toward evening, wounded were reaching our area. I had a chance to talk to a man from Cannon Company. His was the story of a forlorn, desperate little action in the German town of Bleialf, southwest of regiment headquarters and to the rear of our right flank.

"So you wanta know what the hell Cannon Company is doing—fighting in Bleialf," he said as he rubbed the bandage on his right leg. "The goddamned Heinie infantry takes Bleialf in a surprise move. Our rifle companies are too damned busy to do anything about it. Besides, Cannon's run out of ammunition for the guns by now anyway."

He stopped to light a cigarette.

"Understand, I ain't beefin', but hell, village fighting with carbines and damned few grenades ain't no picnic. What the hell, though, somebody's got to try to take the damned town back. Ain't no other way of getting to division at St. Vith."

That explained, I realized, why division headquarters couldn't take our prisoners. We were cut off.

"We take her back," the GI went on. "Don't ask me how. They don't let us keep it long. They come back with artillery fire, and then mortars and then infantry. There's Cannon guys left back there, but they ain't movin'."

The Battle of the Bulge is often referred to as the "Von Rundstedt Offensive," after German Army Generalfeldmarschall Gerd von Rundstedt, although he had little to do with the planning and execution.

He lit another cigarette from his butt. "That's how it is, Mac. But where the hell do we go from here?"

I wondered too. As the white of the snowy hillsides turned to a dirty gray in the evening twilight and then into formless darkness, I ate my last American meal for four months. My K-ration had Camels in it.

That night the crucial situation was reflected in the prisoners. Cowed and obedient for two days, they were getting cocky and talkative. Huddled together in a cold barn, they would erupt into conversation against orders. And it wasn't until Angie fired a burst from his grease gun between the legs of a particularly obnoxious Nordic blond that they shut up.

◆ ◆ ◆

THE NUMBERS OF THE 28TH DIVISION had been terribly depleted in November during the bloody Battle of the Hürtgen Forest, but they still fought on. In the forlorn hope of getting some well-earned R&R, they were moved south to Luxembourg. The rest they so richly deserved would still be a long way off because when the Battle of the Bulge began on December 16, 1944, they unfortunately found themselves in the path of the German Fifth Army commanded by Baron Hasso von Manteuffel. His left two Panzer corps broke through the U.S. 28th Division and reached the outskirts of Houffalize and Bastogne. The 112th plugged the line for two days before pulling north to join the one regiment left of the 106th Infantry Division as a combat team. These men were pushed to the absolute limits of endurance, and after only marginally surviving the terrible Hürtgen Forest debacle, they were once again thrown into the pit of hell to face overwhelming numbers of German troops. The Pennsylvania keystone arm patch would once again earn its title of the "Bloody Bucket."

Five German divisions—Panzer, infantry, and volksgrenadier— hurtled across the Our River the first day of the assault. The 28th Division was severely mauled yet again in its history, but despite repeated German attacks, it still managed to plug the line and fight back. As December 16 wore on, division lines eventually snapped under excessive pressure. In total, nine enemy divisions were identified in the striking force that kept hammering the 28th troopers. Keystone men were outnumbered, overrun, cut off. But despite all the adversity they had to contend with, they refused to panic. Under cool-headed Gen. Norman "Dutch" Cota, the 28th fought, delayed, and fought.

Allan P. Atwell: I was assigned to a rifle company of the 28th Infantry Division on December 16th. The hospital was emptied of all who could walk. I was headed toward Bastogne as a rifleman replacement when asked if I would be interested in becoming a military policeman. I made a quick decision and became one on the spot. Our biggest concern as MPs was to look for Germans dressed up as American soldiers.

If a jeep had black canvas covering the lights, that would give us cause for further investigation. Passwords at roadblocks were a big thing. As I remember, there would not be a particular password but they would ask for a word only an American would normally know. Like players on baseball teams, or what states certain cities were in, or possibly where a river might flow and in what direction. It was a little scary. I, myself, never confronted a German soldier under these conditions . . . that I was aware of, anyway. I saluted General Patton one day as he rode by in his sheepskin jacket and pearl pistols.

Dorothy Barre: I worked as a nurse in the surgical orthopedic wards. We were set up in Liège before the Bulge broke, and we were in tents that would hold thirty patients at a time. In the center of each tent was a pot-belly stove that kept us warm, and we had surgical carts we could use for dressings. When the Bulge broke, Liège was an ammunition dump, so they were sending buzz bombs toward the city. We were in that alley of buzz bombs, and when we heard them, a patient would run out and see what route they were on. There were three routes that they fired over us. Over that period, we were hit three times with the buzz bombs, not where the patients were. We did not have any casualties. We were ten or twelve miles from the fighting.

But one time one of the buzz bombs hit nearby, one of the houses, and we admitted Belgian patients. I had a mother and a daughter, and

On December 17, soldiers of A Company, 38th Regiment, 2nd Infantry Division, deploy southward toward the twin villages of Rocherath and Krinkelt, just a few miles from the German border, as German forces push westward into Belgium. *U.S. Army Signal Corps*

the daughter died. The doctor and I worked together to help them until they could get the mother to the Belgian hospital in Liège.

Before the Bulge, we treated soldiers sometimes, but when the Bulge started, we got them from army trucks or stretchers. They might just be wrapped in blankets, the young fellas, and we got them washed up. Sometimes we would have four nurses to one guy, getting them washed up, pajamas on, their dressings checked. We would ask them if they had pain, and we carried codeine and aspirin in our pockets. I remember sitting on the cots and talking with the guys. They would always ask me where I came from, since I have a Boston accent. Sometimes they would stay with us for just eight or ten hours. The patients would get a good meal and cleaned up and given penicillin too. After they were well enough, they were flown to Paris or London. We had a few specifically from the 101st paratroopers and engineers as well.

I think we knew that the Germans had broken through and the Bulge was getting close to us. We didn't go into the city, about four miles away. We stayed in a chateau, a stone building. I was on the third floor, and there were seven to eight nurses to a room with a potbelly stove in the center. We had showers down in the cellar. Some nights, some of us would go down in the cellar because of those buzz bombs. They would start them about eleven o'clock at night and go until about two or three in the morning, and then they would start again at four in the morning.

Joseph "Joe" Ozimek: At the end of November, they pulled us out of the Hürtgen Forest, and we [Field Artillery, 109th Battalion, Battery C, 28th Infantry Division] were sent to Bocholz [about 40 km south of St. Vith], Luxembourg. We went over there to get some rest and get new replacements. December 16 at 0500 we could hear guns going off over in Germany. Then we had one on the road about one hundred yards from us. It tore up the road and cut our telephone wires. It was my turn to take care of the 50mm _cal._ machine gun on a tripod. I had just checked the gun to make sure it had loaded when one of the regular 50mm guards came up to me and said, "Joe, we're out of touch with headquarters. All lines are cut." So off we went to our truck for some wire, and there were also three other wiremen we had to walk with to the road.

The night was pitch black, and it was difficult to work under these circumstances. Suddenly, a shell exploded, and shortly thereafter we heard singing. The 50mm _cal._ gun went off, and after some light flares were shot in the air. I was just standing in the middle of the road. Now if a flare goes off and you don't move, they can't see you . . . unless you move. It took me five minutes to get to the side of the road.

Thank God the sun started to come out, and it seems our machine gun team took apart a German machine gun group. We found about twelve bodies, all bloodied, and plenty of wounded to carry back. One German was killed trying to hide in the small church door. By 0930 we went back to patching the wires. This is when three Luxembourg freedom fighters showed up who wore "FFI" armbands and carried Belgian 38mm guns. They looked like our 45mm. They pulled about four or five Germans off the road and shot each one in the head. Our captain stopped them and told them to stop with the shooting. It was still dark, and our troops might mistake the noise as coming from the Germans, so we might be hit. That day our captain was shot in the leg about 0545. He maintained his command and used a rifle as a support. He would only be evacuated to the medic station at 1700. He would be out for four months, and the gunner was also hit in the cheek. Five others were shot that day. I can't tell you how many Germans were shot, but they must have had plenty of wounded, judging by all the blood on the road.

We held on to Bocholz until December 18, when we heard over the radio in Wiltz: "We are closing station now. Hope to see you in Bastogne."

John Kline: Because we [M Company, 423rd Regiment, 106th Division] were high atop the Schnee Eifel and out of the mainstream of the German offensive, we were probably the last to know that it had been launched. I cannot remember any evidence or any sounds that would have indicated to us the size of the battle that was to take place.

My division, the 106th Infantry Division, suffered over 416 killed in action, 1,246 wounded, and 7,001 men missing in action in the first days of the Battle of the Bulge. Most of these casualties occurred within the first three days of battle when two of the three regiments were forced to surrender. In all, there were 641 killed in action from our division through to the end of the fighting. In losses, the German Ardennes Offensive, later to become known as the "Battle of the Bulge," was the worst battle for the Americans in World War II.

The original .50-caliber machine gun was developed by John Browning in 1918. An improved version was adopted in 1933 as the Browning M2 water-cooled machine gun. The legendary M2, with nicknames like the "Faithful 50" and "Ma Deuce," is an automatic, belt-fed, recoil-operated, air-cooled, crew-operated machine gun. This versatile and reliable gun had many uses and proved to be a valuable defensive weapon during the winter of 1944–1945.

Our company commander set up his headquarters in one of the enormous Siegfried Line bunkers. The bunker was not completely demolished, as they usually were. The underground rooms were intact and accessible. He had taken a room several flights down. The command bunker was on the crest of a hill. The firing apertures faced west toward Belgium, the backside toward the present German lines. There were steep slopes on either side, with signs and white caution tape warning of mine fields. There was a pistol belt and canteen hanging in one of the trees on the slope. Apparently, some GI had wandered into the minefield.

Albert Tarbell: I was on chute patrol duty with the MPs in the city of Reims. The 82nd was staying in Camp Sissone near Sissone, France. Our job [Company H, 504th Parachute Infantry Regiment, 82nd Airborne Division] was to intervene on behalf of the troopers should they get too rowdy or drunk and get arrested by regular Army MPs. We were usually able to reason with them and bring them back to the truck pickup point and avoid more serious charges. We were to go to the shooting range on the 18th, but when I arrived back at camp late that evening or early morning, there was a lot of activity going on. There were replacements all over the place. I remember hearing one of the replacements telling Sergeant Kogul that he had never fired an M1 before, and the Sergeant replied to him, "That's OK, son, you will learn soon enough."

I still thought we were headed for the firing range.

When I arrived back to my quarters Sergeant Fuller was waiting up for me. I asked him if we were ready and packed for the firing range. He said we surely were ready for the range, and it was then that I first found out about a German counterattack somewhere in Belgium. We did not get much sleep the rest of that night.

W. D. Crittenberger: We [420th Field Artillery Battalion, 10th Armored Division] were north of Metz when the Bulge began, in the small town of Launstraff, France, right on the German border, when we were ordered up to Bastogne, Belgium. We heard about the Bulge because we always tuned our halftrack radios to the BBC. They overlapped, and around 0200 we got a warning order from Division Headquarters saying they were getting ready to go north. Then around 0800 we got our orders to be part of CCB and go to Bastogne. On the 17th we drove about sixty miles up to Luxembourg and stayed overnight.

◆ ◆ ◆

NEWS OF THE GERMAN OFFENSIVE started to spread throughout Allied rest areas in France, but it was not at first clear if the rumors were true.

Clair Bennett: I was in a chateau in Sierck, France. I was told by a runner to return to HQ. I did not pay attention to him, but the second time he told me I did. I had heard that tale before, but this time it was real. Then as we [Company F, 90th Cavalry Reconnaissance Squadron (Mechanized), 10th Armored Division] were moving out, we found out that the Germans were attacking Belgium.

Members of the 630th Tank Destroyer Battalion, Company B, who lost their vehicles during the advance into Belgium, take infantry positions on a hill covering an approach in Wiltz, Bastogne, Belgium, on December 20, 1944.

◆ ◆ ◆

THE SUDDEN DEPLOYMENT OF the 10th Armored Division was a surprise to many of the division's men.

Don Olson: We [Troop C, 90th Cavalry Reconnaissance Squadron, 10th Armored Division] were pulled back to Metz to resupply and rearm, and we expected to spend Christmas there, and then we got the call to move. We had people in Paris on leave, and they had to round them up. We did not know where we were going; we were traveling at night. They did not allow headlights; we drove in the dark, and it was getting colder.

John R. Schaffner: Early in the morning, before dawn, at 0605, our position [Battery B, Survey Team, 106th Division] came under a barrage of German artillery fire. I was on guard at one of our outposts, and though I did not realize it at the time, I was probably better off there than with the rest of the battery. We had a 50-caliber machine gun in a dug-in position, so being somewhat protected, I got down in the lowest possible place and "crawled into my helmet." During the shelling, many rounds exploded real close and showered dirt and tree limbs about, but also there were quite a few duds that only smacked into the ground. Those were the "good" ones as far as I was concerned. After about thirty minutes, the shelling ceased, and before any of the enemy came into sight, I was summoned to return to the battery position. From an inspection of the fragments, somebody determined that the enemy was using 88, 105, and 155mm guns.

Helen Rusz: We [at the 59th Evacuation Hospital, where Rusz was a nurse] were south of Metz, France, in the town of Epinal, when the Battle of the Bulge broke out. We moved towards Metz and stayed near there during the Bulge.

We used to tend the wounded, and when they came into the emergency room, we made sure they had a tetanus shot. The only way we would know if they had had a tetanus shot or not, because half of them were wounded and didn't know what they were saying or doing, was if they had a *TAT* on their forehead. They didn't have the nice markers like we have today; they would put it on with ink or lipstick. If they did not have *TAT* on their forehead we would give them a tetanus shot right away, that was the first thing we did. We would then enter them into the ward, and there was a medical ward, a surgical ward, an intensive care ward, and a cardiac ward, just like a regular hospital. Our unit had about forty doctors and about eighty nurses. The doctors in the emergency room would decide where they would go, and we would take care of them.

We would be on duty for eight hours, and then someone else would take our place. Seven to three and three to eleven and eleven to seven were our hours. We would follow the troops, and we would send the boys away when they were as well as they could be. We mostly treated Americans, but we also treated Englishmen and prisoners of war too. The younger Germans were very nice, but the staunch old German guys did not like it when the German prisoners would communicate with the American wounded.

During the Bulge, there was one fellow who had a very bad eye wound. I really took care of him. I was practically his private nurse; I changed his dressing every day, and I put a solution in his eyes. I think his eye was saved after the doctor told him that it would be all right. Another fellow who was in intensive care, when I was there, this kid, I do not think he was even seventeen, he was crying for his momma. It was so sad; he was absolutely out of his head. He was very confused, he didn't know where he was, he wanted to go home, and he kept crying for his mother. He had a very severe abdominal wound, and we didn't know if he was going to make it or not. We sent him to England, and I do not know what happened to him. I wish I did.

The main thing was in the emergency room: they would come in so awful some of them, but you rarely would see them crying, they were so brave. They would say, "Oh my god, this hurts," and we would give them a shot for their pain, but we did not have any blood for a transfusion. They all needed blood, since they did lose a lot of it. We did have plasma. It wasn't as good as blood, but there was volume.

As soon as they were better, we would have the GIs get up and walk, and I loved walking with the GIs. And once they were walking better, they were sent out to a general hospital.

William W. Fee: We [55th Armored Infantry Battalion, 11th Armored Division] got up about 0600. Sergeant "Doc" Magelli asked me if I'd rolled up my bedroll. Tired of being assigned to work details because I was usually one of the first to be ready for the day's activities, I lied and said, "No." "Good," he replied, "Leave your fatigue [work] uniform out. You're on detail." But the work I was assigned to was not as bad as the detail that Tom Cantrell and others were put on, carrying coal up to the deck. After a while, my partner and I figured out that we could get on deck and avoid additional work by taking up a garbage can to empty it.

As we pulled into the Cherbourg harbor we saw a low, gray stone wall that must have been a breakwater. Farther on, we passed ships of all nationalities. Although we'd been overseas only two months, that old U.S. ensign on the stern of merchant ships made us feel mighty good. We passed a hospital ship with so many men leaning on the side rail that I wondered if it would capsize.

Then we were ordered below deck to put on our stuff. I couldn't find my musette bag [pack] and was horrified because it contained the Colt .45 automatic pistol that my father had sent me at Camp Cooke and Captain Houy had taken overseas for me. To make things worse,

Houy came over and showed me the .45 that Lieutenant Hughston had acquired in exchange for a combat jacket at the Tidworth Ordinance Depot. We had a long conversation about .45s—while I was sweating blood over mine being lost.

Finally I found my musette bag. Some guy had taken it by mistake. We got off the ship onto a pier that was loaded with enormous stacks of C rations guarded by a GI with a carbine [small rifle]. Big "cattle trucks" pulled up, and we loaded up in them. I was lucky enough to be at the side and could see blasted pillboxes [concrete fortifications] on the docks. We turned left and went down a broad street. Here and there were ruined houses all fallen in, sloppy GIs, and some French girls.

We had a hard pull up a steep hill and soon were out of town. The hills were steep, but the scenery was good. Here and there were pill-boxes, and everywhere were hedgerows. We passed little farms and tiny schools. At one house a man threw apples to us. (Hedgerows and apples were well-known features of the Normandy countryside.)

After a ride of about 25 km south from Cherbourg, we unloaded alongside the road in the vicinity of Bricquebec. There was a mad scramble for bedrolls and then Major Blalock came along and got things straightened out. After a tough hike in which many fell out, we came to our bivouac area, a pleasant field surrounded by hedgerows. Our halftracks were there, and we had a reunion with the drivers. Ercil Pennick was wearing a rubber jacket he had swiped from an LST. We pitched our pup tents in rows—it was the first time my buddy Jim Pike had ever pitched a tent! Then he had to dig a latrine.

The chow truck served supper in the dark. As we ate, we watched Bob Holets and Tony Matzie, the company armorers, loading belts of MG ammo by the headlights of their truck. That was an ominous sign, but it still was exciting! After we got back from chow, "Telly," our squad leader, told us what was up: We were headed for St. Nazaire and Lorient, on the coast, where a German garrison had never given up. We would go into the inactive front line that surrounded them and get a mild taste of what war was like—"indoctrination."

"Sack" started moaning and going through his act. I enjoyed being with Phil "Sad Sack" Vornoli (McNulty's squad) in the barracks at Camp

Cooke and in Belgium. He was a faithful soldier and a big asset to our outfit. I and others remember him particularly for his way of expressing the exasperation we all felt about the frustrations of army life. Everybody "griped," but nobody liked to hear others complain. Except "Sack." He had a way of sounding off that made others laugh with him and at him. His buddy Ray Nowicki often responded, "Don't tell me your troubles," and their routine helped to make life bearable. I didn't feel so hot about it either. But we went to our tents full of excitement.

Nelson Charron: On December 16th the weather was cold and damp when we [Company D, 422nd Regiment, 106th Infantry Division] arrived in Germany on the frontlines, but we did not see much snow during the first few days. During the first day we were there we were in foxholes. We were warned that Germans were coming and we had to be quiet and question anybody who walked by. We were awake during the opening morning, and there were buzz bombs going over our heads. We fired quite a lot, but we were just in big trouble because we had no big guns. Our artillery was knocked out, and machine guns against tanks were not going to cut it. There was no way we could have escaped, maybe right off the bat we could have, but we were too weak.

William "Richard" Barrett: We [420th Field Artillery Battalion, 10th Armored Division] pulled out early in the morning on the 16th and moved north in our column. I don't know how much was with us, I could only see what I could see. We spent the night in Belgium in some heavy woods. I stood watch that night with another young fella, and he was scared out of his wits. He fashioned a knife out of wood, and it was so dark that he walked into a tree and stuck a knife in him. It was a little bit scary, he didn't know what he walked into, and it could have been me.

Frank Towers: When the Bulge broke out, I was at Herzogenrath, Germany, and we [Company M, 120th Regiment, 30th Infantry Division] were preparing to cross the Roer River. We did not know what had happened. We were alerted midday on the 16th, I believe, and told to be ready to move out at a moment's notice. We did not know where we were going until late that night, en route to the Bulge area, in the strictest of secrecy that I was ever aware of, when Axis Sally came on the air and said, "The Old Hickory Division is on the way to Malmedy to save the ass of the First Army, most of which has already been captured!" That was the first we knew about where we were going. At the moment, we were a little bit skeptical of this, knowing the source, but by starlight calculations, we determined that we were moving due south. Next morning at Hauset, Belgium, it was revealed to us that the Germans had broken through, but we were not told how badly. We soon determined this as we met convoy after convoy heading *north*! It was the headquarters of the First Army, which had been in the vicinity of Spa, getting the hell out of there. They had left behind all kinds of maps, orders, etc., integral to the battle that was going on. All they wanted was to get out of there and save their asses! We continued on to Malmedy on the 17th and found out from the engineer troops, which were the only ones there, what the situation was. We started deploying from that point onward.

◆ ◆ ◆

A FEW YEARS BACK I (MARTIN) had the honor of accompanying James L. Cooley, a veteran from the 106th, around the places in which he'd fought during that bitterly cold winter of 1944. James went through a whole gamut of emotions that week; nevertheless I'm glad I spent time with him and his family.

I remember James as a soft-spoken, intelligent man who did not say too much about the battle as we drove around in our minibus. Despite my persistent questions, James never gave any indication of the terrible suffering he'd endured as an infantryman of the 106th Division and as a wounded POW. Robert Cooley, James's son, was kind enough to send me the transcript of a tape his father recorded before he passed away to give his family some idea of what he'd experienced during the Battle of the Bulge.

James L. Cooley: I was in Company D, 1st Battalion, 423rd Infantry Regiment, 106th Infantry Division. We left England on a ship from Southampton, and we went over to Le Havre. So we left Le Havre and got into a jeep. I was one of the advanced guard, and we drove through France into Belgium. It was cold, cold, cold. I did everything I could to keep warm, but when you're in the back of a jeep and you have that wind blowing at you for hours at a time, you get past feeling numb. I took my boots off and put my feet in a sleeping bag. I did everything, and I still couldn't get warm. Anyway we went up to the line that was in Belgium. Like I said before, it was just a little inside Germany. The Division HQ was in St. Vith. If you go straight east of St. Vith you come to a town on the border of Germany called Schönberg. I imagine two miles straight east of there is where I was in a foxhole.

The battle started on December 16th at about 0530 in the morning. I mean all kinds of shells and everything else came down on us. It was earth shaking. On our battlefront we were holding twenty-six miles of front for one division. Looking in the book it says we were holding twenty-seven miles of front, but the important thing is that we had up to half-mile gaps in our line. What we did was send patrols back and forth just to patrol it. We were on the hills and sent the patrols back and forth between the hills just to make sure there were no Germans there.

Where we were was supposed to be a quiet place. It was very wooded, and it was very hilly, and you would think that it was impassable. After the Germans attacked us on December 16th I was in heavy weapons. I was in 81mm mortars, which is a shell that you lob over that explodes when it hits the ground. First, I started firing toward our front, then to the left, then toward the right, then in the back of us. As young as we were, we finally figured out that we were surrounded, which we were.

◆ ◆ ◆

THE 424TH COMBAT INFANTRY REGIMENT, one of the three regiments attached to the 106th Infantry Division, survived the initial German onslaught. Some were captured, and the unit suffered

James L. Cooley told his mother he'd be the first American soldier to cross the river Rhine. He was wounded and taken prisoner when the 423rd Infantry Regiment was encircled and cut off from the remainder of the division in the vicinity of Schönberg. They regrouped for a counterattack but were blocked by the enemy and lost to the division on December 18.

heavy casualties during that battle. Nevertheless, it regained its balance and joined forces with the 112th Infantry Regiment of the 28th Infantry Division. The 112th Infantry had been isolated from its parent division by the German thrust toward Bastogne. The two regiments, the 424th and the 112th, continued the fight as a "Combat Team." They succeeded in helping drive the Germans back to the original line during late December and up until January 18, 1945, when they were pulled out of line. Two other converging infantry divisions had "pinched" them out of the line.

By the end of December 16, Maj. Gen. Alan W. Jones had committed all the reserves available to the 106th Division except a battalion of engineers at St. Vith. But reinforcements, hastily gathered by the VIII Corps, First Army, and 12th Army Group, were on the way.

General Hasso von Manteuffel, Commanding Officer, Fifth Panzer Army:
[Note: This is part of the story von Manteuffel recounted to the landlord of a hotel in Weisenbach near St. Vith. The right flank of this army attacked the 106th Division.] The left wing of the LXVI Army Corps was noticeably slower in its advance into the Eifel. This endangered our plan for rapidly sealing off the Schnee Eifel. This, however, was the essential preliminary to the next stage of our advance, which was to be through Schönberg to St. Vith. St. Vith, the center of a considerable road network, was as important a point in this sector as was Bastogne on the army's left flank.

The events of the day (16 Dec) in the area of the army's right-hand corps were disappointing. The corps failed to keep up with the time schedule I had laid down for its advance. I hoped the time lost could be made up by continuation of the attack after dark. I, therefore, spent the night of December 16–17 with the staff of the 18th People's Grenadier Division, which held the key to the operations on this part of the front. Thanks to the energy of the division commander, this division succeeded in capturing Schönberg on the morning of the 17th. This success seemed to show that the corps could now make up the time lost: the events of the day, however, did not realize this hope.

Despite an excellent performance on the part of the troops and the officers of all ranks, the infantry corps was incapable of carrying out the attack with the necessary violence and within the time limit that would ensure cooperation with the army's two Panzer corps. Nor could it quickly capture the vital road junction of St. Vith, which was a pivot in the enemy's defensive position, and which it was essential that we seize for the sake of the operations by the left wing of the Sixth Panzer Army.

The enemy forces threatened with encirclement in the Schnee Eifel attacked westward, straight across the advance of the corps' left-hand battle group. This held the corps up, and it failed to capture St. Vith on the 17th.

Seymour Reitman, 2nd Battalion, 395th Regiment, 99th Division: [Note: Because a majority of the 99th Division sat across a very thin line in the Ardennes region, parts of the 395th Regiment of the 99th were on the offensive. On December 15th, the 395th began its assault on German pillboxes. The soldiers dropped their packs, including their blankets, and took only three days' rations for the attack. Near Rocherath, Germany, the 2nd Battalion of the 395th attacked a group of German pillboxes and managed to capture five of them. Along with the pillboxes, there were thirteen German prisoners taken during the fighting. Reitman describes what happened next after the assault on the pillboxes.] One of our first sergeants said to me, "Take these prisoners back to battalion . . . and I don't care if they get back there."

"Screw you, that's not me," I said.

Troops of the American 7th Armored Division are on the lookout for snipers in the streets of St. Vith, Belgium, January 23, 1945. *Associated Press/U.S. Army Signal Corps*

Three guys took the prisoners, and I never saw any of them again. I would not have shot a prisoner, even if I were ordered to.

During the start of the Bulge, we all heard this tremendous artillery being fired over us at around 0530. We were cut off, and the Germans seemed to ignore us. They knew they had cut off our supplies.

◆ ◆ ◆

FROM THE GERMAN BORDER NEAR Aachen, Germany, to the northern part of France near Metz, American soldiers woke up on December 16, 1944, to the last gamble of the German army. With the green soldiers from the 106th and 99th Divisions fighting in the northern section of the Ardennes against better-equipped and battle-tested German Panzer Divisions, the race to prevent the Germans from making the port of Antwerp began as soon as division commanders received word of the attack.

CHAPTER TWO

THE OFFENSIVE
AND THE ATROCITIES

17 DECEMBER 1944

T HE EVENTS THAT OCCURRED in the small village of
Baugnez, Belgium, are referred to in most history books as the
"Malmedy Massacre," despite the fact that Malmedy is about 5
or 6 kilometers east of the site. Endless testimonies about that particular atrocity have been given, and it has been covered at great length in
many books about the Battle of the Bulge. That the massacre occurred
is an indisputable fact of history, but the circumstances under which it
occurred have been contradicted time and again.

You only have to follow the line of progress (Rollerbhan D) of
Kampfgruppe Peiper to see that it was not an isolated incident; there
were other cold-blooded murders that occurred along the route. In
spite of this, the incident always appears to raise more questions than
answers. Survivors of Battery B of the ill-fated 285th Field Artillery
Observation Battalion have written and rewritten numerous accounts
of their experiences, but what is not so readily available is the testimony of the perpetrators.

The trial—Case Number 6-24 (United States vs. Valentin Bersin
et al.)—was one of the Dachau Trials, which took place at the former
Dachau concentration camp from May 16, 1946, to July 16, 1946. It's
also an indisputable fact that the testimonies of the perpetrators of this
war crime were extracted under duress before the ensuing trial. More
than seventy people were tried and found guilty by the tribunal, and the
court pronounced forty-three death sentences (none of which, incidentally, were carried out) and twenty-two life sentences. Eight other men
were sentenced to shorter prison sentences.

December 3, 1954, little Marie-Claire Bodarwe, daughter of a nearby small café owner and not yet five, puts flowers in the vase at the monument that commemorates the Malmedy massacre. Ten years prior, Nazi storm troopers had shot down disarmed American war prisoners at that spot in Baugnez-Malmedy, Belgium. The slaughter of defenseless soldiers took place after they were captured on December 17, 1944, a day after a German breakthrough marked the start of the Battle of the Bulge, Hitler's final costly attempt to win the war in the West. *Associated Press*

However, after the verdict, the way the court had functioned was disputed, first in Germany (by former Nazi officials who had regained some power due to anti-Communist positions with the occupation forces), then later in the United States (by congressmen from heavily German-American areas of the Midwest). The case was appealed to the Supreme Court, which was unable to make a decision. The case then came under the scrutiny of a subcommittee of the U.S. Senate. A young senator from Wisconsin named Joseph McCarthy used it as an opportunity to raise his political profile. He came to the defense of the convicted men by stating that the court had not given them a fair trial. This drew attention to the trial and some of the judicial irregularities, which had occurred during the interrogations preceding the trial itself.

However, even before the Senate took an interest in this case, most of the death sentences had already been commuted due to a revision of the trial carried out by the U.S. Army. The other life sentences were commuted within the next few years. All the convicted war criminals were released during the 1950s, the last one to leave prison being Jochen Peiper in December 1956.

Manfred Thorn, of the 1st SS Division, Leibstandarte Adolf Hitler, wrote a whole book and released a DVD titled *Mythos Malmedy* in which he claims that the Malmedy Massacre never occurred. After much searching, I (Martin) located him in Nuremberg. His wife, Hazel, a British woman, answered. She seemed to be a very mild-mannered and approachable woman, so I asked if I could speak to Mr. Thorn. I asked him his opinion, which he was quite reluctant to impart when I told him that I was in the process of writing a book with a friend in the United States. He said quite sternly, "The Malmedy Massacre was a setup; it never happened. Those bodies were placed there by U.S. intelligence to appear like they were all massacred. That is the end of it. I don't want to participate further, respect my decision." So ended our discussion.

Some days later, I visited the U.S. cemetery in Neuville-en-Condroz. This cemetery had been the location of the mortuary after the Battle of the Bulge. The bodies of the victims had been brought there for forensic examination and identification. It was more than apparent that many of the victims had been shot at close range due to the nature of the bullet holes in their skulls. Moreover, there's pretty compelling evidence to suggest the 1st SS Division was more than capable of completely ignoring the Geneva Convention rules. The Malmedy Massacre was a pivotal event that changed the psyche of the American soldier during the Battle of the Bulge. There were many massacres during the battle, but when more than eighty-six defenseless soldiers from the 285th Field Artillery Observation Battalion were murdered in a field in Baugnez, Belgium, the war became even more personal for the average GI. The phrase "take no prisoners" became part of the American soldier's motto. Ted Paluch was in one of the halftracks that came under attack while the convoy headed past Baugnez, Belgium, to see how far Peiper's advance had come.

Ted Paluch: On December 17th we [Battery B, 285th Field Artillery Observation Battalion] were in Schevenhutte, Germany, and got our orders to go. We were in the First Army; we got our orders to move to the Third Army. There was a tank column going with us, and they took the northern road and we took the southern road. That would have been something if they had gone with us south. Right before we left, a couple of guys got sick and a couple of trucks dropped out of the convoy, and they were never in the massacre. Also, there were about fifteen sent ahead to give directions and all, and they escaped the massacre.

From the massacre you saw guys . . . they got one guy named Talbert, I remember him, both arms, both legs, across the stomach. He lived to the next day.

We had no idea that it was going to happen. We took a turn, like a "T" turn, and the Germans were coming the other way. We were pretty wide open for I guess maybe half a mile, and their artillery stopped our convoy. We just had trucks, and all we carried was carbines. We might have had a machine gun and a bazooka, but that was about it, we were observation.

They stopped the convoy. We got out, and the ditches were close to five or six feet high because I know when I got in it, the road was right up to my eyes. There was a lot of firing, I don't know what we were firing at or who was firing at anything, but there were a lot of tracer bullets going across the road.

Finally, a tank came down with the SS troopers behind it. They wore black, and on one collar they had a crossbones and skull and the other collar they had lightning. They just got us out, and we went up to the crossroad, and they just searched us there to get anything of value—cigarettes, and I had an extra pair of socks, and my watch, everything like that. They put us in the field there that was their frontline—ours was two and a half miles away in Malmedy. When we were captured and being brought up there, the people who lived there or in that general area brought up a basket. I guess it was bread or something, and they brought it up to them to eat. Every truck and halftrack that passed fired

continued on page 50

JOACHIM "JOCHEN" PEIPER

Joachim "Jochen" Peiper (1915–1976), more often known as Jochen Peiper from the common German nickname for Joachim. Born in Berlin on January 30, 1915, he was a senior Waffen SS officer and commander in the Panzer campaigns of 1939–1945. Initially, he served as an adjutant on Heinrich Himmler's staff before moving on to command various Panzer units within 1st SS "Leibstandarte Adolf Hitler." Himmler was particularly fond of Jochen Peiper and took a keen interest in Peiper's ascension toward command. At age twenty-nine, Peiper was a full colonel of the Waffen SS, well-respected, and holder of one of wartime Germany's highest decorations, the Knight's Cross with Swords, personally awarded to him by Adolf Hitler.

Peiper was a skilled combat leader and took part in a number of major Panzer battles, such as Kursk and Kharkov. His men were fiercely loyal to him; regarded by many as a charismatic leader, he commanded Kampfgruppe Peiper (assigned to the Sixth SS Panzer Army under Sepp Dietrich). During the Battle of the Bulge, Kampfgruppe Peiper advanced to the town of La Gleize, Belgium, before being turned back by American forces and forced to abandon all vehicles, including six Tiger II tanks. Peiper made his way back to German lines on foot with eight hundred men. He was released on parole from prison at the end of December 1956, eventually settling in Traves, Haute-Saône, France, where he worked as a translator. Peiper was murdered in a fire attack on his house on July 13, 1976. The attackers were never prosecuted but were suspected to be French Communists.

Actual location of Malmedy Massacre. *Latchodrom Productions*

Site of the Café Bodarwe. Fifteen-year-old Mr. Pieffer was the only civilian witness to this massacre. Henry Joly was there too, but he sent Pieffer out to see what the situation was as he remained hiding in the cellar of the Café Bodarwe. Some GIs managed to scramble into the café, but the SS set fire to it with flamethrowers and shot them as they attempted to get out of the building. The body of the café owner, Madame Bodarwe, was never recovered. The current resident of this house was married to the widower of Madame Bodarwe, and she clearly remembers hiding in the cellar. Although she didn't see the actual massacre, she gave a detailed account of the events that occurred on December 17. *Latchodrom Productions*

Ted Paluch, 285th Field Artillery Observation Battalion. *Latchodrom Productions*

into the group, and why I didn't get hit too bad . . . I was in the front, right in the front, the first or second or third right in the front. Each track that came around the corner would fire right into the group in the middle so that they wouldn't miss anything, that's why I didn't get too badly hit. We laid there for about an hour, maybe two hours. While we were lying there, they come around, and anyone who was hurt, they just fired and would knock them off.

Someone yelled, "Let's go!" and we took off. I went down the road there, there was a break in the hedgerow, and a German that was stationed there at that house came out and took a couple of shots at me, and I got hit in the hand. If he saw me or not I don't know, he went back and didn't fire me at me anymore. I was watching him come, and there was a well, and I went over there. It was all covered up, and I laid down, and there was a little hill right behind where I was, and I just rolled. I got there, and I started coming in, and I got near a railroad, and I figured it would take us somewhere. I met a guy from my outfit, Bertera, and two other guys—one guy from the 2nd Division, he was shot, and another guy from the 2nd Division. The four of us came in together. It was dark when we got into Malmedy, but we could see some activity.

I thought they would take us back, but they were on the move, so they could not afford to take us back. There were something like seventy-five who were killed right there.

If I had been moaning, I would have been killed then.

◆ ◆ ◆

PALUCH IS ONE OF THE LAST five Malmedy Massacre survivors left in the United States. Later in this volume there's a witness account from a civilian who lived in Stavelot at the time the 1st SS passed through. Read her testimony and draw your own conclusions.

The men who first heard about the massacre were from the 291st Combat Engineer Battalion.

William "Stu" Getz: We [Company C, 291st Combat Engineer Battalion] were at a town called Malmedy, Belgium. There was another outfit coming up, and our colonel told them not to go that way because the Germans were ahead of them. They said they could not disobey their orders. We heard a lot of gunfire for about forty-five minutes, and two or three of the GIs came down from the massacre. They were wounded but survived, and we took them to the medics. Our colonel called up

SHAEF to report what happened. We did not take too many prisoners after that.

◆ ◆ ◆

IT IS NOT OUR INTENTION TO WRITE the definitive account of the events; they've already been covered from virtually every angle. Later in this chapter there are references to the massacre as it was reported to soldiers in the field at the time, and it's their perspective that we want to focus on in this volume.

While the "Battling Babies" of the 99th Division fought with every ounce of strength they could muster in the north, the 106th Infantry Division reported at 1315 that it could no longer maintain contact at the interdivision boundary, and by this time observers had seen strong German forces pouring west through the Lanzerath area. Panic and chaos began to take hold as the young U.S. defenders of a very thinly held line began to feel the extent and ferocity of this German attack.

The intelligence section of the 106th Division staff analyzed the enemy plan correctly in its report on the night of December 16: "The enemy is capable of pinching off the Schnee Eifel." In actual fact, only one German division, the 18th Volksgrenadier, formed the pincers poised to grip the 106th Division. After all, the entire 62nd Volksgrenadier Division stood poised to break through in the Winterspelt area and to strengthen or lengthen the southern jaw of the pincers. Through the early, dark hours of the 17th, the enemy laid down withering mortar and artillery fire on the frontline positions of the 424th Regiment of the 106th Division.

Hubert Laby, a local historian from Stavelot, personally interviewed four U.S. Army survivors of the Malmedy Massacre. He dedicated his life to tracking down the perpetrators of this crime and other members of Kampfgruppe Peiper. *Latchodrom Productions*

While the German forces pounded away relentlessly on the Schnee Eifel and at the harassed defenders of the Elsenborn Ridge, the 1st SS Division poured through the Losheim Gap virtually unmolested. General Courtney Hodges of the First Army decided to plug the southern approaches to the ridge with his tried and tested veterans of many campaigns from North Africa to Normandy. The Germans knew of the 1st Division, the Big Red One. At that moment, they were recuperating after being engaged in heavy fighting during the November offensive and were spread out as far south as Paris. They were hastily summoned to report for duty on the morning of the 17th. By the evening, they were speeding north to protect the southern flank of the Elsenborn Ridge and relieve pressure on the 99th Division.

It should be noted here that one of the most prominent features of the U.S. Army in 1944 was its capacity to displace from one location to another at great speed. Speed and mobility were going to prove key factors in this offensive. The 82d Airborne Division was located at Camps Suippes and Sissonne, France, undertaking normal ground divisional training when, on December 17, 1944, first orders were received to move to the east. Major General James M. Gavin received a phone call while at dinner with his staff, stating that SHAEF considered the situation at the front critical, and that the airborne divisions were to be prepared to move twenty-four hours after daylight, the following day, December 18th.

On both sides of the battle, line reinforcements were on the move, the Germans to close the pincer on the Schnee Eifel troops, the Americans to wedge its jaws apart. The battle had continued all through the night of December 16–17, with results whose impact would only be fully appreciated after daylight on the 17th.

Colonel Mark Devine, the 14th Cavalry Group commander, left the 106th Division command post about 0800 on the morning of December 17 without any specific instructions. The previous evening, V Corps had asked VIII Corps to reestablish contact between the 99th Division and the 14th Cavalry. This call had been routed to Colonel Devine, at St. Vith, who spoke on the phone to the 99th Division headquarters and agreed to regain contact at Wereth. Wereth was to become the scene of one of the most brutal massacres of World War II.

December 17 would go down in history as the day that the Malmedy Massacre occurred, perpetrated by members of

This sequence of photographs shows Kampfgruppe Peiper preparing to move out through the Losheim Gap. Peiper ran into problems soon after he began to move on December 16. Still in Germany, just before the border with Belgium, his route crossed this bridge, which had been blown during the German retreat in September 1944 and hadn't yet been repaired by the engineers. During the night of December 16 and early in the morning of December 17, the Kampfgruppe passed through several small Belgian villages, meeting slight resistance from scattered American forces. Part of Peiper's assigned route consisted of trails that were little more than dirt tracks.

Kampfgruppe Peiper. But that was not the only massacre that occurred on that frozen December day in 1944. Eight GIs were murdered at Ligneuville just outside the Hotel du Moulin, and eleven African-American GIs suffered the same fate at Wereth. (See the table at the end of this chapter.)

Participation by African-American GIs in the Battle of the Bulge is not well known or recognized. The majority of the African-American GIs in World War II, 260,000 in the European Theater of Operations, were simply never acknowledged. They are the "invisible" soldiers of World War II. They include eleven young artillerymen of the 333rd Field Artillery Battalion who were murdered by the SS after surrendering.

The 333rd Field Artillery Battalion was a 155mm howitzer unit that had been in action since coming ashore at Utah Beach on June 29, 1944. Typical of most segregated units in World War II, it had white officers and black enlisted men. At the time of the Battle of the Bulge, the unit was located in the vicinity of St. Vith, Belgium. Specifically it was northeast of Schönberg and west of the Our River in support of the U.S. Army VII Corps and especially the 106th Infantry Division. By the morning of December 17, German troops and armor were penetrating virtually all sectors of the thinly held line. While many personnel tried to escape through Schönberg, eleven men of the Service Battery went overland in a northwest direction in hopes of reaching American lines.

At about 1500 hours, they approached the first house in the nine-house hamlet of Wereth, Belgium, owned by Mathius Langer. The men were cold, hungry, and exhausted after walking cross-country through the deep snow. They had two rifles between them. The family welcomed them and gave them food. But this small part of Belgium did not necessarily welcome Americans as "liberators." This area had been part of Germany before the First World War, and many of its citizens still saw themselves as Germans and not Belgians. The people spoke German but had been forced to become Belgian citizens when their land was given to Belgium as part of the poorly assembled Treaty of Versailles. Unlike the rest of Belgium, many people in this area welcomed the Nazis in 1940,

JAMES GAVIN

In 1942, James Gavin was promoted to lieutenant colonel and attended the Command and General Staff School. Then he joined the United States Army's first paratroop unit. Gavin rose to command the famed 82nd Airborne Division in World War II. Always the first to jump into combat, Gavin led his men on missions in Sicily, Italy, Normandy (providing support behind the German lines for the D-Day invasion), Holland (Operation Market Garden), and the Battle of the Bulge. He became a major general before his thirty-eighth birthday and was widely renowned for his calm leadership in battle.

Some of these captured African-American GIs were savagely executed by the SS in the small Belgian village of Wereth, close to the German border.

and again in 1944, because of their strong ties to Germany. Mathius Langer was not one of these, however. At the time he took the black Americans in he was hiding two Belgian deserters from the German army and had sent a draft-age son into hiding so that the Nazis would not conscript him. A family friend was also at the house when the Americans appeared. Unfortunately, unknown to the Langers, she was a Nazi sympathizer.

About an hour later, a German patrol of the 1st SS Division, belonging to Kampfgruppe Hansen, arrived in Wereth. It is believed that a Nazi sympathizer (possibly the Langer family's friend) informed the SS there were Americans at the Langer house. When the SS troops approached the house, the eleven Americans surrendered quickly, without resistance. The Americans were made to sit on the road, in the cold, until dark. The Germans then marched them down the road. Gunfire was heard during the night. In the morning, villagers saw the bodies of the men in a ditch. Because they were afraid that the Germans might return, they did not touch the dead soldiers. The snow covered the bodies and they remained entombed in the snow until mid-February, when villagers directed a U.S. Army Graves Registration unit to the site. The official report noted that the men had been brutalized, with broken legs, bayonet wounds to the head, and fingers cut off. Prior to their removal, an army photographer took photographs of the bodies to document the brutality and savagery of this massacre.

An investigation began immediately with a "secret" classification. Testimonies were taken of the Graves Registration officers, the army photographer, the Langers, and the woman who had been present when the soldiers arrived. She testified that she told the SS the Americans had left. The case was then forwarded to a War Crimes Investigation unit. However, the investigation showed that no positive identification of the murderers could be found (i.e., no unit patches, vehicle numbers, etc.), only that they were from the 1st SS Panzer Division. By 1948, the "secret" classification was cancelled and the paperwork filed away. The murder of the eleven soldiers in Wereth was seemingly forgotten and unavenged. Seven of these unfortunate men were buried in the American cemetery at Henri-Chapelle, Belgium, and the other four were returned to their families for burial after the war ended. It's remarkable to know that the identities of the Wereth eleven remained unknown, it seemed, to all but their families.

Herman Langer, the son of Mathius Langer, who had given the men food and shelter, erected a small cross with the names of the dead in the corner of the pasture where they were murdered, as a private gesture from the Langer family. But the memorial and the tiny hamlet of Wereth remained basically obscure and were not listed in any guides or maps to the Battle of the Bulge battlefield. Even people looking for it had trouble finding it in the small German-speaking community.

In 2001, three Belgian citizens embarked on the task of creating a fitting memorial to these men and additionally to honor all black GIs of World War II. There are now road signs indicating the location of the memorial.

As the German breakthrough in the Battle of the Bulge got underway, the members of the 291st Engineer Combat Battalion were among the many engineer battalion soldiers who picked up rifles

Hansen's Kampfgruppe did not advance far enough to assist Peiper. The bulk of SS Kampfgruppe Hansen arrived at Petit Spa on December 23, but a Panzerjäger IV accidentally destroyed the bridge by driving over it. After the battle, it was revealed that this group had ordered the massacre of African-American GIs in Wereth.

and fought off the German assault. Throughout the war, the Germans feared and detested the American engineer battalions because not only could they blow up bridges, they could fight off German soldiers just like the infantry. The engineers even had the capacity to take out tanks with explosives and dynamite—these guys implemented multitasking long before it became a contemporary buzzword. After the German army began its thrust through the Ardennes, the 291st was sent to Malmedy, Belgium, and ordered to hold the town at all costs. The engineers set up a series of roadblocks in and around Malmedy, where there were only about 128 men holding the line against the whole Sixth Panzer Army. Their initial roadblocks would be the only barriers between Kampfgruppe Peiper and the roads toward the Meuse River. Since most of the U.S. Army was in disrepair after the first day of the Bulge, the engineers would have to make do with what they had to buy the rest of the American forces time to regroup.

Ralph Ciani swept for mines and was involved in many different actions the 291st took part in during the Battle of the Bulge.

Ralph Ciani: When we [Company C, 291st Engineer Combat Battalion] went into Belgium, we were working at a sawmill in Sourbrodt, and we thought we would be going home for Christmas. In the morning, we saw swastikas on the houses, and we heard shots being fired around but did not know what was happening. When they broke through, we got orders to go to Malmedy and hold it all costs. We went with a company of men, and the heaviest piece of equipment was a bazooka, with only a few mines.

As we were pulling into Malmedy, there was an MP there, and he asked us, "Who are you guys?"

"Engineers," we replied.

"Well, good luck, I am getting the hell out of here," the MP replied.

When we went into Malmedy, we did not know what to expect, and it was scary.

Frank Towers: At about 1000 hours the night of December 17th, our division was ordered to move out—to where, no one seemed to know.

Destroyed buildings create the vista for U.S. First Army soldiers, some in snow camouflage, on reconnaissance in a snowbound street of St. Vith, Belgium, on January 30, 1945, after the city's capture from German forces. *Associated Press*

Just follow the vehicle ahead of you! Soon, we [Company M, 120th Regiment, 30th Infantry Division] were able to realize, by orienting on the stars above, that we were moving south, but to where and why were still big questions.

Finally, in the early hours of the morning, with some of the men still awake and partially conscious and listening to the American Forces Network on their radios, there was a break-in on that frequency by our nemesis and rumor monger, "Axis Sally", the major German propagandist, who informed us, "The 30th Infantry Division, the elite Roosevelt's S/S Troops and Butchers, are en route from Aachen to Spa and Malmedy, Belgium, to try to save the First Army Headquarters, which is trying to retreat from the area, before they are captured by our nice young German boys. You guys of the 30th Division might as well give up now, unless you want to join your comrades of the First Army HQ in a POW camp. We have already captured most of the 106th Division and have already taken St. Vith and Malmedy, and the next will be Liège."

We were stunned, since only then did we have any clue as to where we were going, or the reason for this sudden movement.

The 1st Infantry Division area, U.S. First Army, Sourbrodt, Belgium. Snow and ice have made the roads almost impassable for U.S. Army vehicles. A blizzard was responsible for the gasoline truck (left) skidding off the road, and, as a result, trucks going in the opposite direction are stalled.

John Hillard Dunn: There was a strange quiet Sunday morning the 17th. No rolling thunder of a dawn barrage. A false and temporary optimism . . . from the west we [Company H, 423rd Regiment, 106th Division] heard planes.

A couple of former Air Force men were overjoyed and not above rubbing it in that the planes were coming to our rescue. Then we saw that the P-47s were dumping their loads a long way to our rear. Now we knew that somewhere back there the German spearhead was grinding along. But the P-47s gave us hope that we might be able to break through and reach whatever American forces lay to the west.

Clouds gathered swiftly, and a steady, soaking rain was falling by noon, turning knee-deep snow into ankle-deep mud. Those former Air Force smart alecks didn't have to tell us that ceiling was zero and that the P-47 fliers whose luck hadn't run out were back swigging coffee someplace in France.

Rumors were thicker than rain clouds that afternoon, and as we wallowed about in mud, moving aimlessly from one place to another, we heard that an armored division was battering its way through to us and that we could expect to see Georgie Patton racing around the corner any minute.

By evening the magnitude of the German effort was more apparent. GIs with "rear echelon" patches on their shoulders—and a hunted look in their eyes—begin showing up and offering us the clothes off their backs if we would trade an M-1 for a .45-caliber pistol.

Sunday night is still a nightmare. We holed up in a pinewood, putting our still present prisoners in a three-sided wooden stockade. Two men were assigned to guard them in four-hour reliefs. Another newly made MP and I had a relief to midnight. As we stood there in the drenching rain, he talked almost hysterically of his wife and four children. He's cracking, I thought. Now and then a prisoner wise-cracked in German.

It was necessary for me to leave the stockade to check on our relief. As I returned to the stockade, I could hear muttering and moaning in the darkness. I thought one of the Heinies was sick. But when I drew up to the tall pine that I had used to mark our position, I realized that the moans were from my companion.

He was on his knees in the snow. His hands were raised, and he was crying and praying in a loud, piercing wail. What he had done with his weapon, I don't know. The Heinie prisoners were stirring and jabbering. I had to do it. I swung with my fist as hard as I could on my kneeling buddy.

Harold "Stoney" Stullenberger: Two or three of us [C Company, 55th Armored Engineer Battalion, 10th Armored Division] were in some little town near Metz. It was pretty cold, but we had a chance to take a bath in a stream. It was about three o'clock in the afternoon. A runner came down there and told us we had to get back and get our gear and get ready. We had no idea where we were going.

That first night I stayed in a schoolhouse in Arlon with my platoon, and then the following day, we moved toward Bastogne. We went there around five or six o'clock, and it was quiet. There was no activity at all.

We then moved up to Magaret and stopped between there and Longvilly. The head of the column was all the way up at Longvilly. Our second squad, Wayne Wickert was the sergeant; they were five hundred yards ahead of us. It became dark that first night, and there were a lot of stragglers coming back from the 9th Armored and the 28th Infantry.

They changed the password on us about three or four times, so we figured something was going on, but we still had no idea. So we sat there all night.

John Kline: German activity was reported along our front [M Company, 423rd Regiment, 106th Golden Lion Division] on the 17th (remember the Bulge started on the 16th). The commander called me back to the command post. He informed me that I should be prepared to move my gun to his area to protect the command post. While visiting with him, I noticed that he was very nervous. His .45 Colt pistol was on the table, ready for action. Our master sergeant, who was also present, seemed equally concerned. Later, I was to learn the reason for their anxiety. I suspect, in retrospect, that they had been made aware of the German breakthrough yet did not yet know the importance of the news.

While in the vicinity of the command post bunker, I watched a U.S. Army Air Corps P-47 Thunderbolt chase a German Messerschmitt (ME-109) through the sky. They passed directly in front of us. Our area being one of the highest on the Schnee Eifel gave us a clear view of the surrounding valleys. The P-47 was about two hundred yards behind the ME-109 and was pouring machine gunfire into the German plane. They left our sight as they passed over the edge of the forest. We were told later that the P-47 downed the German ME-109 in the valley.

As it turned out, my machine gun was not moved to the command post. During the night of the 17th we heard gunfire, small arms, mortars, and artillery. We also could hear and see German rocket fire to the south. The German rocket launcher was five-barreled and of large caliber. The rocket launcher is called a "Nebelwerfer." Due to their design, the rockets make a screaming sound as they fly through the air. Using high explosives, but not very accurate, they can be demoralizing if you are in their path of flight.

Clair Bennett: As we [Company F, 90th Cavalry Reconnaissance Squadron (Mechanized), 10th Armored Division] traveled up from Sierck, France, we stopped for about fifteen minutes around 12 o'clock. I did not intend on going to asleep, but I fell asleep. First thing I know someone kicked me in the back down in the turret, I roused, and there's

Longvilly seen from the south. *Public domain*

no doubt that I used the aircom in the tank, which we had for communications, since naturally you can't see each other all the time. With the noise and whatnot it is virtually impossible to hear each other.

I said, "What do you want? What's the problem?"

And George Sutherland, the tank commander, said, "I've been trying to wake you up for the last twenty minutes!" He had his Bostonian slang working on him.

As we continued onward we came to a place, and we were getting pretty darn close to our location. I lost track of the blackout lights, since you can only see for fifty or seventy-five feet. I cut across, and I went through a grove, and I started to go toward a ravine. I went through a German bivouac area, but I finally got back on the road. I could see where other tanks had been, but I was exhausted, there was no question about it.

Nelson Charron: December 17th, we [Company D, 422nd Regiment, 106th Infantry Division] continued to fight; there was nothing else we could do. We all wanted to fight; it was either be captured or killed. The officers told us to surrender, and we had to destroy our weapons. On their tanks they had 88s, and anybody who tried to escape was shot. There was a group who tried to get out, but they did not make it because of those 88s.

At first we walked. There were three thousand of us who were captured, and we walked and walked for about a day and a half, and we were put in boxcars. One night we were bombed by the British, and the Germans locked us in the boxcar, and they left, but they left us to be bombed. Some of the cars were hit, and we lost some men there. The next day, the Germans came back, and then we continued on to Stalag IX-B. They took all the Jewish boys, and they took them down the road and shot them. They massacred them. Just in our barracks there were maybe ten or fifteen of them.

William "Richard" Barrett: The next morning we [420th Field Artillery Battalion, 10th Armored Division] mounted up again and headed out. On the way up there I remember seeing a sign on the side of the road. I was in my machine gun position, and Corporal Dillon was on the other side of the tank. I said, "Dillon that sounds like a name that you might find in a history book, Bastogne, 14 kilometers." That afternoon we pulled through Bastogne, people standing around, watching us drive through, pulled out through town and headed out north and east, set up in the firing position like we normally did out in a field. We got everything set up and got our ammunition ready to go—no firing mission because it was foggy and you couldn't see nothing. They had a sergeant call there. He called all the section chiefs and told them to keep everything because we might have to move fast.

The Nebelwerfer consisted of six barrels on a mobile carriage adapted from the 37mm antitank gun. The six rockets were electrically fired over a period of ten seconds. The weapon was designed to saturate a target with spin-stabilized smoke, explosive, or gas rockets and was used extensively against the 106th Division at the beginning of the battle. GIs referred to them as "Screaming Meemies" and concur that the psychological effect of this weapon was almost as devastating as the physical effect.

John R. Schaffner: The 2nd Battalion of the 423rd Infantry Regiment, in Division Reserve, was ordered to hold positions in front of the 589th [Field Artillery Battalion] while it withdrew to the rear. Meanwhile, the 589th held on in the face of heavy small arms and machine gun fire until the infantry was able to move into position shortly after midnight. About 0400 on the morning of the December 17 our battalion [Battery B, Survey Team] was ordered to move out to the new position. By now the enemy was astride the only exit for the C Battery position so that it was unable to move. The battalion's commanding officer, Lieutenant Colonel Kelly, and his survey officer stayed behind and tried to get infantry support to help extricate this battery, but they were not successful. The infantry had plenty of its own problems.

C Battery was never able to move and was subsequently surrounded, and all were taken prisoner. While all this was happening, I was given orders by Captain Brown to take a bazooka and six rounds and, with Corporal Montinari, go to the road and dig in and wait for the enemy attack from "that" direction. This we did and were there for some time waiting for a target to appear where the road crested. We could hear the action taking place just out of sight, but the battery was moving out before our services with the bazooka were required.

As the trucks came up out of the gun position, we were given the sign to come on, so Montinari and I abandoned our hole and, bringing our bazooka and six rounds, climbed on one of the outbound trucks. I did not know it at the time, but my transfer from A Battery to B Battery was a lucky break for me, since Captain Menke, A Battery's commanding officer, got himself captured right off the bat, and I probably would have been with him. A and B Batteries moved into the new position with four howitzers each, the fourth gun in A Battery not arriving until about 0730. Lieutenant Wood had stayed with the Section as it struggled to extricate the howitzer with the enemy practically breathing on them. Battalion headquarters commenced to set up its command post in a farmhouse almost on the Belgian-German border, having arrived just before daylight.

At about 0715 a call was received from Service Battery saying that they were under attack from enemy tanks and infantry and were surrounded. Shortly after that the lines went out. Immediately after that a truck came up the road from the south, and the driver reported enemy tanks not far behind. All communications went dead, so a messenger was dispatched to tell the A and B Batteries to displace to St. Vith. The batteries were notified, and A Battery, with considerable difficulty, got three sections on the road and started for St. Vith. The fourth piece again, however, was badly stuck, and while attempting to free the piece, the men came under enemy fire. The gun was finally gotten onto the road and proceeded toward Schönberg. Some time had elapsed before this crew was moving.

B Battery then came under enemy fire, and its bogged down howitzers were ordered abandoned, and the personnel of the battery left the position in whatever vehicles could be gotten out. I had dived headfirst out of the three-quarter-ton truck that I was in when we were fired on. I stuck my carbine in the snow, muzzle first. In training we were told that any obstruction of the barrel would cause the weapon to blow up in your face if you tried to fire it. Well, I can tell you it ain't necessarily so. At a time like that I figured I could take the chance. I just held the carbine at arms length, aimed it toward the enemy, closed my eyes, and squeezed. The first round cleaned the barrel and didn't damage anything except whatever it might have hit. As the truck started moving toward the road, I scrambled into the back over the tailgate, and we got the hell out of there.

Headquarters loaded into its vehicles and got out as enemy tanks were detected in the woods about one hundred yards from the battalion command post. Enemy infantry were already closing on the area. The column was disorganized. However, the vehicles got through Schönberg and continued toward St. Vith. The last vehicles in the main column were fired on by small arms and tanks as they withdrew through the town. As the vehicles were passing through Schönberg on the west side, the enemy, with a tank force supported by infantry, was entering the town from the northeast. Before all the vehicles could get through, they came under direct enemy fire.

The A Battery Executive, Lt. Eric Wood, who was with the last section of the battery, almost made it through. However, his vehicle, towing a howitzer, was hit by tank fire, and he and the gun crew bailed out. Some were hit by small arms fire. Sergeant Scannipico tried to take on the tank with a bazooka and was killed in the attempt. The driver, Kenneth Knoll, was also killed there. The rest of the members of the crew were taken prisoner, but Lieutenant Wood made good his escape. His story has been told elsewhere. Several of the other vehicles came down the road loaded with battalion personnel and were fired on before they entered the town. These people abandoned the vehicles and took to the woods, and with few exceptions they were eventually captured.

Robert S. Zimmer: On December 17th, we [1st Platoon, Company A, 22nd Tank Battalion, 11th Armored Division] left our barracks to board a landing ship tank (LST) at the port city of Weymouth. This was our first experience on a U.S. Navy ship. We had bunks with clean sheets and great American chow. Crossing the English Channel was uneventful, with calm seas and clear skies. Entering Cherbourg Harbor, we passed a lot of bomb damage and an American hospital ship loading wounded for evacuation to the States.

Unloading from the LST, our tank had an accident. We were almost the last tank off. The LST carried one company of tanks and being in the 1st Platoon, we were the fourth tank on and the twelfth tank off. The LST, when not carrying cargo, had basketball backboards that swung down so the crew could shoot baskets when not on duty. The vibrations of unloading the tanks caused one backboard to drop down just as our tank was ready to move. Egglington, our gunner, was in the turret and noticed the backboard was down and reached forward to raise it up just as Trevi got the signal to move. Egglington caught his hand between the turret hatch and the backboard. His hand was smashed. He lost three fingers and part of his palm. We had an emergency, as he went into shock. Instead of waiting for an ambulance, we picked up an MP as a motorcycle escort and drove Egglington to the hospital in the tank. What a ride! It was a blackout drive at night. Konigsberg and I held small flashlights to give Trevi what light we could to see where he was going. We had the governor of the tank tied down so our speed wasn't limited to 28 mph. Tankers always tied the governors down because, when we want to move, we want to move! The MPs later said that they didn't know a tank could travel that fast. To make the ride more interesting, the tank had steel tracks. The streets of Cherbourg were cobblestone with streetcar tracks down the center. We made a lot of sparks as we drove through town. At one intersection, another MP was standing astride his motorcycle and put his hand up for us to stop. We couldn't stop and were sliding into him as he scrambled to get out of the way. Then, we had two motorcycle escorts. When we finally got to the hospital, we couldn't find the entrance. We drove around until we found an open door. I carried Egglington up one corridor and down the next until we found someone to take care of him.

When we got back to the company, we found them bivouacked, overlooking the English Channel, opposite the Isle of Jersey. We were there about two days until we got a full load of gas and ammo. We had been half loaded when we left England. We didn't know that the Germans had broken through at what was to become the Battle of the Bulge. We had no news broadcasts or newspapers.

We then began a forced march, which became the longest forced march of any armored division in history. We drove until we ran out of gas. A truck would come up with 5-gallon cans of gas, and we would gas up the tank. The tank held 180 gallons of fuel. We were getting about one mile for every 2 gallons of gas used.

Along the way, we saw many burned out German tanks and artillery pieces. We saw a little train pulled by an engine that burned alcohol. Trevi and I took turns driving. On some hairpin turns, we would spin through a 450-degree turn without even slowing down. We didn't get much sleep. When we got to Paris, they decided to have the division drive through the center of town right up to the Arc de Triumph, where we made a left turn and continued on toward Sissonne. The Germans were broadcasting to the French that they would be in Paris by Christmas.

William W. Fee: We [55th Armored Infantry Battalion, 11th Armored Division] woke up to find it was raining like mad. Our rear tent peg had come out, the back part of the tent had partly collapsed, and some of our stuff had gotten wet. We put on our galoshes, as ordered, and sweated out the chow line in rain and mud. Then we went back and struck our tent, with the rain still coming down heavily. Everything was a sopped, muddy mess, and it was disgusting to roll it all together and cram it and us into the track. I felt terrible, but Wahoo was singing and whistling, making us all feel better. I couldn't understand how anybody could be so cheerful under such conditions.

We rode all day, taking time out at noon for a K ration. It rained at times and was very cloudy the rest of the time. We went through town after town, finally reached the airport at Rennes (the capital of Brittany), and drove down the concrete runways. We pitched our tent right by the track.

As we stood in the chow line, we discussed how long it might be until we'd be dodging bullets. I had a long talk with Wesley Paul, our platoon medic. Nearby, Lt. Charles Hensel was washing up in his helmet with the boys in his platoon. We washed in our helmets, heating the water on the squad's small gasoline stove.

◆ ◆ ◆

SOME YEARS AGO, I (MARTIN) ACCOMPANIED James W. Hanney Jr. and some members of his family back to where he had fought during the Battle of the Bulge. James served with the 168th Engineer Combat Battalion. We even managed to locate what we believed to be the actual foxhole that he dug back in 1944. The soldiers of the battalion were ordered to dig in on the ridge just to the east of St. Vith and hold their positions until they received further orders. I recall asking him how on earth they managed to dig into that frozen ground up there on the ridge. "It was easy," he told me. "We just tossed hand grenades to loosen up the ground and then dug in." For six long days and nights, Hanney and the rest of the 168th resisted sustained attacks of the determined 18th Volksgrenadier Regiment in the most inhumanly cold conditions. It was negative 28 degrees Celsius up there on that small ridge, and they had to contend with a scythe-like wind that skimmed in across the icy hills of the Schnee Eifel. James was eventually wounded and helped down from the ridge by his best friend Frank Galligan.

By December 17, 1944, Allied intelligence had a slightly better idea of the strength and objectives of the attacking German forces. Under mounting pressure, General Eisenhower, at the request of Lt. Gen. Courtney Hodges, the U.S. First Army commander, decided to commit his reserves: the XVIII Airborne Corps. Lieutenant General James Gavin received notification that the 82nd and 101st Airborne Divisions had been alerted to move into action at daylight the following day and head, without delay, toward the town of Bastogne. Lieutenant General Gavin left for Spa, Belgium, and a meeting with Lieutenant General Hodges. On arrival, Gavin received more information regarding the latest situation and was ordered to attach the 82nd Airborne to V Corps and to bolster the defenses in the area of Werbomont, northwest of St. Vith— their mission, to support existing units in the area and block the advance of the Sixth Panzer Army. The 101st Airborne Division, under Brig. Gen. Anthony McAuliffe, established its headquarters in the town of Bastogne to reinforce the defense of this vital location.

For six days and nights, Pvt. James Hanney, along with other members of the 168th Engineer Combat Battalion, resisted sustained attacks by the determined 18th Volksgrenadier Regiment in the most inhumanly cold conditions. It was negative 28 degrees Celsius up there on that small ridge. Hanney was eventually wounded and helped down from the ridge by his best friend, Frank Galligan. For many years after that, Hanney claimed that he still wore three pairs of socks and that his feet hadn't been warm since that long week in 1944. The unit received a Belgian Croix de Guerre and a Presidential Unit Citation.

The troops in Reims boarded trucks and departed with all haste to their allocated positions. Many men were pulled from leave, and many others were devoid of proper equipment or arms, but they were notified that these would be collected at their destination, so they departed with all speed. By 2000 hours on December 18, the lead

Frank Galligan, James Hanney, and Robert Zimman Learning How to Dig In

It was a gloriously warm summer's day as we stood together on the Prumerberg Ridge looking out between the trees at the Schnee Eifel in the distance. He did not actually say much, but he was obviously deep in thought, and his eyes said everything. I recall James telling me that he was a Boston man and not afraid of the cold but that the cold he endured back in 1944 was unlike anything he'd ever experienced. Some years after he had returned to the States, he and his wife moved down to Florida to escape the cold north. Nevertheless, sixty-two years after the battle he still wore three pairs of socks because, according to him, "My feet haven't been warm since the longest week of my life back in 1944." The 168th Engineer Combat Battalion was awarded the Croix de Guerre by Charles, the Prince of Belgium (of the leader after Leopold's abdication for suspected collaboration with the Germans), along with a distinguished unit citation.

We found the name of one of Hanney's friends from the 168th, Robert Zimman, on the MIA wall at Hamm Cemetery. Zimman died while crossing the Rhine River in March 1945. His listing in the American Battle Monuments Commission reads as follows:

Robert Zimman
Private, U.S. Army
Service #31363645
168th Engineer Combat Battalion
Entered the Service from: Massachusetts
Died: 27-Mar-46
Missing in Action or Buried at Sea
Tablets of the Missing at Luxembourg American Cemetery
Luxembourg City, Luxembourg
Awards: Purple Heart with Oak Leaf Cluster

elements of the 82nd had arrived in Werbomont, where they trudged through blizzard conditions along muddy, snow-blocked roads toward their defensive positions.

William Hannigan: I was a member of H Company, 504 Parachute Infantry Regiment [82nd Airborne Division], and we had come off the line for rest and kind of repair. We were in [*sic*] Ramerville in

Donald Zimmerman, 82nd Airborne Division, arrived at the village of Werbomont late in the evening. The thirteen-hour drive in an open truck had made him feel ill. After a few days on the line, he was taken down with appendicitis and removed to an aid station for an emergency operation. *Latchodrom Productions*

William Hannigan, H Company, 82nd Airborne Division. *Latchodrom Productions*

France when the Germans invaded the forest. And we were pulled out on trucks; inadequately armed and given, you know, clothes. We were just pulled out in necessity in this thing. Wasn't well thought out, but we did get up on these trucks and were taken right up to Bastogne.

My brother was at Bastogne, and I always told him that we saved his skinny little butt, but maybe we shouldn't have. And he later on, you know, being a paratrooper and in the 101st and me in the competitive 82nd, whenever he asked how many jumps I'd made, whatever I said, he would add one. Whatever he said, I would add one. And we bought it so many years that we kind of don't know.

Now we went up there and were put in there. We had leadership in Lieutenant Megellas, another special officer named La Riveriera, and Jack Rivers, and we had Ted Finkbeiner, an excellent leader. I asked him just recently, "How come you never had the fear that the rest of us had, normal fear?" and he said, "I grew up in the swamps in Louisiana with a gun in my hand in the woods and the rivers hunting all the time." And he said he found great joy in it. And I thought, well, these people didn't send us into battle . . . they led us, that was important.

Now the battle is a confusion of things that I just know a very small amount about. A couple of things I remember are that toward the end we captured some Germans who'd been pulling back from the Battle of the Bulge, and I asked a noncommissioned officer (NCO) in the German army, "Why when you knew you lost the war did you fight so viciously?" And he said, "My family." He said, "For eight or ten years that's all we had, one another, so we protected and fought viciously for one another." I thought it was interesting. First we got off the trucks in Werbomont and started moving north, and we had engagements then.

It was a question of survival and lack of equipment, and they talked about getting two guys in a hole in the ground. They called it "dig a foxhole." Well, if three guys got in there and you slept "spoon fashion," the guy in the middle got warm, and you did that and turned it over. Now it sounds a little out of sync, but you did some things you normally wouldn't do in order to survive. And I want to tell you that I spent a lot of years trying to forget this and I succeeded.

You know, I went into the war, I went into school for four years and got a degree at the University of St. Thomas. I did forget. Now three movies, *The Longest Day*, *A Bridge Too Far*, and one more, and of course *Band of Brothers*, they stirred up things that I hadn't thought about in years. And I come to this when people ask me and wanna know about how I felt. Well, I buried most of that, and now I'm eating better.

◆ ◆ ◆

THE 101ST ARRIVED AT 1145 on December 18, and at daylight the next morning the soldiers began taking up positions at the roadblocks around Bastogne in support of Team Cherry, Team O'Hara, and Team Desobry at Noville under the command of the distinguished William R. Desobry. The 501st arrived first and moved into areas around Longvilly. The unit proved to be a stubborn barrier that would allow the necessary time to build Bastogne's defenses.

Ralph K. Manley: I was in Paris on a twenty-four-hour pass after we [501st Parachute Infantry Regiment, 101st Airborne Division] just returned from Holland, and a loudspeaker came on saying, "All units report to your units immediately, as quickly as possible, any way possible." So, we returned then from Paris back to our unit and immediately got on what clothes we had. I still had on my class A, of course, for being in Paris, and we loaded onto port battalion trucks—these semi trucks that had four-foot sidewalls on them and open tops—loaded onto those without overcoats and without overshoes and headed toward the Bulge, and it was very cold.

We met troops that were coming out, wounded (this, that, and the other), walking as we crossed paths, us going in, and them coming out—those who were disenchanted, having been overrun by the Germans and so on—a truck with maybe a series of bodies on it, and as one rounded the corner, some of the pieces of bodies fell off the truck. At that time they had grouped together clerks, anybody who was a soldier, to go to the front, and some of those not having seen that just keeled over in their tracks because they had not seen that type of wartime before.

We did not know actually what was going on. As we got back to our unit in Mourmelon, France, then we got our equipment and our guns, and what have you and were on trucks in minutes, headed off to Bastogne. We didn't know the situation, we just knew it was cold, and we had to go as we were without overshoes or overcoats. Again, with zero degrees, you can imagine—in open-air trucks, going there, put in like cattle you might say, on trucks that weren't covered. They were actually port battalion trucks that were used to haul merchandise from the ships out to the warehousing areas, so that's what we rode to Bastogne on. Once we got there, of course, it was just dismount and head up the road to the city, on foot. We just missed others as they were coming out—both wounded, disabled, and what have you, who were hobbling and going out in trucks coming out hauling bodies that had been killed and so on. That's what we met as we were going into Bastogne.

Being a demolitionist, I was out on the edge, in a foxhole. In this case, the ground was frozen, but we were in a barn lot with all the feces and cattle stuff that was coming out, so it was easier to dig a foxhole there. You can imagine what I must have smelled like. We disabled some tanks that were coming through with the bazooka, but they got very close. Often times you maybe had two in a foxhole, but in this case it was just one because the ground was so hard to dig, at least on the surface with the snow. Also, you didn't want to reveal your position because of the black dirt on top of

James Megellas, 82nd Airborne Division, and Ralph K. Manley, 101st Airborne Division. *Latchodrom Productions*

the white snow, so you had to get snow and cover over the soil that you had dug out of the foxhole.

◆ ◆ ◆

OUT ON THE FREEZING PRUMERBERG just east of St. Vith, a few hundred members of the 168th Combat Engineers were fighting tooth and nail against the whole 18th Volksgrenadier, who were attacking their position with devastating ferocity. They had no idea how long they were going to have to hold that ridge. Down in Luxembourg at the Schuman Crossroads, members of the "Bloody Bucket" 28th Division were tenaciously holding back elements of the German Seventh Army. The 28th had been badly mauled in the Hürtgen Forest just weeks previous to the massed attacks into the Ardennes and were due for some seriously needed R&R. They had even spent some time out on the Schnee Eifel before being replaced by the 106th Division in early December. The pace was by now seriously gathering momentum.

The German Sixth Army was responsible for most of the atrocities committed against both U.S. service personnel and civilians in December 1944. By December 20, Peiper's command had murdered approximately 350 American prisoners of war and at least 100 unarmed Belgian civilians, this total derived from killings at twelve different locations along Peiper's line of march.

So far as can be determined, the Peiper killings represent the only organized and directed murder of prisoners of war by either side during the Ardennes battle. The commander of the 6th SS Panzer Army said under oath during the trials of 1946 that, acting on Hitler's orders, he issued a directive stating that the German troops should be preceded "by a wave of terror and fright and that no human inhibitions should be shown."

Place	Prisoners of war killed	Civilians killed
Honsfeld	19	
Büllingen	59	1
Baugnez	86	
Ligneuville	58	
Stavelot	8	93
Chêneux	31	
La Gleize	45	
Stoumont	44	1
Wanne		5
Trois-Ponts	11	10
Lutrebois		1
Parfondruy		24
Petit-Thier	1	

CHAPTER THREE

WE'RE ON THE MOVE

18 DECEMBER 1944

NEWS OF THE MALMEDY MASSACRE had spread like wildfire among the ranks, and some reports stated that rather than frighten the GIs into submission, it had caused the reverse effect. It had galvanized the U.S. troops to put up an even more determined resistance to this massive attack by German forces, and there would be reprisals. Out on the Schnee Eifel, the situation became even more precarious for the 106th Division, which was now almost completely surrounded. Back in Belgium, there was fevered activity as units rushed to plug gaps, stabilize defenses, and bring up reinforcements.

German failure to break through the 99th Division defenses at the twin villages of Rocherath and Krinkelt on December 18 had repercussions all through the successive layers of German command on the Western Front. Realizing that the road system and the terrain in front of the Sixth Panzer Army presented more difficulties than those confronting the Fifth, it had been agreed to narrow the Sixth Panzer Army zone of attack and, in effect, ram through the American front by placing two Panzer corps in column. The southern wing of the 1st SS Panzer Corps, in the Sixth Panzer Army van, had speedily punched a hole between the 106th and 99th American divisions, and by December 18 the leading tank columns of the 1st SS Panzer Division were deep in the American rear areas.

Down in the southern half of the Bulge, rumbling trucks, halftracks, and tanks of the 10th Armored Division entered Luxembourg. They were the first reinforcements who would try to push back the German army's last offensive of World War II. The 10th Armored became the "Ghost Division"; they were not allowed to wear any of their patches on their arms or the insignia that gave away their identities. The Allies wanted to prevent the Germans from discovering that one of Patton's armored units was arriving before the Third Army.

The men of the 10th Armored Division had already faced their baptism by fire in November 1944 in Metz, France, helping take back the city from German control. The 10th Armored "Tiger" Division was due for a rest after fighting in Metz, but once the Germans broke through on December 16, their rest was short-lived indeed. General Patton did not like the fact that he was losing one of his armored divisions, which was ordered to go up and help slow down the German advance before the whole Ardennes region was overrun. The Tiger Division showed its tenacity and held off a larger German force that had already smashed through the initial American lines on December 16 and 17.

On December 18, Col. William Roberts, in charge of Combat Command B, arrived in Bastogne and reported to Maj. Gen. Troy Middleton, commander of Bastogne. Middleton ordered Roberts to block the three most dangerous accesses to the city. As the 10th Armored arrived in Belgium and Luxembourg, the main section of the division was split into three separate teams to help stop the German advance toward the crossroads town of Bastogne, Belgium. The three teams named after their respective commanders were dispatched with all haste. Major William R. Desobry went north to Noville, while a similar group under Lt. Col. Henry T. Cherry wheeled east to Longvilly. Lieutenant Colonel James O'Hara's group shifted southeast to Bras. The rest of the 10th Armored Division was kept in Luxembourg to prevent the Germans from swinging into Bastogne from the south. These three teams would be the first line of defense until reinforcements from the 101st Airborne arrived. The 10th Armored initially faced the full force of that German onslaught alone in those dark December days, before the 101st could get there. Those soldiers displayed remarkable ingenuity and resilience in the most inhumane conditions. They were there for the duration. Wayne Wickert (C Company, 55th Armored Engineer Battalion,10th Armored Division) made the journey up to Luxembourg and spent time in Longvilly, Belgium, with Team Cherry (even though he was part of Combat Command R).

Wayne Wickert: First thing we knew we were in Luxembourg and went to a house and stayed on the third floor. Morning came, and we were on our way. We did not know where, but we found out it was Bastogne. There was always a square in every city, and my truck had to stop, since we were bumper to bumper for quite a few miles. Next thing we knew it was dark, and we did not know where we were, but the German planes were coming over, and they kept telling us, "Don't shoot or else they will drop their bombs on us."

When we arrived to the area around Longvilly, a captain asked me, "Are you an engineer?"

"Yes, sir," I replied

"I may have a bridge for you to blow up," he said.

We slept in the truck during the night and got up in the morning and had our K rations. I walked down the road toward Longvilly, since I wanted to see if I could get my truck down there. I needed the TNT and other equipment down by the bridge. I saw a row of Biblical statues with bars on them on the hillside, and I went to look to see what my approach was and if there was a road to go on. In my truck I had about twenty-five landmines with eight pounds of TNT, and pipes full of TNT in it to shove into roadblocks to clear the way, also a couple of five-gallon cans of TNT for bridges.

When I got back there was not one of my men there. I knew my platoon sergeant was back in Mageret, Belgium. I thought, *If I stay by these vehicles I may get picked off*, because I was visible. I went across the road to a real steep hill, and I got up on the hill so that I was high enough up. I knew they were aiming at my truck because it was full of TNT. I got behind an evergreen tree, and I lay down in a prone position with my rifle up, watching. Next thing I knew I felt something on my neck, and I thought that someone was behind me because I fell asleep, and I was going to get the bayonet. When I pulled myself up my arm started flapping around because of shrapnel.

Along came a medic, and he said, "Did you take your pill?"

"No," I said.

I took the sulfur tablet; I do not know why he did not put a tourniquet on it. The medic said he would send men to get me, and here came a couple of men to come and get me. Then there was small arms fire around. They just grabbed my shirt and started running down the hill, and they were not a bit careful. I was holding my arm, and the bone was sticking out of my arm, and as they carried me the bone got stuck on a tree.

I jumped on a halftrack and held on but asked if I could sit down, I was exhausted. I backed up to the door, and all the blood had accumulated in my sleeve from my elbow. There was a solid clot of blood that slid out of my sleeve, and when it hit the floor, the radioman got sick. He jumped outside, and a machine gun cut loose, and I could hear the tinning on the side of the halftrack. There was a tank there, a Sherman, which shut up the machine gun. When I got to an aid station in a house, they put some dressing on it, put a steel rod on it, and wrapped my arm up close to my body.

They were putting the wounded into the ambulance. The worst were on first, but I was not the worst, so I was not first. All the other wounded were on stretchers, but they were not strapped down, and I was holding on. We were going down the road at sixty miles per hour, and then we heard the sound of a machine gun, sounded like we went about a hundred yards or so and down through the ditch. We went up into the woods and hit a tree, and the ambulance ended up sitting on its left front fender.

I was behind the driver and went flying ahead sixty miles per hour, hit the windshield with my head, and slid underneath the steering wheel with my head resting on the driver's chest. My body was pinning his head over, and I saw that the driver had been shot through his chest, and he was breathing through the holes in his chest since his trachea was pinched. I wanted to get off him, but I could not. The medic could not get the door open, but finally they got it off.

Another man was shot up in the ambulance, and a tank driver was burned so much you could not see any skin on his face, just rawhide. They carried me to a lone brush pile and put brush on me and said they would come back to get me. From noon until about four or five p.m. I slept. I woke up and felt someone pulling off the brush, and Lieutenant Nalsinger from the Recon was there. They put me on a jeep to take me back, and the next thing I knew they were digging for my dog tags, and I could not talk because my mouth was so dry. It was four a.m. I could not talk, so I jerked the guy's pant leg, and he said, "Hey, this one's still alive!"

Due to poor access to provisions during the Battle of the Bulge, German troops often resorted to foraging what they could from POWs and the civilian population of the Ardennes.

They picked me up and said, "We were taking these bodies to the cemetery."

They put me in a room, and they took me out immediately and put me in a German ambulance, which we had captured. We were brought to a house, and right when we were put into the house they gave the order to evacuate immediately, take your wounded and best equipment, and get out of here. Then they brought us to another house where in the living room and in the corner they were sawing off some guy's leg.

A major and captain came back, and I was sitting in a chair when I was in the makeshift hospital, and I was still a bit groggy. They took off the dressing, and they cleaned it up and set the bone back in my arm, and then one doctor said to another, "Where are we going to take it off?"

A medic also had a needle in my vein that was spurting, and I was going to ask him about the needle, but I passed out. When I woke up, the first thing I looked for was my arm, which thankfully was still attached. I received seven pints of blood after that and was transferred to England.

◆ ◆ ◆

THE BATTLE OF THE BULGE WAS OVER for Wayne, but for others it was still going strong. Meanwhile, the situation for the 106th Division was becoming increasingly desperate.

John Hillard Dunn: Monday the 18th, a magic word spread through our bewildered but still hopeful ranks [Company H, 423rd Regiment, 106th Division]—Schönberg. This is a tiny town on the Belgian border. We heard that our 424th—the regiment in reserve—was still holding Schönberg and that there was an escape path from it to the main American forces. So Monday night we sloshed around in a cold rain. Toward dawn we were concentrated on a twisting mountain road that led to Schönberg. But here occurred one of those freaks of battle. Somehow, "Recon" had overlooked a demolished bridge across a narrow mountain run—hardly more than a ditch but deep enough and full enough to stop even a jeep. Our escape to Schönberg was off.

Albert Tarbell: Early in the morning of the 18th, the trucks started arriving and lining up on the company streets. The trucks were Army Air Forces semi-tractor trailer trucks with open tops. We [Company H, 504th Parachute Infantry Regiment, 82nd Airborne Division] started loading onto the trucks, and in no time at all we were out of the area and on our way. Where? We did not know.

What a ride it was. There were a lot of rumors and stories going around. It was shortly after that when it started to rain and sleet. It was a very miserable ride to say the least. We went through villages, towns, and countrysides. All we really knew was that we were on our way back into combat. It was cold and miserable riding in those trucks. We tried to crack jokes and make light of our situation. As we were going through the town, the streets were very narrow, and the buildings were so close together that one could look right into the windows of the homes. There were a lot of people with their heads out of the windows of the homes. I guess they were really encouraging us. There were some young girls looking at us, giggling and pointing to my buddy and me. Our Tommy guns were slung over our shoulders with barrels up. We usually had the tip of the barrel covered with a condom to keep the barrel dry and clean. We had completely forgotten about that, but it sure caught the eyes and attention of the girls. Everyone started laughing, and that kind of took the chill off our minds for a while.

We arrived in Werbomont, Belgium, amid a lot of confusion. It was still daylight, and our trucks were idling until we could move on. We noticed some soldiers coming out of the woods here and there onto the road. There was one NCO, and we tried to get some information from him. He just looked at us, threw his helmet to the ground, and walked off on the road away from us. We figured he was running away from his unit. We eventually ended up around Rahier and set up our CP until we received more orders.

William "Richard" Barrett: On the 18th, we [420th Field Artillery Battalion, 10th Armored Division] moved back through town, and we were moving alongside two-story buildings, and we had some shell fire. They hit a building, and that wounded two or three people. We moved out of our position on the north side of Bastogne. When we left, we left at night. We set up our firing position, but we did not have a lot of firing missions because our forward observers couldn't see anything. You don't know with that bank of fog if you are looking at the muzzle of an 88 or a squad of infantry. So, you're a little on edge. Finally, we got a few missions. Then we got back to where we were, but we were too close—we had to back up, we had to get high so our shell would drop back on the point we wanted to put it.

Troops from H Company, 82nd Airborne Division advance in a snowstorm behind a tank. The packhorse, which was not U.S. government issue, was likely "borrowed" from a local farm. It is a Brabander, a Flemish workhorse, the same breed as was used by Napoleon for his heavy cavalry.

John Kline: Our column [M Company, 423rd Regiment, 106th Division] did not come under fire until we were near our destination, a heavily wooded area (Hill 504) southeast of Schönberg. As we approached the logging trail, near Radscheid, we were shelled by German 88s. My driver drove the jeep into the ditch on the right side of the road. A bazooka-man had hitched a ride on the jeep over the right rear wheel. As we hit the ditch, his weapon fell apart. The rocket fell out and landed in the mud alongside of me, where I had fallen. Fortunately, the bazooka rocket did not arm itself. As I picked myself up, I noticed a pair of German binoculars lying in the ditch. I picked them up and hung them around my neck. They were probably left there by German troops who had been patrolling in this area. I have often thought, "What if they had been booby trapped?"

A point where my memory fails is that I cannot remember what happened during the night of December 18. It would have been logical to set up defensive positions and sleep in shifts, which we probably did. However, my mind is completely blank about the events of that night. M Company men I have met in recent years, 1988 and 1989, tell me that we spent most of the night trying to get our jeeps out of the mud. The number of vehicles on the road and an unusually warm spell caused the fields to be very muddy. The weather turned much colder and stayed that way.

Phil Burge: I remember going through the town of Arlon in the afternoon of December 18. It was a scene out of a Christmas card. It was snowing, but the Christmas lights were on, people were shopping, and it was about the prettiest scene you could ever imagine. After passing through Arlon, we [Company C, 55th Armored Engineer Battalion, 10th Armored Division] made a turn in the road, and the truck headlights showed a sign saying *Bastogne*—white letters on a dark blue background. I had never heard of Bastogne, but something told me that it was a name that I would never forget. We drove through the snow and reached Bastogne by seven or eight p.m., and we spent the first night in the railroad station.

Frank Towers: We [Company M, 120th Regiment, 30th Infantry Division] arrived at the prescribed destination on the afternoon of December 18, and light defensive positions had already been established all around.

Malmedy had not been taken, as Axis Sally had said, and we found that Malmedy had been our objective destination. Malmedy was in our defensive sector, but St. Vith was not, being just south of our sector. However, St. Vith had been captured by the Germans.

Prior to our arrival in Malmedy, it had been hurriedly occupied by the 291st Engineer Combat Battalion, which had hastily erected roadblocks on the most strategic roads and approaches to the town.

Colonel Joachim Peiper was the commander of the 1st SS Regiment, of the 1st SS Panzer Division, the spearhead that was to attack Malmedy. Due to the many defensive roadblocks established by the 291st and the 120th Regiment, Peiper was unable to get into Malmedy, and then he opted to skirt the area to the south and make a dash for Stavelot and Stoumont by "backroads." The main incentive for this routing was to reach our First Army fuel depot at Stavelot, where there were over one million gallons of gasoline. Had they attained their goal, we could not have stopped them, and they would have been on their merry way to Liège and Antwerp. There were no reserve troops in this area to block his advance.

Some of the most intense and vicious fighting of the entire war took place in this area due to the cold weather and lack of warm clothing, food, supplies, and ammunition. Temperatures hovered below freezing during the day, windy and with snow falling on many days, and temperatures running as low as negative 20 degrees Celsius at night.

Seymour Reitman: I marched at 0700, dug in at 1000, did a perimeter defense, and awaited orders. Then I marched two more miles to the rear and did not have any water or rations. We [2nd Battalion, 395th Regiment, 99th Division] set up another perimeter defense, and we marched to Elsenborn Ridge and then marched back. What happened was that the Germans had gotten a hold of our communications and sent us to the Elsenborn Ridge which opened up a large hole for the Germans to go through. There was a tremendous tank battle in Krinkeldt and it was a brutal tank battle to see from a distance. Half the town of Krinkeldt was blown away.

Early on the morning of December 18, Peiper advanced toward Stavelot and then decided to halt for the night. He was probably surprised to find the bridge over the Amblève still intact. Several U.S. units defended Stavelot, but the Germans were able to gain the main road west. The original bridge over the river Amblève at Stavelot was badly damaged during the fighting.

Hans Baumann, 12th SS Hitler Jugend.
Latchodrom Productions

Hans Baumann: Two days into the battle, we [Jagd Panzer IV for the 12th SS Panzer Division "Hitler Jugend"] were getting tired and weary. Most of us hadn't slept since we set off on December 16. Some of us were stuck on the other side of the Elsenborn Ridge. My company encountered very strong resistance at Krinkelt and Rocherath and suffered many casualties there. The 12th SS had been on the move for quite a few days. I recall that it was some time in the late afternoon on December 18 when we advanced again in the direction of these villages.

Almost immediately we came under sustained artillery fire. I was driving a heavy Jagd Panzer and clearly heard the shells whizzing past. Some exploded close by and shook my vehicle. We were very well trained to deal with these situations but didn't expect such a strong fight from the Amis (Americans). Suddenly, I felt a tremendous crash as a shell impacted. I don't know what fired the shell, whether it was artillery or a Sherman. I still don't know.

The small compartment in the Jagd Panzer began to fill with black, choking smoke. I knew that we had been hit. I struggled to open the hatch and free myself. My crew and myself managed to jump out and run for cover. Eventually, we got to the German lines and dressed our wounds. That was the closest that I came to being killed in the battle. Soon after, I was assigned to another vehicle. I spent the next few days driving inside the German lines attempting to procure fuel, but there was none to be had. I even approached some men from the 2nd SS in Noville, but they said that they didn't have any fuel to spare.

Harold "Stoney" Stullenberger: At daylight, the column started to move toward Longvilly, and we [3rd Squad, 3rd Platoon, C Company, 55th Engineers, 10th Armored Division] must have gone a couple of hundred yards before they turned the column around and we parked exactly where we spent the night. We spent the whole day there. We had a trailer that we pulled on the back of the truck that we dumped that because we couldn't turn our vehicle around. We began to get small arms fire off to our southern direction during the day, and we took the .50-caliber off the truck. We also had a lightweight .30-caliber. On the right side there were high-tension poles of cement. We put the guns on the backside of the slope. I could see the German infantry off there, a couple of hundred of yards away. Our squad leader told me to go back to the truck to get a bazooka.

Now, I had never fired a bazooka except for basic training. They don't have much distance, and we had twelve rounds of bazooka we carried. Guys were firing the .50 and .30, so I was firing this bazooka. Half of them were coming in short; we had the thing at big arc to reach the woods. Finally four or five of them went off in the woods; some of them would not even explode when I fired them because they were used for antitank.

We were there all day, till about four o'clock in the afternoon. They started moving toward Magaret, and that's when they found out they could not get in because the column was caught. There was a lieutenant from the artillery, and he told us that if we couldn't move any of the vehicles to put thermite grenades in them. If there were any vehicles there that were abandoned, we could take them. There was an abandoned 90th Reconnaissance Armored car there, and the fellow who usually drove our two and a half ton truck, he said he would drive it if someone drove our truck. They told me to get in with him and get on the .50.

There was a little dirt road that went up toward Bizory. We got up there, and we were bumper to bumper. It was ten or eleven at night, and they threw up flares that lit up like daylight, and they were shelling the heck out of the column. The driver and myself, we were lying under the armored car, and I don't know where this fella came from, but he dove under with us. He was a chaplain who was about my age—I was young at nineteen years old. All at once, I saw our platoon sergeant was in the vehicle behind us, our truck, and he started going forward.

"Where are you going?" I asked.

"I'm going up to find out why we're not moving. We can't just sit here," he said.

We never saw him again. I got a letter from him in April or May, and I found out later that he was taken prisoner that night. There was a lot of shelling for the rest of the night.

Charles Hensel: We [Company C, 291st Combat Engineer Battalion] got up around 0600, got the trucks loaded up with our stuff, and went down the road. We got to the underpass to get to Stavelot, and it was full of tanks of the 7th Armored. I argued with my colonel that they were running away, but he said they were going to another location.

We got down to the underpass, and I told my truck driver to back up and wait for a break in the traffic. And after staying there for a few hours, we finally decided to go back to the chateau.

We pulled up to the chateau, and I got into the chateau, and a lieutenant came out and said, "Boy, am I glad to see you!"

"What?" I said.

"I want you load up into your trucks everything that you can out of the chateau and follow me," he explained.

"We can do that," I replied.

We then pulled behind and followed the jeep and went about ten miles behind where we were, and we arrived in a schoolyard. The lieutenant gave us our orders to be on guard duty for twenty-four hours on and twenty-four hours off. During our off time, we would go to a farmhouse and chase the farmers and stay there during the night, and in the morning we'd return to the schoolhouse where our food was. We stayed there until about January 5th.

Clair Bennett: When we [Company F, 90th Cavalry Reconnaissance Squadron (Mechanized), 10th Armored Division] drove onto the road between Magaret and Longvilly, we arrived near the town of Longvilly around 1600 to find the entrance blocked with the abandoned tanks of the 9th Armored Division. After we helped clear the path, my platoon, first platoon, and another reconnaissance platoon were assigned to do recon work around the Longvilly area. The terrain at that time was muddy and swampy, which was not a problem for our tanks, but the armored cars and the jeep became stuck in the mud, and we had to pull them out of the mud all day long. We arrived at village and began to set up our defenses on the eastern outskirts.

Charles Haug: It was now the morning of December 18. Most of us [112th Regiment, 28th Infantry Division] had lost overcoats on the first day of the attack, and the light jackets we were wearing had no lining. The Germans were now beginning the third day of their attack.

As we sat in our holes, we watched a patrol of about twelve Germans pass through the woods a short distance from us. We were told to hold our fire, and the Jerries didn't spot us. As soon as they were gone, one of our officers told us to crawl out of our holes and head west once more. It would soon be light, and we had to go someplace where we would have more cover. We started walking. About 0600, we came to a small town, and three of our men went into the town to see who was in it. After about twenty minutes, they came back all excited. They said that there were about a hundred men from our division in the town and our morale was lifted 100 percent. Once we were in there, we found that our battalion commander, Colonel Nelson, was in charge of these men. They had been driven from another town the day before, and they were happy to have us join them. We now had a few men from almost every company in our 112th Regiment. Everyone told the same story. They had all been attacked on the first morning, December 16, and most of their men had been either killed or captured.

It didn't take long before it was daylight again. Colonel Nelson and his men had managed to save two of their machine guns, and they set one up at each side of the town. He ordered nearly all of the men to dig in around the town, and the rest of us were to stay in town and help him. Twelve of us were ordered to take care of the ammunition he had saved for the machine guns. He told us that in case we were attacked, it was our job to see to it that we carried plenty of ammunition out to the machine guns. By 0800 everything was still quiet, and we thought our job was going to be easy. The twelve of us started to hunt around in the house where the ammunition was stored. We found a trap door that led to a basement. In the basement we found a wine cellar. Everybody had a drink.

While we were in the cellar, we heard our machine gun on the far side of the town start firing. This meant that the Jerries must be coming again. Wouldn't they give us any peace? Must they attack all the time?

It wasn't long until we heard big shells coming into the town and our riflemen opened up near the machine gun that was firing. We knew now that the Germans were close. We soon found ourselves running and crawling toward the machine gun with extra belts of ammunition.

We got to the machine gun all right, but what we saw coming was not a very pleasant sight. We saw German tanks coming up a road directly in front of us, and German infantry were headed for our town on foot to our left.

Our riflemen and machine guns were firing everything they had at the infantrymen coming across the field, but they kept advancing steadily. By the time the twelve of us were back in town to get our next load of ammunition, the Krauts had knocked out our machine guns. Our colonel could tell that we were outnumbered about ten to one, and it wasn't long until our whole outfit was once more on the retreat. The

Two regiments of the 26th Volksgrenadier Division circled through Longvilly and Luzery with the intention of entering Bastogne from the north via the Noville road. This village was the location of Team Desobry, supported by elements of the 101st Airborne Division.

tanks rolled into town from one side, and we withdrew into the woods on the other. We lost many men.

We made our way into the woods behind the town, and the Germans lost contact with us. Our colonel led us through the woods for about five miles before we stopped to rest. It was now about three o'clock in the afternoon. We all threw ourselves on the ground, and no words were spoken. As we lay there we realized for the first time that we were mighty hungry. Some of our guys had not had a bite to eat for three days now. Many of the rest of us had found food in the basements of the houses in the town we had just been in. Some of us still had hunks of bologna stuffed in our pockets, and we had been eating it as we had been walking. Our colonel decided that each of us should share alike. He made everyone empty all the food we were carrying in our pockets into one pile. He then split it up and each of us got a little something to chew on.

It was now drawing near to the third evening of the German breakthrough. Our colonel told us that we would have to spend the night in the woods. Each of us started to dig a shallow hole. We were in a small wooded area that was surrounded by fields on three sides. In the field were standing many grain shocks that had never been taken in from the last harvest season. Each of us got ourselves one of these grain shocks and dragged it into the woods. We lined the bottoms of our holes with the straw, and as we crawled into the hole, we pulled the remainder of the straw over us to serve as a blanket. We knew that we were going to have another cold night ahead of us.

Just as we were settled for the night, we saw about five GIs coming on foot across the open field. As they got nearer, I suddenly recognized Frankie as one of them, and I ran out to meet them. When I got to them I found that they were five guys from my old company. Besides Frankie, there was Quimby, our first sergeant, and a couple of others. We were all together once again. They told Ken and me that the Germans had attacked them just a short time after we had left on the patrol to the artillery, and also that they were the only ones who managed to keep from getting captured. They had been running and walking now for nearly twenty-four hours straight, and they were completely exhausted. When they got into our woods they just fell on the ground and went to sleep without even digging a hole.

◆ ◆ ◆

JUST SOUTH OF WAYNE WICKERT and "Stoney" Stullenberger, Donald Nichols, attached to Team O'Hara with the 21st Tank Battalion, arrived in the Bastogne area.

Donald Nichols: The next day, December 18, we [Company C, 21st Tank Battalion, 10th Armored Division] traveled on toward our destination, which was to be Wardin, Belgium, passing through Bastogne to get there. We had to pull over to the side of the road during the night to let other units traveling to the rear escape the German drive from their front. We asked where they were going, but the reply was, "Give them Hell Yank!"—our only communication with the retreating soldiers. We did not know it at the time, but the combat command had split the command into three separate task forces, one northeast of Bastogne, one to the east, and one to the southeast in the Wardin area (Task Force O'Hara, the task force that C Company, 21st Tank Battalion was assigned to). The

On December 16, 1944, at 0400, Kampfgruppe Peiper attacked Honsfeld. Opposition had evaporated, and German paratroopers easily took the village. This photograph was taken before the German vehicles ran over and mutilated the bodies.

O'Hara Task Force was in better shape, as far as being up to strength, than the other two. Combat Command B's commander's information was that the main German forces would hit in that area. Fortunately for Task Force O'Hara, the hardest hit was Task Force Cherry to the northeast. C Company, with armored infantry attached, pulled into the Wardin area after dark on December 18 and set up our road-blocking area. The night was uneventful.

William W. Fee: We [55th Armored Infantry Battalion, 11th Armored Division] got up early, took down our wet tent (not as wet as before), and had breakfast in the dark. As we were getting ready to leave, Sergeant Magelli came around and said, "Unload. We may be here as long as a week." (We didn't know about the German offensive and how it had thrown Allied planning into confusion.)

All day long it rained intermittently. In the morning, I cleaned the .50-caliber MG that was mounted on the halftrack. In the afternoon, we were moved twice to nearby locations, and as we were pitching our tent I saw General Kilburn by the tracks. As Jim and I finished putting up our tent, we noticed GIs with large pieces of beaverboard that they were going to sleep on. Lee Hens (Sergeant Ramsay's squad) and I went after some. We went up a gravel field and through an orchard to the highway. There was a house full of bomb casings and another farther on, full of MG ammo for airplanes. I got a wood slab from a bomb crate for me and a piece of tin for Jim. The word came around that we could write letters. After washing up, I wrote in the tent, by candlelight.

W. D. Crittenberger: On the 18th, we [420th Field Artillery Battalion, 10th Armored Division] continued on up to Bastogne. One of the exciting things was that we were given a goose egg, which meant taking a grease pencil on a map and drawing circles around different points we found out. We sent a reconnaissance party into Bastogne, which had been corps headquarters for the Red Cross. They had stripped their classified maps off the wall, but they had left the 1/100,000, which are similar to Esso road maps, and that is what we used to fight with. We were on the east side of Bastogne when we arrived. We had plenty of ammo and refitted some of our weapons, including adding a second machine gun onto our halftrack We were in a position that we could fire support for the three task forces: Desobry, Cherry, and O'Hara. We knew it was going to be a tough fight because the maps were so large, and we sent a chief messenger to each task force to see what was going on. Two of the messengers were fired on with small arms, but they got out. We fought that night and put a minefield out in front of our battalion just in case the Germans kept coming.

Zeke Prust: I was a member of a tank retriever crew [Service Company, 54th Armored Infantry Battalion, 10th Armored Division]. We were supposed to have four men in the crew, but we had three. We had one person who wasn't in combat who fell off the tank and broke his leg. On December 18th, I remember we were about seventy, seventy-five miles south of Bastogne. We were actually going to go to the east, but we were pulled back, and we arrived, specifically my tank, we arrived at four o'clock in the afternoon. We parked the tank next to the hospital on December 18. So then around four o'clock we were just going to get our stuff out of the tank, our sleeping bags to go sleep in beds. Well, we no more got to the steps when all hell broke loose. The shells starting coming in and so forth from the Germans. We did not sleep that night in nice beds; we were actually outside of Bastogne, to the southeast of Bastogne. We hardly moved during the whole time. We maybe moved a mile or two back and forth during the whole month.

Most of them were very concerned because of the ammo. We didn't have ammo, well, we were running out. We also didn't move our tanks as much. We didn't have fuel. We were actually hoping that we got ammo and we got fuel. We were afraid we were going to run out.

The 101st arrived, and I was in the Bastogne area when they came in. We were glad to see them. They were, of course, as I recall, head-quartered in the same place that we were.

We did actually repair and get some jeeps, but we were under cover a lot of the time. We got shelled a lot. We were next to a brick house that had a great brick wall around it, and we thought it was good place to be, even though we slept on the ground and sometimes in the home, which we felt was the safest place. There wasn't anything in the house. The people took everything with them. There was a basement, but we didn't get any large artillery fire, much more small arms fire.

◆ ◆ ◆

PRIVATE FIRST CLASS MASON ARMSTRONG served with F Company, 119th Regiment, 30th Infantry Division. The 30th Division had a bit of a reputation and was occasionally referred to by Mildred Gillars—aka "Axis Sally," who broadcast on German radio during the campaign (the Battle of the Bulge equivalent of "Hanoi Hanna")—as Roosevelt's SS. There is no doubt that Mason Armstrong was an exceptional hero. What he did actually halted one of Peiper's columns in their

A group of refugees heading out of Bastogne. Notice the bomb-damaged buildings behind them. This photograph was probably taken some time after the siege had ended.

tracks, or rather halftracks. We knew that using his bazooka, he'd personally taken out two halftracks belonging to Kampfgruppe Peiper, it says as much on the plaque that extols his action, but that was more or less all we knew about him. Who was he? Our initial research on him did not yield any fruit, but we kept digging.

As with many different armored, infantry, and engineering units during the opening days of Battle of the Bulge, the 30th Division had been rushed in to help stabilize the many different areas in and around the area stretching from just south of Aachen, Germany, all the way down to Wardin, Belgium, just over the Luxembourg border. The 119th Regiment of the 30th Division was one of three infantry regiments, including the 117th and 120th Regiments, sent down to the Malmedy, Stavelot, and Stoumont area of Belgium. With the engineers of the 291st Combat Engineers holding several roadblocks along the main roads, which ran through Stavelot and Malmedy, the 30th Division began to arrive as reinforcements to take over for the engineers. The engineers delayed Peiper long enough for them to blow the Neufmoulin Bridge across Lienne Creek and cause him to split up his tanks in order to get to the Meuse quickly.

As the 30th Division split up to cover the three towns, Company F of the 119th Regiment was sent to prevent one part of Peiper's column from advancing along one of the main roads in the small hamlet of Neufmoulin, which in those days contained only four houses. As night approached, Capt. Edward Arn had his men of Company F set up a roadblock and waited for the German armored vehicles to arrive. Mason Armstrong, a young bazooka man had a machine gunner set up in a window next to him on the second floor of one of the homes (now called Lambotte House), and Armstrong managed to fire three

Lambotte House, Neufmoulin.
Latchodrom Productions

shots as a group of three halftracks full of German infantry came around the corner toward the roadblock. The machine gunner who gave Armstrong cover was killed after one of the halftracks fired at the house. Armstrong survived and managed to take out two of the halftracks and disable the third halftrack. Armstrong's action helped prevent one of Peiper's spearheads from advancing, and once again another part of the German thrust was stopped by a small group of soldiers who were considered by the Germans to be inferior fighters. Captain Arn was commended for the roadblock by Gen. James "Slim Jim" Gavin of the 82nd Airborne, who was keeping tabs on how the 30th Infantry was doing. Arn would submit Armstrong for a Distinguished Service Cross for action, and he would receive it. Even though Armstrong did not talk much about his experiences, Company F would continue to face more action after December 18, and many men were lost, but Armstrong survived. His action on that fateful night changed how the German army its continue their doomed crusade toward the Meuse River.

The battalion report of F Company, 119th Regiment for December 18, 1944 read as follows:

Dec. 18—Bn entrucked and crossed BN IP at 1315 and moved approximately 50 miles to Stoumont, Belgium.
2100—Arrived at the Bn CP in above town.

On December 18, Peiper was forced to divide his armies at Stoumont in a desperate attempt to reach the river Meuse in the west.

Despite having been almost completely destroyed by the Allies during the battle that raged there in September 1944, fighting continued in and around Aachen from September 1944 through February 1945.

Edward C. Arn: Within seconds, I heard a blast from one of the company's bazookas in Neufmoulin. And then another. I discovered later that one of Beaudoin's bazooka men, Pfc. Mason Armstrong, had worked his way from the wooded high ground north of town into the second story of a residence and had fired down on two Kraut half-tracks . . . knocking out both. Several weeks later, by the way, I put Armstrong in for the Distinguished Service Cross (DSC), the nation's second highest award, for this particular action. He got it too. I heard a jeep coming down the highway behind me. I nearly fell down into the Grand Mont rivulet when it pulled up and a tall, lean paratroop officer—with two stars on his helmet—leaped out. "Who's in command here?"

"I am, sir, Lieutenant Arn, F Company, 119th Regiment, 30th Division . . . at your service!" I was flabbergasted and showed it.

"I am Jim Gavin of the 82nd Airborne Division." He waved away my salute, which I brought up from about thirty feet under that road, with a grin. "Looks to me, Lieutenant, as if you've had quite a night of it."

"Yes, sir, we have, but my men have secured Neufmoulin, and we are about to complete its occupation. We have also set up a roadblock."

"Good! You'll be pleased to know that my people will be relieving you here and moving through your positions. We're on the ground now in this emergency. I'll go on up ahead and have a look around if that's all right with you, Lieutenant."

"Yes, Sir!" I responded, with wide-eyed admiration. Major General James Gavin, commanding officer of the very famous 82nd Airborne Division, out ahead of the whole division with a jeep and a driver! I was dumfounded, and so were my men with me.

Just a few yards up the road from that farmhouse there's a monument that was placed by the Belgian government.

This is the only known photograph of Pfc. Mason Armstrong receiving his Distinguished Service Cross. Most members of his family didn't even know he'd earned it because, after he returned to the United States, he very rarely mentioned his exploits.

It reads something like: *Ici l'envahisseur fut arrêté l'hiver 1944 (Here the invader was stopped in the Winter of '44).*

Mason Armstrong was personally responsible for that. One man *can* make a difference.

◆ ◆ ◆

ON DECEMBER 18, EISENHOWER ASKED Patton how long it would take to wheel his Third Army around ninety degrees and attack the Germans to relieve Bastogne. Patton shocked everyone present by announcing confidently that he would attack in forty-eight hours. The Third Army, led by the 4th Armored Division, moved through the Ardennes in a lighting maneuver. It would take them six days to reach Bastogne. Six days was a very long time back in the winter of 1944. In the battle zone the situation was becoming critical. On December 18, the 1st Panzer SS Division, commanded by Obersturmbannführer Peiper, broke through American lines and headed toward Stavelot, Recht, and La Gleize. Neverthless, Peiper's desperate attempts to move on toward Neufmoulin, Trois Ponts, and Stoumont failed because of the heroic resistance of the 119th Regiment, 30th Infantry Division. The 82nd Division had left the base camps at Sissonne and Suippes, France, at 0900 hours. Combat team component march units met at Sedan, France, and proceeded toward Bastogne, Belgium. At Sprimont, Belgium, the head of the division column was directed to proceed to Werbomont. Higher Headquarters had then decided that the division would hold the northern flank of the penetration and that the 101st Airborne Division would hold the southern flank at Bastogne. Roads were clogged with vehicles and refugees. The locations of the German advance breakthrough elements were uncertain. A screening force from the 119th Infantry Regiment (30th Infantry Division) was deployed in the vicinity of Habiémont to cover the assembly of the 82nd Division. Those soldiers arrived at Werbomont at 1730 hours. Defensive positions were organized without delay by each unit upon its arrival. Security and reconnaissance measures were established immediately. The defenses around Bastogne were in place by December 18. Each team was named after its commander.

The battle for Clervaux was a vicious street-to-street battle. The men of the 110th Regiment, 28th Division were well and truly trapped in Clervaux. The Germans were hoping that the encircled Americans would simply surrender, but much to their dismay those U.S. soldiers were more than prepared to fight to the bitter end. By the morning of the 17th, the leading vehicles of the 2nd Panzer were on the ridge that overlooked Clervaux. After a quick review of the situation, their commander decided to bombard the low-lying town from the ridge while other elements of his regiment conducted a double envelopment, capturing the crucial bridge and suppressing any enemy antitank fire.

German shells rained down on the town. Desperate, the town's U.S. commander called in what artillery he could from the 28th Division and ordered his four Shermans to try and silence at least some of the assault guns, which were now among the buildings of the town and were cutting down all in their sights.

Sergeant Frank Kushnir exacted some revenge on the Germans, who were now firing point-blank into American positions. Armed with

On the morning of December 18, 1944, on the road between Poteau and Recht, the U.S. Army 14th Cavalry Group was ambushed by Joachim Pieper's friend, Kurt Hansen, of Kampfgruppe Hansen. Propaganda movies were made by the Germans shortly after this encounter and are still widely used to depict German activity during the Battle of the Bulge.

a bolt-action M1903 Springfield sniper rifle in a tower of the chateau, Kushnir took the opportunity to kill a few careless Germans who were "smoking and joking" outside their armored vehicles instead of being safely inside with the hatches shut.

The struggle intensified, but the Americans refused to surrender as fighting moved like a tidal wave from street to street, house to house, room to room. The fighting continued off and on all day. Still, the Americans held the town. The Germans would push down a block, and the Americans would respond with a withering fire that would slow the advancing German infantry. The Germans would then call up supporting armored vehicles and push back the Americans. Eventually, it became apparent that the Germans were slowly gaining the upper hand.

A monument in Stavelot bears the names of 133 civilian victims of Nazi brutality. These murders occurred in and around Stavelot and were perpetrated by members of Kampfgruppe Peiper. Peiper himself vehemently denied any knowledge or complicity in these acts.

Totally cut off, overwhelmed, and out of ammunition, some of the defenders of Clervaux managed to escape from the battle. There was no formal order of retreat.

Clervaux, however, was not yet completely in German hands. The chateau was still held by fifty or so stalwart souls under Capt. Clark Mackey, commander of the 110th's Headquarters Company, and Capt. John Aiken, Fuller's signal officer. By the afternoon of December 18, totally out of ammunition and with the chateau burning and crumbling around them, the gallant defenders of "Fort Clervaux" finally surrendered.

CHAPTER FOUR

A ROCK AND
A HARD PLACE

19 DECEMBER 1944

BACK IN THE WINTER OF 1944–1945, the GIs of the 106th Golden Lion Division and the 7th Armored discovered that the German border was actually a little too close for comfort. St. Vith is in the German-speaking region of Belgium. It was geographically within the boundaries of Germany until 1919 when the treaty of Versailles allocated it to Belgium. In 1940 it became German again until 1944, and consequently the people of St. Vith were denied all civil rights until 1968. The town was completely devastated during the Battle of the Bulge. Today, if you walk around in St. Vith, there are notice boards displaying before and after photographs of how it looked before the battle and so on.

The monument to the 106th is a little misleading because the 106th was not really in the Ardennes Forest. Most of those soldiers were out on the Schnee Eifel. Although some did make it as far west as Baraque de Fraiture, the bulk of the division was strung out between Schönberg and the Siegfreid Line. Courtney Hodges in the north had somewhat underestimated the situation and stated categorically, "Our position is not critical," but by December 19, this was most definitely not the case. The situation *was* critical, and worsening by the hour. A torrent of information was streaming into the SHAEF HQ in Versailles. The German Fifth Army, lead by Baron Hasso von Manteuffel, was striking with great ferocity against St. Vith, Bastogne, and Houffalize while, slowly but surely, General Eisenhower was beginning to grasp the magnitude of the offensive. These were dark days indeed for the U.S. forces

Trianon Palace Hotel, Paris, France;
SHAEF headquarters in Versailles.
© *Kevin George/Alamy*

in the Ardennes and just over the border in Germany. It was at this point that Eisenhower decided to divide the battlefield in two. He drew a line from Givet beside the Meuse River in the west to Prüm in Germany. All forces north of that line would be allocated to the 21st Army Group commanded by Sir Bernard L. Montgomery while the south side of the line would remain under the command of Gen. Omar Bradley. It's reasonable to state that the appointment of "Monty" in the north did not go down particularly well in some departments.

In the Ardennes, the German attack was gathering pace and momentum. At dawn on December 19, Kampfgruppe Peiper attacked Stoumont. Farther back along the kampfgruppe's route, the fight for Stavelot continued. Both Peiper and his division commander realized that Stavelot was a critical point that must be kept open and under German control at all costs. The 2nd SS Panzer was ordered to attack through Stavelot from the east. Peiper withdrew back into Stoumont during the night of December 19, having been turned back from the alternate route he had tried to reach. He was now essentially cut off in the area of Stoumont and La Gleize, with insufficient fuel to take him farther. He was forced to defend this area and rely on the rest of the division to break through Stavelot and Trois-Ponts to reinforce him. The U.S. Army was feeding more units into the battle to contain and restrain Peiper. While elements of the 30th Infantry Division continued to attack Stoumont from the west, the 3rd Armored Division now entered the battle from the north. Combat Command B of the 3rd Armored operated in three battalion task forces. Task Force Jordan moved toward Stoumont from the north, while Task Force McGeorge and the strongest element, Task Force Lovelady, approached La Gleize along narrow roads from the north and northeast.

Peiper countered the forces approaching La Gleize by pushing out Tigers and PzKw IVs in blocking positions. Task Force McGeorge ran into one of these positions about two kilometers (1.2 miles) north of La Gleize on the road to Bourgomont, where they were prevented from advancing farther. Another German outpost took up a strong position at the Marechal mill south of La Gleize along the road from Trois-Ponts. A German survivor of the encounter recalled after the war that dense, freezing fog severely hampered visibility. At one point, an American dismounted element approached close to the mill, only to be driven back. In the afternoon, the group discovered

During the Battle of the Bulge, Gen. Omar Bradley was the commander of the 12th Army Group. Widely admired and respected by the men under his command, he was often berated by General Patton, who criticized Bradley's close relationship with Eisenhower, with whom he'd attended West Point. Promoted to four-star general on March 12, 1945, he succeeded Eisenhower as army chief of staff in 1948.

Task Force Lovelady moving south on the road from Francorchamps, just to the east of their position. The tank-driver-turned-scout suggested that the Tiger pick off the first tank while the PzKw IV destroyed the last, which would prevent the rest of the tanks from deploying and make them easy targets. Despite this temporary setback, Task Force Lovelady pushed on toward Trois-Ponts, ambushing several vehicles along the way that were moving north to reinforce Peiper. When the lead Shermans of E Company, 33rd Armored Regiment tried to move from Trois-Ponts toward Stavelot, they were driven back by antitank guns and King Tigers, four of which were destroyed.

The Germans fared better in the center (the 20-mile-wide Schnee Eifel sector) as the Fifth Panzer Army attacked positions held by the U.S. 28th and 106th Infantry Divisions. Although the Germans lacked the overwhelming strength that had been deployed in the north, they still succeeded in surrounding two regiments (422nd and 423rd) of the 106th Division in a pincer movement and forcing their surrender. By December 19, the division had been on the continent a little over two weeks, and most of the soldiers were as green as they come. In addition to this, the division had minimal supplies and ammunition, the soldiers were in a forest with small roads and little terrain, and the regiments lacked armored support. Though they regrouped for counterattack, they were blocked by the enemy, and consequently the division suffered 641 killed and 1,200 wounded in these early actions. Around 6,800 soldiers were captured and sent to various POW camps throughout Germany. One of the division's losses in this action was Kurt Vonnegut, who suffered the rest of the war as a prisoner in Dresden and later drew upon his experiences to write his novel *Slaughterhouse Five*. John Hillard Dunn and the 423rd would spend their last days fighting on the Bulge.

John Hillard Dunn: At daybreak of Tuesday the 19th, the 423rd's vehicles were lined up, bumper to bumper, along this narrow road. I lay on the side of the ridge, and in the open. A few of us [Company H, 423rd Regiment, 106th Division] were still guarding the German prisoners. There was a sharp, brisk crack. And I remember asking no one in particular, "Do they know what they're shooting at?" An ex-artilleryman just grunted. But when the second report split the air, his face turned a light shade of chartreuse, and he yelped, "Them ain't 105s, Mac." He scrambled to his feet and dashed into a clump of pine saplings. I lay still, quite unable to believe that the third crack was from an 88 and that treetops were exploding in the woods across the ravine.

I followed the Heinie prisoners into a fire ditch instead of chasing my ex-artillery friend into the pines. By this time, the earth was shaking and the air screaming. The shells came on and on. We were fish in a wide-open barrel. After a lifetime, somebody started shaking me by the shoulder. He started laughing hysterically and asked me in a strangely high voice, "You jerk, can't you hear how quiet it is? Get up. We've surrendered." Down at the bottom of the draw, I came across a truck driver shoving a tracer bullet into his M-1 chamber and backing off to the rear of his truck. Just as he

M3 Halftrack, Stavelot. *Latchodrom Productions*

took a bead on the gasoline tank, a young officer, his face drained to a light yellow, barked, "Stop that, you goddamned fool. You want to get us killed?"

The truck driver and I both gulped and said nothing. But the driver did not lower his M-1.

The officer swung his own carbine.

"Fire into that tank and I'll shoot you," he said nervously.

The truck driver lowered his M-1.

The officer held his carbine to his shoulder and went on, nervously trying to restrain the shrillness of his voice, "The Heinies can see us. And if we start blowing up this equipment, they'll open up on us again, sure as hell."

The driver dropped the M-1. His face was white and his hands fumbled for a cigarette. He tried to spit at the officer's feet, but his mouth was too dry.

This wasn't typical of all our officers; a lot of them died with empty .45s.

Slowly we assembled. Our German prisoners now took over. One of them offered to lead us to the German headquarters, and we took off up the other side of the draw. I fell into step with a staff sergeant. He told me that he had been captured Friday night, had escaped, and had been recaptured Sunday night, only to make his second escape.

A group of dead Belgian civilians. Age and gender were no deterrent to Kampfgruppe Peiper's men. This photograph was probably taken by French war correspondent Jean Marin.

"It's a wonder the Heinies don't shoot me, I'm such a nuisance," he said and grinned.

The words had hardly left his lips when I heard the crack of an 88. Up ahead, as though in slow motion, men tumbled to the ground and there was a horrible scream. Till the day I die, I shall shiver when I remember that I took another step before diving for a rut. I'll never know if this firing was an accident—certainly they didn't annihilate us—but not so long ago a German colonel was executed for the massacre of American prisoners at the same time and only a few miles away at the Belgian town of Malmedy.

It was not until the next day that we knew that our division, as a fighting unit, had been wiped out. All Tuesday night prisoners from the 422nd and the 423rd streamed into the village of Bleialf until it seemed there were thousands there. Subsequently Secretary of War Henry L. Stimson broke all precedent by announcing in January that the 106th Division had suffered 8,663 casualties between December 16th and 21st.

We expected our division general to join us in the Bleialf pigpen any minute. He didn't, but two of his regimental commanders and a lot of other brass did.

Donald Nichols: At daybreak a very heavy fog had moved in, and visibility was very limited, seventy-five to a hundred yards. About 1000 hours, the fog would lift and come back down. At this time, when it lifted again, the forward observer tank, about seventy-five yards to my right front, burst into flames. Sergeant Bulano, the loader, climbed out of our turret running toward this burning tank to help its crew. Due to the enemy fire at this time, we [Company C, 21st Tank Battalion, 10th Armored Division] yelled for him to return, since we needed him also. The tank to my left front about seventy-five yards was hit as it was backing up, and its gunner was killed. It stalled out as it hit a small building behind it, and its crew bailed out and went to the rear.

No one in my tank had observed any enemy tank or force. We were slightly hidden because the terrain was not completely flat but slightly rolling, as farm country is. As mentioned, the fog would rise and fall. At one point in searching with my gunner scopes, I saw a Tiger tank point its nose out of the pine woods about six hundred yards to my front, fire, and back up. I told other crewmembers, but they were unable to see or identify it. After several times of this happening, the tank commander told me to fire on it and adjust my own fire. My first round was a little short, and he (the Tiger) backed up again. My next rounds were over or ricocheted off the trees. One hit the Tiger turret and bounced off but did not explode. These were high explosive shells. I finally told the loader, Sergeant Bulano, to load the HEAT (high explosive antitank), fired, and hit the Tiger as it was rolling back into its pine tree hideout. Saw black smoke and figured it was out. Did not see it or hear from it again. Kill was later confirmed.

More and more enemy fire was coming across our front at the five-hundred-yard distance from a hidden position. We had other C Company tanks ahead and to my right front. To my left front at several hundred yards was a line of trees that hid another road or trail. I began to see vehicle movement, but the vehicles were too obscured to identify whose they were.

We reported by radio and were soon told to move our position to the road and to the rear. Probably moved about a mile or less back and set up a roadblock on the side of the road with the other C Company tanks joining us. We could still see the smoke and explosions from the burning forward observer's tank.

After a short while, there was a German tank firing his 88 shot down the road, narrowly missing our tank. Eighty-eight near misses sound like a freight train passing by at high speed. We were ordered to pull back to a new position at Marvie, which was a small village close to and east of Bastogne. We were posted on one of the main roads into Bastogne. Task Force O'Hara was located in a farmhouse across the road close to where my tank was positioned, to guard that road. One other C Company tank was posted next to me and across the road, and several more were posted as well.

Not much activity the rest of that day or the next, since the Germans were trying to gain access to Bastogne on the other routes. Within a couple of days, probably the 20th or 21st, they mounted an attacking force on Marvie. This was on the other side of the road from me in more of a hidden position, and some trees were between me and that battle. Although I could hear it, I could not see it.

One of our tanks was hit and knocked out with casualties. However, the enemy column of a couple of tanks and a halftrack with infantry was destroyed. One German lead vehicle was able to get into Marvie but had to retire from there. Meanwhile we, or Bastogne, were being surrounded, and some of our tanks were deployed to other hot spots for defense of that area. There were more C Company casualties of men and materials.

One of my friends was in the area, and his tank had to report to O'Hara's command post for orders. He came over to see me and wanted to know if I knew that we were surrounded. I said, "Yes." We talked for a few minutes and decided we

A rare photograph of a King Tiger II with a Henschel turret and a Jagdtiger. The latter was used extensively during the Battle of the Bulge.

Task Force Collins at a farmhouse in Chenogne, north of Sibret. The American column took shelter here while under enfilading fire from a small woodlot close to the road. A nearby tank company turned to deal with this menace and finally suppressed the German fire.

should feel sorry for the "poor bastards" who had us surrounded. We got a laugh out of that.

John Kline: In early morning of the 19th I received orders to position my .30-cal water-cooled machine gun in the edge of the woods overlooking Schönberg. I was high on a hill, several hundred yards from Schönberg overlooking a slope leading into a valley. I could see the housetops of the town.

Company M, 423rd Regiment [106th Division], my unit, was assigned to support the soldiers of L Company, a rifle company, who were preparing to enter Schönberg. They were advancing down the slope, attempting to enter Schönberg along the Bleialf–Schönberg road, which was several hundred yards in front of my gun position in the edge of the woods. The town and area were infested with Germans, but from my position I saw no sign of them. I saw little, except the rooftops of Schönberg ahead of us and a few of our troops on the slope below us.

A rifle company to our rear, I Company, 423rd Regiment, was waiting on orders to proceed down the hill in support of L Company. It was about 0900 when we were suddenly hit by very heavy artillery fire. It seemed that all hell had broken loose. The shells were exploding all around us, on the ground and in the trees. Men were screaming for medics. I heard during the day that M Company's commander, Captain Hardy, had been killed and the executive officer, Captain Wiegers, was blinded by a tree burst. There was a terrible lot of confusion at that time. I thought to myself that the officers could be from one of the rifle companies. That was not so, it was our officers that were hit by tree bursts.

Captain James Hardy, M Company commander, was killed by the very first tree burst as the German shells landed in the woods around us. Captain Wiegers, M Company executive officer, although hit, was not blinded. I learned in 1988 that he rode a tank out of the officer's camp, Oflag 13C, Hammelburg, during an attempted breakout.

During the day, December 19, 1944, Smitty, my gunner, was injured in the leg by an artillery shell. I was hit on the backside of my right boot with the same burst. My right overshoe and combat boot were ripped. I sustained a small wound in the area of the right Achilles tendon. (In the excitement and trauma that followed, I did not realize I had been hit.) It was not serious enough to prevent me from walking and eventually healed. I learned later, in 1987, that Smitty had his leg amputated in a German hospital and had also suffered stomach wounds. His stomach wounds caused him to be unable to continue to work after 1963.

The first hostile artillery barrage, at 0900, was unbelievable in its magnitude. It seemed that every square yard of ground was being covered. The initial barrage slackened after forty-five minutes or an hour. I could hear the men from K and L Companies on the slopes below, screaming for medics. Shortly after that the shelling started again. The woods were being raked throughout the day by a constant barrage of small arms and artillery fire. We were pinned down in the edge of the woods and could not move. I found some protection in a small trench, by a tree, as the shelling started. It must have been scooped out by one of the riflemen the night before. The front of the trench, pointing toward Schönberg, was deeper than the back. My feet stuck up above the ground. I suppose that was the reason I suffered a leg wound. At one point during the shelling, I heard a piece of metal hit the ground. It was a large, jagged, hot, smoking piece of shrapnel, about eighteen inches long and four inches wide. It landed a foot or two from my head. After it cooled off, I reached out and picked it up. I don't think it was a mortar or an 88mm shell. It might have been flak from an antiaircraft shell.

James L. Cooley: So we [423rd regiment, 106th Division] fought there until the morning of December 19th, then we got orders to fight our way out. I guess we were about five miles behind German lines, maybe more. At this time the Germans shelled us, and I got wounded in my left upper arm. I was lucky, of course, during the shelling. I was lying flat on my stomach, and I had my arms over my head. I was lucky it hit my arm instead of my face or something, or going into some other part of my body. So a medic came by in the afternoon and cut off my sleeve and gave me a shot of morphine. But we were out there in the cold, and it was really cold, and on the battlefield and bleeding for the rest of the day. This was also December 19th. About 1730 or 1800 that afternoon or night (Dec 19th) they (the officers) decided to give up. So we destroyed what weapons we had and we gave up. To show the intensity of the battle, I'll kind of go up the line. My captain, Captain Clarkson, was killed. My battalion commander, a lieutenant colonel, was killed. And I'd say we had about oh, 35 percent casualties in our outfit. Anyway, I was captured and I was marched. I don't know, of course, but the body does wonderful things when you have something happen to it. You reach the point where you're just numb. They marched me into kind of a, not a hospital, just a barn where German medics were working on wounded people. I stayed there a day; two days, something like that. They wouldn't look at any Americans. They would look at Germans regardless, and if they got through with Germans, they would start on us. Finally, they took me in and poked around with a needle to find the shrapnel or whatever was in there and could not find it.

Phil Burge: The next morning it continued to snow, and I saw paratroopers from the 101st Airborne Division marching in. They had come in by truck, since it was impossible to drop them in by air. Eventually the whole division of the 101st Airborne was in Bastogne. But we [Company C, 55th Armored Engineer Battalion, 10th Armored Division] were there first, by a matter of hours.

Because I was with the headquarters, supplies were an issue, since they were very low. The 101st set up quarters in a hotel that was already being shelled by German artillery, and since we needed supplies, my friend Ray "Flash" Villard and I were ordered to go there to see what could be done to get us needed supplies. On the way to the 101st's headquarters, I saw something I could not imagine. Remnants of the 28th Division from Pennsylvania were going to the rear, opposite the direction that we were going. Many of the soldiers were wounded and were bandaged up, and almost all of them looked as if they were in shock!

On November 19, 1964, General McAuliffe stands outside the barracks that served as his command post in Bastogne, Belgium. The peaceful fields and quiet villages of Belgium still bear some of scars of the Battle of the Bulge, the costliest battle ever fought by U.S. soldiers in any war. *Associated Press*

When we arrived at 101st Airborne's headquarters I saw General McAuliffe, a one-star general at the time, chewing out some paratrooper who apparently was not in proper uniform. It was something about the tie or neckerchief he was wearing. "Who is this guy?" we both thought, not knowing that he would be a national hero for telling the Germans, "Nuts!"

After we left the 101st headquarters, the shelling in Bastogne became much more serious, and my buddy "Flash" Villard, who was a very devout Catholic, insisted that we stop at a Catholic church so that he could make peace with his maker. He said to me, "Burge, this is our last day on earth, and I'm going to church, no matter

U.S. and Belgian World War II veterans salute during a wreath-laying ceremony at the General Anthony C. McAuliffe memorial in Bastogne, Belgium, December 18, 2004. Belgium and Luxembourg commemorate the Battle of the Bulge, a last-ditch German offensive on December 16, 1944, which was the bloodiest land battle of World War II involving U.S. troops, who suffered some 80,000 casualties, of which 19,000 were killed. *Associated Press/Geert Vanden Wijngaert*

what." So he and I went to church, which was crowded with civilians, even though it was early in the evening. They knew more than we did about the German offensive, since they were all in church.

Harold "Stoney" Stullenberger: We [C Company, 55th Armored Engineer Battalion, 10th Armored Division] got separated, three or four of us from our squad got separated from the ones behind us, it ended up there were about seventeen of us that got together over the hill into a valley away from the column. We decided we would go west, but we started north, where the road was going. I know it was still dark, about four o'clock in the morning, and we were going across this open field, and off in the distance there was woods and a big old barn or house. And somebody shined a flashlight from over in the building. We all hit the ground out in this open field. There was a staff sergeant there, and he was the highest ranked guy.

He said, "I'll circle around and try and find out what it is. If I whistle it's alright to come in."

It turned out it was an aid station for the 101st Airborne, and there was a guy on sentry duty with the flashlight. We went in there. They took care of the wounded, and I slept there.

When daylight came, we walked back to Bastogne, and I found my company headquarters, along with the 1st Squad, which was in reserve with the headquarters. Christmas Day I received my Christmas package: my parents sent me an expensive pen and pencil set.

John R. Schaffner: On December 19, 1944, in the afternoon, what was remaining of the 589th Field Artillery Battalion arrived at the crossroads at Baraque de Fraiture to establish some kind of blocking force against the German advance. There were approximately one hundred men and three 105mm howitzers to set up the defense at this time.

The weather was cold, wet, and foggy, with some snow already on the ground. Visibility was variable, clearing from maybe fifty yards to two or three hundred on occasion.

I didn't know who was in charge of the rag-tag group that I was with until I saw Maj. Elliot Goldstein out in the open, verbally bombasting the enemy (whereever they were) with all the curse words he could think of and at the top of his booming voice. I thought at the moment, *He won't be around too long if there are any Germans out there to hear him.* Apparently there were none, since he drew no fire. I was taking cover behind the rear wheel of one of our trucks and felt rather naked.

The three howitzers were ordered into position to defend the crossroad, and I was told to go out "there" and dig in and look for an attack from "that" direction, still having no idea of the situation. Most of the night we spent in the foxhole. All was quiet on the frontline. When I was relieved during the night to get some rest, I tried to find a dry place in the stone barn to lie down. The floor was deep in muck, but the hay rack on the wall was full of dry hay, so I accepted that as a good place to sleep. Pushing the cows aside, I climbed into the hay. I guess that the cows just didn't understand because they kept pulling the hay out from under me until I became the next course on their menu. Anyway,

Baraque de Fraiture, "Parker's Crossroads," 105mm howitzer. *Latchodrom Productions*

it wasn't long until I was outside in another hole in the ground.

Charles Haug: This night seemed to go by exceptionally slow, and it was the coldest one we [112th Regiment, 28th Infantry Division] had had so far. We all tried to doze off now and then, but it was no use. It was too cold to sleep. It was too cold to do anything. About four o'clock in the morning it started to snow, and it kept getting heavier all the time. By the time it was daylight, there was a real snowstorm on. There wasn't much of a wind, but the snow was

Baraque de Fraiture, 105mm howitzer and monument to the defense of "Parker's Crossroads." *Latchodrom Productions*

coming down so heavy that you couldn't see over a hundred yards in front of you. Our colonel in charge said that this was the chance we had been waiting for. Now we could start moving in the daylight, and the Krauts wouldn't be able to see us.

We had close to two hundred men in our little group now, and soon we were headed west again on the first road we came to. We thought we would keep going until we ran into something. By noon we were still going, and we had not seen any signs of any Germans or any Americans. But all of a sudden, the snow quit falling. We didn't dare stay on the road any longer, and we didn't want to take the chance of getting caught in another town. We came upon a huge chateau, just a few hundred feet from the road, so we moved in and took the place over. There were no civilians around anyplace, so we weren't able to get any information as to whether the Germans had been there or not. We were now back in Belgium, and all of the civilians had been fleeing with the Americans rather than be captured by the Germans again.

We stayed in this old chateau for the remainder of the day and the next night. During the night, we could hear a lot of small arms fire in the distance. This meant that there were other GIs still resisting the Germans close to us. Our colonel sent out a patrol to contact them, and they reported back that these GIs needed help desperately. By dawn we were on our way to help them. We had had no food since the couple bites of bologna the day before, and our stomachs were aching. We soon got to the town they were in, and once more our men started to dig in positions around the town. This time the Germans weren't attacking yet. They were dug in on a hillside about three quarters of a mile from our town, and the only action there was the exchange of small arms fire between our troops and theirs. I went back to my old job as a messenger for our first sergeant, and we organized ourselves as best we could.

We stayed in this town until about noon the following day.

William "Richard" Barrett: The 19th was when the paratroopers came in on trucks. In our course of combat, we [420th Field Artillery Battalion, 10th Armored Division] had been to a lot of battlefields, and we found a lot of extra equipment. Most of our guys would rather have an M1 Garand than their carbines that they carried. So we had a lot of extra guns. The 101st come in, and some of them were picked up off of leave. One paratrooper jumped off a truck wearing his dress uniform and carrying a .45; he jumped off into the snow. We chucked down extra blankets, digging out these extra guns. Our sergeant said load up everything. We had extra ammunition. We had extra everything. We were more than glad to share it, and we did share it. From the 19th, we had firing missions all around, and our observer told us that our last mission that day was for the road we came in on. We had to move, since the enemy was getting close, so we backed off a mile or two.

When we would fire, they told us to look through our barrels. If we saw our tank, they said do not fire, but we were firing between our tanks at a range of six hundred miles. We fired everywhere we could in support, and we were running long on everything, since we were there for so long. We were waiting for the weather to clear and hearing stories about help breaking through. We heard that Patton was supposed to be coming up from the south with a unit to break through to us. We were sending out a unit to get through the lines to get help.

William W. Fee: It was very cold. As Jim [Gavin, 82nd Airborne Division] and I huddled in the front seat of the track, he said that Father Galvin, the Catholic chaplain, had said that we should regard the coming hardships as penance for our sins. We spent the morning straightening up the track. In the afternoon, they tried to keep us busy with drill and PT (physical training—i.e., calisthenics), but I got out of it by cleaning the .50-caliber MG. That night we got the first news of the German breakthrough in the *Stars and Stripes* Army newspaper. I read it by the light of a track's headlight while Lieutenant Murphy shaved by the other.

◆ ◆ ◆

HANS HERBST IS THE MOST energetic veteran we've ever met. He spoke for nearly twelve hours nonstop during our interview. We were all exhausted at that point, but Hans wanted to keep going with his story, below.

Hans Herbst: "The "Windhund" Division [116th German Panzer Division] was one of the most respected divisions in the German army. When we set off, I vividly remember seeing Hasso von Manteuffel standing on a Panther shouting, "Schneller, schneller!" ("Faster, faster!") as we passed toward the Belgian border. It was bitterly cold, and there was no heating in our halftrack, so we did as best we could to keep warm. Shortly after crossing the border, we picked up supplies abandoned by the Amis [U.S. Army]. We had plenty to eat, and I had many cartons of "Lucky Strikes" in the halftrack. We were about a mile from Wibrin heading direct west when the Panther G in front spotted a Sherman beside the church in Wibrin. He fired a round that glanced off the front of the Sherman. Through my field glasses, I saw the whole action.

My platoon disembarked from the halftrack and moved in the direction of the Sherman. As we closed in, the Panther fired another round and another that both missed the target. The Sherman then turned to return fire; the turret slowly turned, and it pointed directly at us, and then there was a huge explosion. The Sherman was out of action. We didn't know what had caused it, though. It was only when I got closer to inspect the damage that I saw what had happened. The first shot had glanced off the front and slightly bent the cannon on the turret of the Sherman so that when he attempted to return fire, his shell got stuck and exploded the turret. It was a very lucky escape. We continued west after that. Our division was one of the few that almost made it to the river Meuse. We also fought the British near Hotton. It was a savage firefight there, and many of our comrades were killed. That was the worst fighting we encountered during the whole offensive.

◆ ◆ ◆

TASK FORCE LOVELADY, comprising 2nd Battalion, 33rd Armored Regiment; 2nd Battalion, 13th Infantry Regiment; 3rd Platoon, B Company, 23rd Armored Engineer Battalion; 1st Platoon, B Co, 703rd Tank Destroyer Battalion; 2nd Platoon, Reconnaissance Company, 33rd Armored Regiment; and 391st Armored Field Artillery Battalion (Direct Support), attached to the 30th Infantry Division (December 19, 1944) in action on the La Gleize road assisting in the capture of Stavelot.

Bob Withers: As the task force moved south, they were met by an enemy convoy of several ammunition trucks, two 150mm towed guns, and a 75mm field piece at the junction of the La Gleize–Stavelot highway. This convoy was destroyed, and a block was established as ordered. The task force then continued south and reached a road junction near Trois-Ponts, where they intended to turn east toward Malmedy. Here they met enemy tank fire and lost the four leading tanks of the column. Since the enemy seemed to be concentrated in some strength between this point and Malmedy, Lovelady set up another roadblock here and left Major Stallings, his executive officer, in charge of this critical position.

So, that's the big picture. Here is my "little picture" within the big picture. This may be a lot about me, but how else can I tell it? This is how I remember it.

As our task force moved south on a small road paralleling the La Gleize highway, we were met and advised by a small group of local men that the Germans were using the La Gleize–Stavelot highway for a supply route. They led us along a paved road to a point intercepting the highway. Sure enough, our timing was, luckily, just right. As my squad and I stood with several of the natives, there on a knoll overlooking the road, we were watching a German convoy passing by. We had no idea how much of it had already gone by and was already way up the road. No way could we resist the opportunity. Without waiting for backup from the task force coming in right behind us, we all opened fire—six carbines, two .30-cal peep-mounted machine guns [*peep* is an earlier term for *jeep*], all pumping gunfire into the German supply trucks. Out of the canvas-covered truck beds came a small stream of enemy soldiers whom we had rudely interrupted on their expected quiet ride back to the rear. They appeared to be unarmed, and as they hit the road they scattered to the far side between the few houses there and disappeared down toward the riverbank. A short description of the area would be a big help here.

The La Gleize–Stavelot highway would be better described as the Spa–La Gleize–Vielsalm highway running from north to south. It is intersected by the Bra–Stavelot–Malmedy road running generally north from Bra. That intersection must have been Trois-Ponts, which is where we lost the four tanks, were stopped dead in our tracks, and were ordered to stay and set up a roadblock. From the map you can see a railroad running alongside the La Gleize road. Not shown on the map is the raging, shallow, narrow, rock-strewn river that also paralleled the road on its east side with grassy, green banks that sloped up into green, forested hills on both sides of the river and road. The terrain strictly limited wheeled vehicles to the road.

At Trois-Ponts, the railroad and the highway had at some time in the past crossed the river and continued on toward Veilsalm, except the bridges were now missing, thanks obviously to a thorough bombing job by our air force. Just before the missing bridges, there was a road junction, a sharp left turn toward Stavelot. The highway tunneled under the railroad by virtue of a rugged stone underpass. This is where we lost our four tanks as they emerged from the tunnel pursuing the enemy convoy and ran unexpectedly into the German antitank guns.

So, there we stayed put for three days. At some time during that first day at Trois-Ponts, we were informed that a unit of the 81st Airborne Antiaircraft Battalion had occupied a village atop the hill across the river and looking right down on us, probably less than half a mile away. They had good news, they had artillery in place some distance to the rear, and they offered us covering fire if needed, in case the enemy was desperate enough to send infantry over the hill to overwhelm us and reopen the road for them.

The bad news was that in order to be effective, they had to have a forward observer in position to observe, and therefore he had to be with us at Trois-Ponts. Even worse, he had to be hard-wired, i.e., by telephone, and connected to his artillery. Radio communication was terrible due to the hilly terrain.

It was our turn again (Recon) to do something useful. Our scout section leader, Second Lieutenant "X" (name long forgotten) was ordered to take two peeps [jeeps], himself, me, and our crews and go back the way we had come to find a way across the river to pick up the artillery observer and also set up the telephone line. It was by then probably late afternoon. All went well. We backtracked past the burnt-out, shot-up convoy, past our entry point, and found a perfectly good stone bridge spanning the river. The highway turned sharply left over the bridge and then sharp right to again follow the river. Right there on the far side was another little village, just a few houses apparently deserted and, fortunately for us, no convoy in sight. Over the bridge, we left the road, turned left, and drove the riverbank back to where we had come from, except across the river. There we found a nice, wide trail through the trees and leading up to the hilltop village occupied by the paratroopers, where we were to pick up the artillery observer. The observer, a captain, was waiting for us, and this is where I got much more personally involved. I got left behind.

The captain was alone and apparently anticipating a long stay, judging by the size of his backpack and bedroll. He immediately commandeered *my* seat in *my* peep. With hindsight, I afterward realized, I was the logical one to leave behind, but at the time I sort of remember my reaction was, "Holy . . . not me!" The plan was this: The observer would be transported back to Trois-Ponts to set up his observation post. I would remain behind till some time after dark and then would guide a wire team down to the riverbank. At a prearranged time, we were to be visually contacted by a group from our task force on the banks of the river, except they would be on the other side about fifty yards away. Major Stallings was to be one of them. Supposedly, before his army career, he was a budding pro baseball player, a pitcher, and his job on this night was to throw a stone attached to a light line across the river à la George Washington and the Potomac. Our job was to retrieve the line, attach the telephone wire, and play it out as it was pulled across the river and onto the observer's telephone. That was the plan. It didn't work out quite like that!

Can you imagine the sinking feeling of loneliness that engulfed me as I stood there in that little town on the hill and watched my squad ride away without me, back home to Trois-Ponts, which at that moment was the only home I knew, temporary as it might be. Anyway, the paratroopers treated me well, fed me, and allowed me to nap indoors. No complaints, baby, it was cold outside.

Sometime before our designated meeting hour, I was awakened with a nudge from a GI boot and brought outside to meet my two companions for the night: two wiremen from the artillery company. They had with them a good-sized reel of telephone wire, its outer end already tied into the wire network connected back at the artillery battery. Compliments of the Airborne kitchen, we got acquainted over a cup of hot coffee before it was time to depart for our rendezvous with Major Stallings.

Anyone who might have been watching would never have been even minutely impressed with our little parade as we marched down the path to the river . . . me in front, leading the way, armed to the hilt, my carbine slung over my shoulder and my .45, unholstered, cocked and at the ready, just in case. The two wiremen, each carrying a .45 but holstered because they needed both hands to shoulder the steel pipe upon which the reel of telephone wire rotated, playing out the wire as we descended down the path through the woods. It was dark in there, just barely enough moonlight filtering through the trees to guide us down. As we emerged from the dark pathway and onto the riverbank, we were suddenly aware that this was a beautiful, clear, cold, bright, moonlit night, and visibility was excellent, so much so that it made us feel like a new actor must feel, spotlighted, in full view of a vast, unseen audience; in our case, not friendly! So, there we were, on the riverbank at the appointed hour, right on plan, except . . . no one showed up on the other bank!

We yelled, we screamed to get attention, all in vain. The rushing river made far too much noise. We had to talk real loud just to hear ourselves. We waited, probably ten minutes. It seemed like an hour as we hunched down trying to be as unnoticeable as possible in the bright moonlight. Still, no one showed up on the other bank. Enough's enough, we were ready to pack it in, call it off, get out of there.

Then, unexpectedly, across the river a back door opened on one of the houses, and a sleepy GI stumbled out onto the deck, slouched up to the railing, zipped open his fly, and proceeded to pee into the yard. We yelled, we screamed, we jumped up and down frantically waving our arms. He never even once looked our way. As he turned and started back toward his waiting, warm bedroll, one of my new companions grabbed my carbine and, cursing like the true paratrooper he was, took aim at the retreating pee-er. I was too numb to even think about stopping this angry, needless killing, but I was wrong about him. It wasn't the GI he took out, it was a windowpane, and it took a couple of rounds to do it, but he got their attention. Our GI disappeared in a flash, well trained as he was. We retreated to the cover of the trees in case they got mad at us and started shooting back. Five minutes later, give or take a few, a small group had assembled on their side of the river. I never found out why they muffed the appointed hour, but they were prepared with Major Stallings on hand with a ball of twine and a preselected missile. There was no shortage of rocks on that crazy river.

So, it was time for the big heave. We couldn't hear each other, but they were only about fifty yards away, and on this bright night we could clearly watch it all. More like an outfielder than a pitcher, Major Stallings, missile in hand, took several running steps forward to gain momentum and with a mighty heave, launched the stone, trailing its long umbilical cord on a high and swift flight toward us. It never made it, falling into the river only a few yards short. Without that trailing cord, it would have been an easy throw for the major, but with that handicap it was impossible. They tried pulling the cord back, but the stone and cord quickly became entangled in the rocky river. Evidently, there was not enough cord left for another try, so that was the end of the mission . . . but only temporarily.

My two companions again came to our rescue. One took off, up the path to the town. His buddy, using hand and body gestures, managed to get his message understood on the other side, that was to stay put, in place until his buddy returned. While we waited, he explained to me that they had done this sort of thing before. They had a grenade launcher, an old rifle, fitted at the muzzle with a cage to hold the grenade and fired by a blank shell. They had left it behind, in the town. Being assured that the major had everything under control, they assumed he had a grenade launcher, not knowing he planned to do it à la George Washington.

We sat there and looked at each other across the river. About fifteen minutes later, the trooper was back, rifle in hand and a tin can full of neatly coiled, fine, strong line. In no time at all, those two were ready to launch the line attached to the dummy grenade. Everything was in place. With the barrel pointed out over the river, the trigger was tripped, and with one sharp crack, away went the grenade, arching out over the river. No problem; it landed way up the bank and was quickly retrieved. On our side the line was cut and securely tied to the telephone wire, a nice smooth join—no knots or protruding bumps that might snag on the rocks. It worked! We made it! On the other side, they hauled it all in, picked it up, and disappeared again, doling out the wire as they went. Mission accomplished . . . but not over.

We three still had a journey ahead of us, to return to our bases. No problem for the other two, they had only to trek back up the hill. They hid the big, wooden wire reel in the trees and tried to make the telephone line as inconspicuous as possible in the grass. With all the cleanup details attended to, we stood there at the foot of the trail, shook hands, and said goodbye. They disappeared! "Cripes!" (That's not what I really said to myself.) "Alone again!"

Back on stage, back in the spotlight . . . how many times must an actor do this before it becomes nonthreatening? I joined the wire reel in the trees and hid in the shadows. The plan was for my peep to come back for me, and it did. I saw them depart, two peeps moving across the spaces between the houses. Did I mention it was cold? No problem staying warm while we were busy, but alone in the shady wood it was frigid. To generate some heat I got moving, back up the river, inside the treeline and out of the moonlight where we had lingered far too long. It took a while, seemed like forever, but my pickup did make it back to me. What a relief! I was heading back home to a house and warm blankets. Oh joy! What a wonderful life . . . in the army and a war on and thinking of a temporary shelter as "home." My poor brain must have been truly running in low gear right then.

So, mission accomplished. Only a couple of gunshots, and they shouldn't count because we were only shooting at ourselves. No enemy encountered, no one even scratched. We were lucky, our timing excellent, for just the next day the German convoy was back and set up its own roadblock, trapping us in Trois-Ponts for the next two days. Our forward observer never once had to order covering artillery fire, the enemy never once came over the hill, but all that should not diminish the deed. We did what was expected of us. 'Nuff said!

Our relief came in the form of infantry. Up the road they came, on both sides, in single file, made the turn under the railroad and kept right on going. Our roadblock mission was over.

So that's my not-so-little story within the big picture.

W. D. Crittenberger: The next afternoon [December 19] after we [420th Field Artillery Battalion, 10th Armored Division] had been fighting there for eighteen or twenty hours, the 101st Airborne dismounted and started marching along, and we saw them marching by. These guys walked into battle with no helmets or overboots, and some of them didn't even have weapons, so we tried to help them. They were gung-ho fighters, but so were we! The first couple of days, we had support from the rear and were resupplied. They liked the armor a lot because we had tanks, jeeps, trucks, and gasoline. We had a good relationship with the 101st.

We were lucky in the armored division, we had gasoline and an engine, so you could stick your C-ration on the manifold to warm it up. It was the poor infantry who had it tough.

Around Christmastime, we only have five or six rounds per gun, so we could only shoot when we had to. What we did to fox the Germans was that we used our colored smoke normally for marking targets for the air force to scare off the Germans, and we used white phosphorus too.

The 101st looked around the town to see what was there, and they found the Red Cross donut supply place. They issued donut flour to all the mess halls and the troops on Christmas morning.

◆ ◆ ◆

NOT ALL THE REGIMENTS attached to the 106th were captured by the Germans. Some individuals took incredible risks to extricate themselves from the situation. On December 19, 1944, elements from the 589th Field Artillery Battalion (106th Division) withdrawing from St. Vith reached the crossroads around 1600 hours. There were just about a hundred men, three 105 howitzer guns, and a few vehicles. The German forces were hot on their trail. Major Arthur C. Parker, who was in charge of this group, immediately understood the strategic importance of this crossroads not only between Vielsalm and Laroche but also between Houffalize (Bastogne) and Manhay, on a wide road that also lead to Liège. Can you imagine the mindset of his troops, though? They'd disentangled themselves from the precarious Schnee Eifel against incredible odds, and now, just as they were heading to safety in the west, Major Parker was asking them to dig in and make a stand! Here Major Parker said, "We will run no more. Here we will stand and fight, and here we will make a difference."

A 7th Armored Division antitank gun covers the approach at a railroad crossing near Vielsalm, Belgium, where the 106th Division has established a new headquarters, December 23, 1944.

Because of the weather conditions and the precariousness of the Ardennes road network, bordered with pine trees or even sometimes swamps, that kind of wide "smooth" road was most important, especially for tanks and hauling vehicles.

So, Parker decided to make a stand there, and the group quickly started to dig in, binding telephone lines, arranging the guns and equipment, laying mines lines, and so on.

In the next hours, Parker and his men got reinforcement from several units on the run, whoever they could convince to start fighting there, right in the middle of nowhere. Among them, a few tanks from the 3rd Armored Division; some paratroopers from the 509th Parachute Infantry Battalion as well as paratroopers from F Company, 325th Glider Infantry Regiment (82nd Airborne); GIs and M8 armored vehicles from the 87th Reconnaissance Squadron, 7th Armored Division; a few halftracks from the 203rd Antiaircraft Artillery, 7th Armored Division; and several 76mm guns from the 643rd Tank Destroyer Battalion. From the 19th until the 23rd of December, the GIs bravely fought off elements of the 560th Volksgrenadier Division and managed to keep the Germans at bay. Ammunition was running low. Parker had been wounded, and against his wishes he had to be driven away from the action.

Then, the 2nd SS Panzer Division "Das Reich" arrived on the scene.

On December 23rd, after a heavy artillery bombardment, the 7th Company, 2nd SS Panzer Regiment, supported by Panzer IV and Sturmgeschütze tanks, launched a final attack. The 2nd and 3rd Battalions of the 4th SS Panzer Regiment "DF" joined then to overwhelm the U.S. positions. At 1900 hours, it was all over. The roads were littered with the wreckage of burning and smoldering vehicles, and during that night a group of GIs surrendered to the German forces. Many had lost their lives during the previous day's encounters.

Nevertheless, a handful of determined GIs had held back the powerful 2nd SS Panzer Division for over twenty-four hours, enough time to save the lives of many other GIs and allow them to organize yet another stand. Many years after the war was over, Gen. James Gavin, who commanded the 82nd Airborne, wrote a personal letter to Major Parker:

The stand that your defenders made at the crossroads was one of the great actions of the war. It gave us at least twenty-four hours' respite, so I thank you for that, and all the brave soldiers who were under your command.

Following is an excerpt from "Morning Reports" of D Troop, 87th Cavalry Reconnaissance Squadron relating to the battle at Baraque de Fraiture, Belgium (Parker's Crossroads) in December 1944:

23 December 1944
Werbomont, Belgium VP5499

Moved CP fr Malempre, Belgium to coordinates VP 5489 at 0800. Moved CP at 1530 [could be 1330] to Manhay, Belgium. At 2300 moved CP to Werbomont. The position at 578852 [WJ: road junction at Baraque de Fraiture] was maintained and held under 8 heavy enemy counter attacks. On the 9th attack it was abandoned by order. All vehicles had been destroyed by enemy action and those still able to leave the position on foot were to do so. The 3 Rcn Platoons held to the last minute, without a man leaving his post till ordered. The MIA list is being held up in hopes some 50 men may return. Though each and every man of this unit knew the fullness of this suicide mission, credit must be given to the fullest extent to the O's and EM for thier [sic] loyalty to dy [sic] in this action as they fully knew that nothing but death awaited them. When the order to abandon post was given they were surrounded on all sides. This unit held this post for 4 days. While there they were under constant small arms and Arty fire. On this date they were subjected to the fury of a full Div.

◆ ◆ ◆

ON THE NORTHERN SHOULDER of the Bulge, previously untried troops of the 99th Division were earning their nickname the "Battling Babies." The nickname was largely due to the young ages of these indomitable men and the fact that they were putting up a major fight against overwhelming odds. Their remarkable defense at the twin villages of Krinkelt and Rocherath was frustrating the German advance and causing them to reroute. At first light on December 19, their movements masked by thick fog, the German grenadiers advanced on Krinkelt and Rocherath. The batteries back on Elsenborn Ridge once again laid down a defensive barrage, ending the attack before it could make any headway. Another advance, rolling forward under an incoming fog at about 1000 hours, placed enemy snipers and machine gunners close to the American positions.

Shortly after noon, a few German tanks churned toward the villages and unloaded machine gunners to work the weapons on derelict tanks that had been abandoned close to the American foxhole line. Apparently the enemy infantry were edging in as close as they could in preparation for a final night assault. Headlong assault tactics were no longer in evidence, however. In the meantime, the defenders picked up the sounds of extensive motorized movements (representing the departing elements of the 12th SS Panzer Division), and a platoon of tanks appeared northeast of Rocherath but quickly retired when artillery concentrations and direct fire were brought to bear.

On December 23, the Seventh Panzer Army was given the task of seizing the important crossroads at Baraque de Fraiture. Ostuf Gresiak led eight Panzer IVs north to the crossroads just after 1620 hours. This location was fiercely defended for four crucial days and nights by U.S. troops and became known as Parker's Crossroads.

Inside the twin villages' perimeter, the defenders were aware that a phase of the battle was ending. Colonel Stokes, the assistant division commander, was preparing plans for a withdrawal to the Elsenborn lines. Finally, at 1345, the withdrawal order was issued and put into action commencing at 1730. The 395th Infantry was to retire from its lines north of the villages and move cross-country west to Elsenborn. The 38th Infantry and its attached units, more closely engaged and in actual physical contact with the enemy, would break away from the villages, fall back west through Wirtzfeld, then move along the temporary road that the 2nd Division engineers had constructed between Wirtzfeld and Berg. Once the 38th had cleared through the Wirtzfeld position, now held by elements of the 9th Infantry and a battalion of the 23rd, it would occupy a new defensive line west and northwest of Wirtzfeld, while the 9th Infantry, in turn, evacuated that village.

The 19th had been a black day indeed for the badly mauled 106th Division. Despite its stubborn defense, things were not looking too good. Elsewhere, the 82nd and the 101st were in position and providing much-needed aid to beleaguered GIs of various other regiments and divisions. Down in Bastogne, the situation was becoming critical. Colonel Cherry had waited through the small hours of December 19 with the comforting assurance that troops of the 101st Airborne Division were moving through Bastogne and would arrive to the east sometime that day. At first light a detachment of tanks and infantry from the *Panzer Lehr* hit the Reconnaissance Platoon, 3rd Tank Battalion, at the Neffe crossroads. The platoon stopped one tank with a bazooka round but then broke under heavy fire and headed down the Bastogne road. One of the two American headquarters tanks in support of the roadblock got away, as did a handful of troopers, and fell back to Cherry's command post, a stone château three hundred yards to the south. Over on the road to Bastogne, the 2nd German Panzer Division clashed with the Noville defenses early on the 19th.

When the 101st was sent into Bastogne, the 2nd Battalion was sent into reserve between Bastogne and Foy, with 3rd Battalion on the left (west) flank. The 1st Battalion got rushed north through Foy into Noville, where the group was joined by Major Desobry of the 10th Armored Division, who was already engaged with his Shermans and tank destroyers from the 709th with several Panzer groups. They repulsed several attacks at the crossroad, including a bitter coordinated tank-infantry charge.

Major Desobry and his tankers cleaned up the German tanks but took horrible losses of their own. The tankers fought almost point blank against Tigers, Mark IVs, and Panthers, all the while under constant artillery barrages. They were flanked a couple of times, but they held the town for two full days, holding up the Germans long enough for the other units to dig in around Bastogne. After those two days of horrible fighting, the surviving Americans were ordered to pull back to the American lines in the Bois Jacques. One of the last things they did before they left was to blow the steeple off the church so that the Germans could not use it to direct fire onto the Americans to the south.

Team Cherry repairing the broken tracks of a temporarily disabled Sherman somewhere near Longvilly. Team Cherry soon discovered elements of the Panzer Lehr on the team's rear. Longvilly was isolated, and it became imperative for Team Cherry to attempt a breakthrough and reopen the road to Bastogne.

During the night of December 19, the 326th Medical Company was overrun by six German vehicles (halftracks and tanks) supported by 100 infantrymen. In that action, the Germans captured 18 American officers and 124 enlisted men, as well as most of the unit's medical equipment and supplies. Major Desobry of the 10th Armored was severely wounded, and his adjutant, Lieutenant La Prade, was killed when an artillery blast sent shrapnel into Desobry's HQ. Desobry was brought to a hospital that had been overrun by the Germans.

As Teams Desobry and Cherry continued to fight the German forces in Noville and Longvilly, the third team of the 10th Armored Division's Combat Command fought just to the southeast of Bastogne. Team O'Hara set up roadblocks around the towns of Wardin and Bras.

On December 19, the senior Allied commanders met in a bunker in Verdun. Eisenhower, realizing that the Allies could destroy German forces much more easily when they were out in the open and on the offensive than if they were on the defensive, told the generals, "The present situation is to be regarded as one of opportunity for us and

This King Tiger II was one of the six left behind by Kampfgruppe Peiper. This sixty-eight-ton tank had a road speed of 35 kilometers per hour and a range of 170 kilometers. It was armed with a 88mm KwK 43 and was protected by 150mm of armor at the front and up to 185mm on the turret. This was most definitely not the right terrain for this tank, and it proved an easy target.

not of disaster. There will be only cheerful faces at this table." Patton, realizing what Eisenhower implied, responded, "Hell, let's have the guts to let the bastards go all the way to Paris. Then, we'll really cut 'em off and chew 'em up." Eisenhower asked Patton how long it would take to turn his Third Army (then located in south-central France) north to counterattack. He said he could do it in forty-eight hours, to the disbelief of the other generals present. Before he had gone to the meeting, in fact, Patton had ordered his staff to prepare to turn north; by the time Eisenhower asked him how long it would take, the movement was already under way. Patton's great counterweight on the British side, Montgomery, was also getting into the picture. To protect the crossings on the Meuse at Givet, Dinant, and Namur, on December 19, Montgomery ordered those few units available to hold the bridges. This led to a hastily assembled force, including rear echelon troops, military police, and Air Corps personnel. The British 29th Armoured Brigade, which had turned in its tanks for re-equipping, was told to take back those tanks and head to the area. XXX Corps in Holland began its move to the area as well.

When CCB of the 10th arrived in Bastogne and was divided into three teams, each named after its leader, Team Desobry was given the task of heading to the northeast and stopping the enemy advance from that direction.

Colonel Roberts, commander of CCB, spoke to the young Maj. William R. Desobry prior to his leaving. Desobry had known Colonel

Roberts well for a number of years and looked upon him as a kind of father figure.

"It will be a close race to get there before the enemy. You are young, and by tomorrow morning you will probably be nervous. By midmorning the idea will probably come to you that it would be better to withdraw from Noville. When you begin thinking that, remember that I told you that it would be best not to withdraw until I order you to do so," encouraged Colonel Roberts

Savage battles around Noville continued for two long days and nights. Fighting from the shelter of the buildings of Noville, Desobry's tanks and infantry exacted a heavy toll on the encroaching enemy forces. During that time, the arrival of a platoon of M-18 Hellcats of the 609th Tank Destroyer Battalion strengthened the sagging American defenses.

After two days of vicious fighting, seventeen German tanks littered the countryside and roadways. Desobry's losses were a handful of tanks and other vehicles. He still held the town, however, though his instincts were telling him it was time to withdraw.

Then the words of his mentor came into his head, "Remember that I told you that it would be best not to withdraw until I order you to do so." He radioed the colonel for that permission. Instead of permission to withdraw, he received news of reinforcement. This included tank destroyers from the 705th Tank Destroyer Battalion and the 1st Battalion, 506th Infantry, 101st Airborne, under Colonel La Prade. He would stay a little while longer.

In total, Desobry's group lost eleven tanks, five tank destroyers, a number of smaller vehicles, as well as two hundred men, half of whom were taken prisoner. The losses they imposed on the 2nd Panzer were impressive. The Germans lost over thirty tanks and an estimated six hundred casualties.

Even more important, their heroic, sacrificial stand at Noville had caused an irretrievable delay of two valuable days in the German schedule.

CHAPTER FIVE

FIGHTING BACK

20 DECEMBER 1944

O N THE MORNING OF December 20, the Americans defending St. Vith held the easternmost position of any organized nature in the center sector of the Ardennes battleground. The most advanced elements of the German drive by this time were twenty-five miles to the southwest of St. Vith. The St. Vith perimeter, now of substantial size, continued to act as a breakwater while other German units forged westward past its northern and southern extensions. As yet, the enemy forces passing to the north and south failed to coalesce to the west of the St. Vith perimeter. The northern penetration, represented at its tip by the 1st SS Panzer Division, remained narrow and road-bound. Well to the rear of the 1st SS, the 9th SS Panzer Division, reinforced by the 519th Heavy Antitank Battalion, was toiling slowly westward on the single free main road, which served as the main supply route for two armored and two infantry divisions. The advance guard had arrived near Recht the previous evening.

The southern advance, which had carried a mass of German armor and infantry from the 47th and 58th Panzer Corps toward Bastogne and Houffalize, had the troops and the maneuver room to constitute a real threat to the southern and western sections of the St. Vith perimeter. The German successes in this area had already isolated the St. Vith forces from the remainder of VIII Corps, although a slim connection remained between the 7th Armored Division rear installations at La Roche and the VIII Corps headquarters at Bastogne. Communication between the 7th Armored rear headquarters and the St. Vith command post (thirty-five miles by road) was extremely difficult. Communication

La Roche-en-Ardenne, like many other towns in southern Belgium, has the distinction of being twice liberated during World War II. The beautiful old town found its river path crossroads right in the middle of the Battle of the Bulge and was liberated once by the Americans in the September 1944 Allied advance, then retaken by the Germans in the Ardennes offensive and re-liberated by the British and Americans in January 1945.

between the VIII Corps headquarters and the St. Vith command post was almost nonexistent, even by radio.

The road to Spa and the First Army headquarters, albeit roundabout and hazardous, remained open on the morning of the 20th. When the 7th Armored Division was decimated by taking on the German armor face to face at St. Vith, the response of the Allied military to the German offensive changed and was, in fact, quite brilliant. Instead of trying to meet the German offensive head on, the plan was to allow the Germans to create an even deeper horseshoe-shaped bulge in the Allied positions while making sure the Allied units on the flanks of the horseshoe were well supplied. Each mile gained in depth by the Germans meant longer supply lines and increased harassment from the lengthening flanks of the horseshoe, which meant that the Germans were forced to use more and more of their resources to guard against attacks on the supply columns.

In the northern sector out on the Elsenborn Ridge, the 2nd Division was holding its own against the 12th SS, and the 99th Infantry Regiment

"Battling Babies" fought hard as well. The battle for Stavelot continued on December 20. Kampfgruppe Sandig attacked repeatedly from the south but could not cross the river. While supporting these attacks, a Tiger was knocked out by an antitank round at the southern approach to the bridge. Since the tank did not catch fire, the crew remained inside until they could escape under cover of darkness. This is almost certainly the same action described by Captain Raney of the 823rd Tank Destroyer Battalion, whose M-10 tank destroyers were firing at the Tigers:

> We saw the long tube of the Tiger's 88mm gun emerge from behind the last building. The M-10 gunner must have been tracking the tank with his telescopic sight, for as the Tiger cleared the building, the M-10 fired one round of armor piercing shot which penetrated the armor on the right side above the track, about 14 inches under the turret and four to five feet to the rear of the front glacis plate. The Tiger stopped in its tracks. . . . Surprisingly the tank did not burn.

Soldiers from the 30th Division inspecting the frozen hulk of an abandoned King Tiger somewhere near Malmedy. Kampfgruppe Peiper had been forced into this area primarily due to concerted defensive actions on the northern shoulder of the battle.

One by one, a few Tigers continued to arrive at Stavelot and assist the battle. However, most were still broken down far behind. Spare parts and fuel were in short supply. Peiper would get no further reinforcements from his heavy tank battalion.

This tank was developed to stop the German Panther and Tiger tanks at long range. Basically, it was an M-10 with a new turret and more powerful gun. The "Slugger" was first used in late 1944 in the Battle of the Bulge, where it notched up impressive scores. Only about 1,500 of these were ever built.

The Germans made a mad dash for an Allied fuel storage facility at Stavelot, where three million gallons of gasoline were stored. The 3rd Armored Division and the 30th Infantry Division beat them to the dump and successfully removed all the gasoline within twenty-four hours. By December 20, the Germans had increased the depth of the horseshoe to fifty miles and the width to thirty miles. On the 20th, German infantry made repeated counterattacks in a desperate effort to recapture Stavelot. Here, the GIs pitted themselves against the 1st SS Panzer Division.

Also on the 20th, General Gavin's 82nd Airborne Division deployed its four regiments along the front lines to the east of Werbomont and immediately went into action. At 1950 hours over in Oufny, the 376th opened fire in the direction of the village of Chêneux. The 319th Battalion moved out at 1900 hours to Goronne, in support of the 508th Regiment, while the 320th Glider Battalion redeployed to the town of Brux near Lierneux during the afternoon, in support of the 325th Glider Regiment. Finally, the heavy howitzers of the 254th Battalion left Werbomont at 1815 hours to settle in position in the vicinity of the town of Lavaux, also in the Lierneux area.

Seymour Reitman: I saw that a few stragglers had joined up with us [2nd Battalion, 395th Regiment, 99th Division], some tankers and anti-aircraftmen. I found a blanket along the way and a large can of string

Close-up of James Megellas' medals. He is the "most-decorated officer in the history of the 82nd Airborne Division," having received a Distinguished Service Cross and a Silver Star and been nominated for the Medal of Honor. As a lieutenant during the Battle of the Bulge, he commanded H Company. *Latchodrom Productions*

beans, which was a whole meal for all of us in the five-man squad. During the offensive, we only had three rations, and that was it. We reached Elsenborn Ridge at night because the 2nd Division opened a line for us. I remember we ended up on a hill, and they drove these mess trucks right on the top of the hill and started to serve breakfast. I dug in a slit trench with another guy, a straggler we picked up as a replacement. Well, the artillery began to fall, and this replacement from St. Louis started shivering because he was so fearful. He was not the only one, but I was used to artillery being fired. I stood up and I said, "Nothing's happening, and if something is going to happen . . ."

Then a shell hit nearby, and I slid back down in the trench. I saw the food was still there, and I said, "To hell with this, I am going to get some food." The replacement had not been with us, so he was not as hungry as I was. I went up with my mess kit and got what they were serving, and when the artillery started up again, I dove underneath the truck. When it ended, I jumped back in my trench and ate my breakfast.

John Hillard Dunn: Early in the morning of Wednesday the 20th, we [Company H, 423rd Regiment, 106th Division] were started on a march to Gerolstein. The Heinies told us that it would take only a few hours. It took eighteen hours, and the distance covered was forty-two kilometers. Because they had no place to confine us at Gerolstein, the Heinies forced us to stand in the cold mud of the road all night. Late Thursday afternoon, December 21, we were finally fed, a bag of hard crackers and cheese; eight men to a twelve-ounce can of what smelled like limburger and tasted as if it had been made in a sewer.

Soldiers from Company C, 1st Battalion, 325th Glider Regiment, 82nd Airborne Division drag a heavily loaded ammunition sled through the snow as they move up for an attack on Herresbach, Belgium.

Thursday evening, we were herded into "40 by 8" cars—sixty men to a car. The most recent passengers had been horses, and nobody had cleaned out after them.

We received no more food nor water for two days—until our train laid over in Limburg. We also had something else that night, Saturday the 23rd—a visit from the RAF. Sweating out a night bombing locked up in a boxcar is no way to enjoy the holiday season, I assure you. The RAF did enough damage to the Limburg railroad yards to hold up our train for another twenty-four hours, but the bombs missed the train. Eight GIs were killed and twenty wounded in another car because they didn't believe a warning that the Heinie machine guns would open up if they tried to break out during the bombing.

Sunday night was Christmas Eve, and we waited—not for Santa Claus, but for the RAF. Limburg wasn't on the schedule, though, and as the weary hours wore on, we took to singing all the Christmas carols and hymns we could remember.

The next morning, we were on our way again and after a few hours reached Bad Orb, Germany, where 1,800 of us from the 106th and 1,400 from the 28th Division were to stay 106 days before our liberation by the Seventh Army in April.

These modified M-10s were faster and more maneuverable than the German Tigers and Panthers, and, carrying a 75mm cannon, they proved to be more than a match for them.

As we marched into Stalag IX-B on a bright, clear Christmas afternoon, somebody recalled the common nickname of the 106th—the "Hungry and Sick." And a soft-voiced Southerner, who was given to leading the hymns and to chewing the tobacco from our soggy butts, said with a disarming solemnity, "Well, I reckon we can always say the Hungry and Sick was the first American division to cross the Rhine."

Many soldiers from the 106th were destined to spend the remaining months of World War II not in the Stalags reserved for POWs. Several hundred who were Jewish or who "looked" Jewish were sent to Berga, a notorious concentration camp of the Third Reich.

Frank Forcinella: We [2nd Regiment, 5th Infantry Division] got notice about the Bulge the day after the Bulge began. It was very snowy and cold in the trucks, and we were up against each other to try and keep warm. We got used to the weather. We were pretty well equipped with ammunition, but we were not prepared for the cold. We had a raincoat, and in the wintertime it would stiffen up. It was not too bad in the rain or snow because you would have a little bit of protection. We did not have white uniforms, but we later received white sheets, and they did work a little bit, but the minute you hit the ground they turned black from the mud.

When we arrived in Luxembourg, we were not far from the front, and we were moving. The area that we hit was defensive because they had foxholes there with logs on top.

John Kline: Left Bleialf at 0630. We [M Company, 423rd Regiment, 106th "Golden Lion" Division] were on the road until 2300 that night. We had no water or food except for the snow from the ground. During the march,

In February 1945, 350 of these American POWs were singled out by the Nazis because they were Jews or were thought to resemble Jews. They were transported in cattle cars to Berga, a concentration camp in eastern Germany, and put to work as slave laborers, mining tunnels for a planned underground synthetic-fuel factory. This was the only incident of its kind during World War II. Starved and brutalized, the GIs were denied their rights as prisoners of war, their ordeal culminating in a death march that was halted by liberation near the Czech border. Twenty percent of these soldiers—more than seventy of them—perished. After the war, Berga was virtually forgotten, and the experiences of these Americans were buried.

as we were going through a very small village, the Germans stopped us in front of some civilians. They made us take off our overshoes and give them to the civilians. That was when I discovered that my right overshoe had been ripped open on the backside by shrapnel. The shrapnel had cut through my backside of my rubber overshoe, leather combat boot, and heavy sock. It had then cut around but not through my Achilles tendon. It was a small wound, but had it gone any deeper it would have cut my tendon, and I would have been unable to walk. There was much evidence, in the area, that a large-scale battle had taken place. I remember, as we were leaving Bleialf, walking through a small village. It could have been outskirts of Bleialf, or some small village nearby. There were German troops in American jeeps.

They were opening ration boxes and meat cans. They were eating our Christmas dinner. My guess is that this had been our battalion supply depot. As we walked through the area, I was surprised to see my jeep with four Germans in it. I was positive it was mine. I had personally painted my son's name, *Teddie*, on the jeep, and the name was there. There had been a real shootout, with hand-to-hand fighting. There were dead Americans and Germans lying in doors and ditches and hanging out of windows. The infighting must have been fierce, for some of the bodies were on top of each other.

As we left the town and just before we made a slight right turn that led us into the country, I saw a two-story stone building. Its upper floor was occupied by several young women, who waved at us through the open windows as we went by. I have often wondered if they were brought along by the Germans. The road we were on eventually took us through Prüm, Germany, the town that I could see from our positions on the Schnee Eifel. We ended up that evening sleeping in an open field near Gerolstein, Germany.

Charles Haug: Several waves of Germans hit our positions [112th Regiment, 28th Infantry Division] on the edge of town during this time, but all of them were repelled by our troops. On one attack, our men captured about ten Krauts, and they were brought into the town for questioning. The guys we were helping in the town still had a radio

These 101st Engineers are moving up through a wooded area in northern Luxembourg. Dense forests and steep hills are typical characteristics of this area.

set with them, and they were constantly trying to contact some of our troops in the rear to see if there was any help headed in our direction. Several times they were able to contact other outfits, but each time they would contact one, they would always report that their opposition was too great and they were pulling out for the rear. There seemed to be no help coming from anywhere. We ourselves had now retreated about thirty miles since the first day of the attack, and it looked as if the only thing we could do was start retreating again. Finally, our radiomen contacted some tank outfit, and they said they would come and help us. They ran out of gas before they ever got to us, though, and they were caught helplessly by some attacking Krauts.

During the forenoon of this second day, two of our men in the holes at the edge of town shot themselves through the foot. They said it had happened accidentally, but our officers knew better. These guys just couldn't take it any longer, so they figured if they shot themselves, the medics would see to it that they got safely to the rear. Had they known that they would be left in the town when we started to retreat again at noon, I'm sure they would have pointed their guns in some other direction.

Yes, by noon of this day, we were once more on the retreat. The Germans had pulled up with heavy forces and tanks to the edge of our town. Our officers knew it was useless for our few men to try to hold against them as they started to attack, so we all moved into the thick woods behind the town. I have no idea as to how far we walked, but I know that by this time the morale of our remaining men was very low. Everyone was hungry and tired and cold. Whenever two or three of us got together, we would always find ourselves talking about one subject. That was the big question as to whether or not we should give ourselves up the next time we were attacked. For the past week, we had only had a few bites to eat, and our stomachs ached. We had been beaten every time we had met the Krauts, and they seemed to be getting more powerful all the time. We knew of no help coming from the rear, and we thought that the American lines must have crumbled throughout all of Europe. We thought the Germans were winning the war.

Zeke Prust: December 20th. At the edge of Bastogne, there was a vehicle that had been hit, and we [Service Company, 54th Armored Infantry Battalion, 10th Armored Division] were to go down and retrieve it.

The driver told the captain, "Jam it! That's just like digging our own grave."

So the captain said, "You're no longer the driver."

He pointed to me and said, "You drive."

From that time on I drove the tank. That was something I did not anticipate, but I was happy that I was driving the tank.

William W. Fee: In the morning, we [55th Armored Infantry Battalion, 11th Armored Division] had PT and a class by Lieutenant Been on mine detection. At noon, we got the word that we would move out the next morning. We still thought we were going to St. Nazaire and Lorient. I noticed Tony Petrelli testing the radios. In the afternoon, Technical Sergeant McClain gave a lecture on scouting and patrolling. I took pictures of Jim Pike, Ed Bergh, Lee Hens, and myself by our pup tents, and then Lee and I went over to the houses and took pictures of each other there, wrapped in MG ammo and sitting on bomb casings.

W. D. Crittenberger: December 20th: When the Germans kept coming in, we [420th Field Artillery Battalion, 10th Armored Division] had to raise our artillery high to hit them, so we moved across Bastogne out to the west to a small town called Senonchamps. We could reach the whole perimeter from there. It was a good location. The Germans who were trying to get by the armor and the airborne on the east side of town, they started to come around, and they tried to come in the back door, that was where we were. We had two or three firefights everyday, but we could hold them off, since we had machine guns on our halftracks and vehicles. We also had a battery of triple-A, self-propelled, four-guns mounted on a track. We called them woodchoppers because when they swept the woods, the trees fell down. We had those, 105mm howitzers, and halftracks, so we could handle the Germans until the 101st came.

◆ ◆ ◆

GENERAL JAMES M. GAVIN PLAYED a central role in integrating the U.S. military, beginning with his incorporation of the all-black 555th Parachute Infantry Battalion into the 82nd Airborne Division. The 555th commander, Col. Bradley Biggs, referred to Gavin as perhaps the most "color-blind" army officer in the service. A major general before his thirty-eighth birthday, he was widely renowned for his calm leadership in battle. He showed great skill and resourcefulness in dealing with the precarious situations that confronted the 82nd Airborne Division during the Battle of the Bulge. Never content to stay behind the lines, Gavin would "go and see for himself" at every opportunity. German intelligence had set December 20 as the expected date for the start of the upcoming Soviet offensive, aimed at crushing what was left of German resistance on the Eastern Front and thereby opening the way to Berlin. It was hoped that Stalin would delay the start of the operation once the German assault in the Ardennes had begun and wait for the outcome before continuing. By December 20, General Eisenhower had developed a counterstrategy and modified

This photo was taken while Bastogne was still under siege. These troops of the 101st Airborne are moving up to dislodge the Germans who had surrounded them for over ten days.

his command structure to meet the threat. Eisenhower focused on confining the penetration to as narrow a front as possible, holding the crossroads at St. Vith and Bastogne to slow down the German timetable and threaten their supply lines. Montgomery's 21st Army Group established a blocking position to limit the depth of the bulge at Givet and Maastricht and to deny the Meuse River crossings. Patton's Third Army was turned against the southern side of the bulge and ordered to break through to relieve Bastogne with a drive to start December 23. Also on December 20, Eisenhower removed the First and Ninth American Armies from Bradley's 12th Army Group and placed them under Montgomery's 21st Army Group command. The decision to do this was not received well by certain U.S. generals in the field at the time. Most military strategists agree that it was imperative to coordinate forces in the north where the greatest concentration of German troops was assembled. Omar Bradley was too far from the scene of the crisis to gauge the situation adequately, therefore Montgomery was an obvious choice. By December 20, Bastogne was a city under siege, and a complete victory for the Allies was still a long way off.

CHAPTER SIX

DIGGING IN AND
HOLDING ON

21 DECEMBER 1944

B Y DECEMBER 21, St. Vith had fallen to the Germans, and Peiper decided to withdraw all of his forces to the immediate area of La Gleize. With ever-dwindling hopes of relief from his division, his only possible course of action was to fiercely defend his position. The problem was that behind him, the U.S. Army had captured Stavelot, effectively severing his supply line to the bulk of the Sixth Army in the east. The American pincers continued to close on the isolated kampfgruppe: the 30th Infantry Division hammered away from the west, the 3rd Armored Division approached from the north and northeast, and the 82nd Airborne Division attacked Peiper from the southwest. With increasing fury, the Americans brought the power of their artillery to bear. Peiper's artillery was almost out of ammunition and virtually silent. The King Tigers defended an arc that covered the northeastern to southeastern approaches to La Gleize. One estimate states that the 30th Infantry Division's artillery poured over fifty-seven thousand shells into the area. The constant bombardment aggravated the Germans' lack of sleep, and food was in as short supply as was ammunition and fuel.

Such was the volatility of Hitler's mind back in 1944 that by December 21, he'd decided on a new offensive, this time in the Alsace region, in effect selecting one of the options he had ruled out earlier in favor of the Ardennes. The desperate and ill-advised Operation *Nordwind* (North Wind), planned for December 31, was effectively to be the Germans last-ditch attempt to harass the Allies in the West.

With Dietrich's failure to break the northern shoulder, and with little hope of attaining their original objectives, both Hitler and Rundstedt agreed that an attack on the southern Allied front might take advantage of Patton's shift north to the Ardennes.

The German main advance through the center of the Ardennes sector moved into a narrow corridor northwest to Marche after bypassing Bastogne. By December 21, Bastogne was a city under siege. German forces had completely surrounded it. Conditions inside the perimeter were really difficult. Most of the medical supplies and medical personnel had been captured at Noville a day or two previously. Food was becoming scarce, and ammunition was so low that artillery crews were forbidden to fire on advancing Germans unless there was a large concentration of them. Despite determined and sustained German attacks, however, the perimeter appeared to be holding.

In an attempt to alleviate the suffering in the 12th Army Group on December 21, an order was issued confirming prospective airdrops. A day later, the commanding officer of the Communications Zone, Lt. Gen. John C. H. Lee, requested SHAEF to prepare stocks of ready-packed supplies, capable of air delivery, at airfields strategically located on the continent. This proposal was accepted in its entirety.

Meanwhile, elsewhere on the Bulge, the beleaguered Gen. Norman "Dutch" Cota, commanding the 28th Division, had issued the order: "Nobody comes back." Despite the fact that the 28th had taken over 1,500 casualties in the Battle of the Hürtgen Forest one month before, they were still a force to be reckoned with. The 28th's portion of the front was a twenty-five-mile-long sector that was more than three times the area an infantry division was normally expected to defend. The 106th Golden Lion Division had been charged with an

Joseph "Sepp" Dietrich discussing tactics with a junior officer. Joachim Pieper, who regarded Dietrich as a "yes" man, did not hold his commanding officer in particularly high regard.

equally arduous task of holding a large frontline that far outreached the division's parameters. The division's fate had been sealed two days previous. The 28th fought on using all available personnel and seriously disrupted the enemy timetable before being forced to withdraw to Neufchâteau the following day for reorganization, which, in fact, is a polite way of saying that the division had taken yet another hammering and was in dire need of attention.

Meanwhile, on December 21 behind the U.S. lines, there was another problem to contend with: Operation *Greif* (Griffon). Hitler had promoted Skorzeny to lieutenant colonel and given him a new mission. As part of the planned German offensive in the Ardennes in the last days of 1944 (the Battle of the Bulge), Hitler suggested that Skorzeny's English-speaking men infiltrate behind Allied lines dressed and equipped as American soldiers in order to create mass confusion. In addition to captured Allied jeeps, the Germans used Panther tanks and other German vehicles repainted and modified to look like Allied vehicles. Otto Skorzeny's Trojan horse, the 150th Panzer Brigade, attacked Malmedy. He did not manage to actually get into Malmedy, but that was his intention nonetheless. A lot has been written about this man and his hand-picked band of saboteurs, but in retrospect, was Skorzeny *really* the most dangerous man in Europe? And how successful was Operation *Greif*?

Hitler's idea was successful to some extent at least. In addition to the direct damage caused by the actions of Skorzeny's phony American soldiers, the news and rumors of their activity spread rapidly among Allied units and caused a reaction that was in fact much more damaging. Traffic of Allied officers of all ranks, and of reinforcements and supplies, was seriously slowed down by the sudden need to repeatedly stop at checkpoint after checkpoint and identify as genuine Americans, and not just by presenting identification papers but also by having to answer American trivia questions because of the obvious suspicion that the disguised Germans carried fake American papers.

When some of Skorzeny's soldiers were captured, they told their interrogators that their mission was to reach Paris and assassinate the Allied supreme commander, General Eisenhower. This was an

After the bitter and bloody struggle in the Hürtgen Forest, the 60th Infantry Regiment displayed its immense courage and steadfastness by winning another Presidential Unit Citation in the snow and bitter cold of the Battle of the Bulge.

intentional direct lie perpetuated to sow concern among the higher echelons, but they also divulged that their commander was Skorzeny, which was indeed true, and since Skorzeny's record with regard to foreign leaders was well known, it was immediately believed that Skorzeny was trying to get to Eisenhower. As a result, Eisenhower was confined to his office for a long time under close security.

It's interesting to note that Skorzeny personally considered Operation Greif a failure. Because of delays, only a small number of his men actually infiltrated behind the Allied lines, and the rest, most of his unit, had to fight as regular soldiers. Furthermore, their command of the English language was not as good as initially assumed. Nevertheless, the psychological effects on the U.S. forces were powerful indeed, and the ensuing paranoia is proof of that.

Charles Haug: About this time our officers [112th Regiment, 28th Infantry Division] decided that they would try retreating as we had learned while training in the States. This was known as "rear guard action." It meant that as we retreated, our officers would leave about twelve men at each big crossroad we came to. These men were to stay at this spot and hold up the Germans for as long as they could—or until they ran out of ammunition. This would give the main body of our group more time in which to get back. It meant certain death or capture for the men left behind, though.

We started retreating on the roads once again, and the officers started to leave a few men at each crossroad. By the time we got to the

---

OTTO SKORZENY

A particular favorite of Adolf Hitler and once reputed to be the "most dangerous man in Europe," Otto Skorzeny (June 12, 1908–July 5, 1975) was a colonel in the Waffen SS during World War II and is considered by many to be the best commando in the history of modern warfare. During the Battle of the Bulge, Skorzeny led the 150th Panzer Brigade in Operation *Greif* (Griffon). Some of these men were dressed in U.S. military police uniforms in an attempt to confuse the Allies. They were allegedly perfect English speakers, although after the war, Skorzeny denied this. Those who were captured by the Americans spread a rumor that Skorzeny was leading a raid on Paris to kill or capture General Eisenhower.

This was definitely not the case. Nevertheless, Eisenhower was confined to his headquarters for weeks. Skorzeny personally regarded the operation as an abject failure. Because of various delays, only a small number of his men actually infiltrated behind the American lines, and the rest, most of his unit, had to fight as regular soldiers. If it had been fully implemented, Operation *Greif* could have caused far greater damage behind the American lines. The special force intended to capture the vital Meuse bridges in advance of the main German army.

fourth crossroad, it was Company B's turn to leave twelve men. Frankie, Quimby, and I were three of the twelve men ordered to stay behind. We were scared, and as we watched the rest of the guys head down the road, we were wishing we could be going with them. Soon they were out of sight and we were left to our fate.

We started digging holes with our helmets, but the ground was frozen, and we couldn't make much progress. We felt helpless, and we all had lumps in our throats. The longer we stayed here, the more nervous we got. We tried to figure out how in the devil twelve GIs armed with only rifles could hold up a whole German army. There seemed to be no answer, and our only hope was that no Germans would come up our road. We must have stayed there about two hours without seeing or hearing anything. Suddenly, we spotted a halftrack coming down the road to our right. It was coming very fast, and we got ourselves into position to do the job we had been left to do. As it got near to us, we saw that it was an American halftrack, but to play it safe, we kept our rifles pointed

Only four of Skorzeny's men were court-martialed and shot as spies at Henri-Chapelle on December 23, 1944: Wilhelm Schmidt, Günther Billing, Manfred Pernass, and a fourth German soldier whose name is not known. A second squad was reported as missing in action. The other six squads succeeded in returning to German lines. The squad pictured in this photograph almost managed to cross the Meuse River.

toward it. The driver spotted us as he came to our crossroad, and he waved his arm. He stopped, and he had five GIs with him. Three of them had been wounded badly and were lying in the back. He told us which outfit they were with and that the Germans had just attacked them about two miles down the road. They said that most of their men had been captured, but they had got away and were headed for the rear as fast as possible. They told us that we were crazy if we stayed here and waited for them to attack us, but we had been ordered to stay here, so we stayed. They took off again, and it wasn't long until they were out of sight also.

General Norman "Dutch" Cota's 28th Infantry Division, the first troops in Bastogne, marching down a street. Some of these soldiers lost their weapons during the German advance in this area. Their numbers had been seriously depleted during the preceding Battle of the Hürtgen Forest.

We didn't have to wait long before we heard many vehicles coming down this same road the halftrack had just come. As they got closer, we could see that it was the Germans who were coming this time. We could see a long column of German trucks, headed by three huge tanks. Each of the trucks was loaded with German infantrymen. They were out to lick the Americans. The closer they got, the more scared we got. The rumble from the tanks and trucks got louder and louder. When they got about five hundred yards from us, the lead tank spotted us and opened up with its machine gun. Our rifles were useless against the tanks. We were soon driven from the crossroad and into the woods again. We retreated until we spotted a small town at the foot of the hill in back of us. We could see no activity in the town, but we spotted a couple of jeeps standing by one of the buildings. We ran into the town and up to the building where we saw the jeeps.

Inside we found four soldiers who were waiting and were in the same boat we were. They knew the Germans were coming, but they didn't know which way to retreat in order to get away from them. We told them about the long column of Krauts that we had just seen coming in this direction, and we all decided to get out of town before we were caught. By this time, we were getting desperate. We decided we would keep running as long as we had any breath left in us. As we came out of the building, we once more spotted the same long column of tanks and trucks. They were headed directly for our little town. The twelve of us ran for the woods on the far side of the town, and the rest of the GIs jumped in their jeep and headed out of town in the same direction on the road. Once more the tanks stopped and started to fire at us as we ran from the town. This time they scored some hits. Two of our guys were hit, and they fell face first into the snow.

As soon as we were in the woods the Krauts pulled into the town. We kept running because we knew that they were at our heels. I ran into a branch once and lost my helmet, but I didn't take time to stop and pick it up because every second counted. I remember Frankie ran into another branch once and hooked his jacket. He gave one tug and kept going. The whole back of his jacket got left hanging on the branch, and all he had left was the front and two sleeves. We must have run for an hour steady, and then we were so exhausted that we all stopped, threw ourselves on the ground, and rested. Our lungs ached from lack of wind.

By now it was dark again, and as we lay there, we suddenly realized that it was Christmas Eve. We didn't have the slightest idea where we were, and none of us seemed to care whether it was Christmas Eve or not. All we knew was that it was cold, and we wanted something to eat. We lay there for about half an hour, then we decided we would try once more to see if we could find our way out of this mess. We started walking. I had a compass that we could see at night, so we set our course due west. We walked for about an hour, and we came to a river about a hundred yards wide. By now it was nine o'clock at night. There was a full moon out, and there were millions of stars overhead. On the far side of the river it was all open country with no trees. We could see a road running parallel with the river about two hundred yards on the other side of the river. It was cold, but the river was still running. There was just a little ice near each bank. We knew we had to

Skorzeny's men also proliferated rumors that German paratroopers were going to be dropped behind Allied lines. This didn't occur, but the suggestion alone did damage.

get across the river, but we could see no bridge, so we stopped again to figure out our next move.

L. B. Clark: On the 21st of December, we [37th Tank Battalion] moved again to a position a few hundred yards southwest of Arlon and covered three roadblocks consisting of trees prepared for demolition by corps and Communication Zone engineers. The lack of definite information about the situation of the German offensive had made the troops in this area very jittery. These troops had already blown up several bridges and were preparing to blow several others until stopped by various officers in the battalion who were on forward reconnaissance.

Albert Tarbell: We [Company H, 504th Parachute Infantry Regiment, 82nd Airborne Division] moved into the Monceau area, northeast of Cheneault. We were moving up onto a hill or knoll when we noticed two flak wagons to our right. At the time, we thought they were abandoned vehicles. Just then, Lieutenant Rivers started yelling to get those German soldiers who were heading for the flak wagons. We ran down toward the hill shooting at them but were unable to get them. Once they got into the flak wagons, they turned the weapons on us. By hitting the trees above our heads they really raised hell with us. We had a lot of casualties from that encounter. There was a captain from Service

Members of the 101st Airborne Division walk past dead comrades, killed during the Christmas Eve bombing. The water tower was demolished after the siege. After the siege was lifted, fighting actually intensified as more German units were dispatched to the Bastogne area.

Company who was severely wounded and eventually died. Another of our men was wounded in the leg (Stover) and was yelling like a stuck pig. The officer told him to quiet down, that he was not hurt that bad. I helped with the wounded by getting them out of the line of fire and onto the trucks that were parked nearby to get them to the medical station. We were pinned down for a while from the 20mm shrapnel. The trucks with the wounded were unable to move for quite a while. Just before dark, I walked over to see some of the wounded, since they had not moved out yet. All of our casualties were wounded, except for the one captain from Service Company. There again, a lot of the casualties were unknown to us, having just joined us as replacements for our losses in Holland. The same thing always enters your mind after things cool down a little, *When is my time coming?* Men are getting hit all around you and you do not get hit. You worry about the law of averages.

William W. Fee: We [55th Armored Infantry Battalion, 11th Armored Division] left Rennes early in the morning. Wahoo always came piling in at the last moment, and this time we almost lost him. He always occupied one of the two rear seats so he could see everything. As we rode along, he used to yell back to Pete Valdez, in Staff Sergeant Torok's mortar squad, which followed us, "Hey, Pedro." Pete would answer, "Whadaya want, Chief?" knowing that Wahoo would reply, "Nothin'. Just checkin' up on my list." When we stopped for a K ration at noon, Wahoo was so dirty that Pete yelled at him, "Hey, Chief, smile so I can see you." And so it went as we rolled along.

We stopped at Le Mans, almost halfway to Paris. We were in a dark, bushy area, and we had to use the squad's machete to clear spaces for our pup tents. We heard Lieutenant Fagan giving instructions to the squad leaders: This would be the last night without guard duty and the next-to-last night for fires. The .50-caliber MGs would be half loaded. We were issued armor-piercing rifle ammo and put mines on the rack on the outside of the halftrack. As usual, Magelli checked the guys in the chow line to be sure they were wearing a helmet and carrying a weapon. Connie Rienstra and Douglas Black illuminated their tent with the light that was connected to the track's battery by a long wire.

John Kline: At Gerolstein, we [M Company, 423rd Regiment, 106th Division] were awakened at 0600 and given our first food since breakfast on December 18th. They fed us hard crackers and cheese. Seven men to one can of cheese. We left Gerolstein during the evening, arrived in Dockweiler Dreis around 2300, and billeted in an old German barracks. During the three and one-half days there, we were fed one ration of very weak potato stew. We received two bread rations of one loaf split between five men, one ration of cheese in one small tin can between four men. We were each given two old German army blankets. They were old and worn but did give us some warmth. They would prove to be lifesavers as time went on.

Meanwhile, near the German border in Luxembourg, the 10th Armored Division continued to fight pockets of German soldiers.

Robert T. Miller: We [B Company, 21st Tank Battalion, 10th Armored Division] were traveling at night, and it was dark, and you couldn't see nothing. I did not even know where it was; you couldn't see the signs for the towns. I was a gunner for the 75mm gun on a Sherman. On December 21st, our tank was the lead tank going into the town of Longvilly, and when we got to the end of the little village of Waldbillig, Luxembourg, we found out that nobody else was following us. We had three tanks, and the rest of the column didn't follow us for some reason. So we were actually stranded in the middle of the village, and the Germans were in the back of us and all around us. The two tanks following our tank got hit by bazookas, and several men were killed, and my tank commander got out of the tank and checked out in front of us to see what was happening. He saw that the tanks in back of us had been hit and that nobody was following us and we were by ourselves. He tried to back the tank up to a safe place, and he was sitting on top of the tank when a German sniper hit him in the head and killed him. With the other two tanks there, we got together. I don't remember how many men had been killed. The platoon leader of the third tank, he disappeared and was taken a prisoner of war. The tank commander of the second tank in back of us, he jumped out of the tank because he was hit. He jumped into a beef pen and stayed there until the rest of us who were left got back together. We captured some Germans in one of the houses there; we put some of the wounded on the back of our tank, and we made the Germans walk in front of us. When we got out of town then, somebody else took care of the prisoners. We acted as a block for the Germans until they brought up the tank destroyers, who relieved us.

◆ ◆ ◆

FRANCIS CURREY OF THE 120th Regiment, Company K, in the 30th Infantry Division, along with his platoon, talked about his experiences of holding down a position outside of the town of Malmedy the morning of December 21st. Currey's small detachment of troops included Warren Shinn, Raymond Gould, Raymond Snow, Gordon Gunderson, and Adam Lucero. They positioned themselves outside of Malmedy to hold off the German advance of Joachim Peiper and helped prevent the capture of Liège, which was located behind Malmedy and was important to the German attack.

Francis Currey: The next morning at 0400, an antitank outfit, just a platoon with a halftrack, came through us. We were chatting, and they went out and made a roadblock in front of us, but that lasted about three seconds before the Germans hit them and ran right over it. To our flank way up there was a railroad embankment where there was a Norwegian battalion dug in. They were up high, and they had machine guns.

Francis Currey, 30th Division.
Latchodrom Productions

We had heard that antitank gun cool off once since they apparently had gotten a shot off that missed the tank. The tanks just ran over them. They were out in front of us five hundred yards or so. This Norwegian outfit had held, but they kept funneling the Germans toward us. Next thing we knew, two tanks were coming, and one ran right through us. I saw a German coming down the street, and I buttoned him up with my Browning (BAR). He went right across the bridge. We had a company command post across the bridge, and we had a forward observer who took out a tank with a bazooka. Next thing you knew, we had another German tank coming through, and they flanked to the side of us to guard the high way coming in from Malmedy. We got a bazooka and took care of that tank. Then the German infantry started to come in, and we started to fire on them. This action took a period of twenty-four hours. We were fighting all day long. During the course of that day, I found out the guys from the AT were trapped out there, three tanks had them boxed in. I managed to crawl out to one of their holes and said, "What the hell is going on here?"

"We can't move with them damn tanks there. How the hell did you get up here?" one of the tank destroyer men said.

"Well, infantry, you know," I said.

"If you can, get us out of here," the tank destroyer man stated.

A young Pfc. Francis S. Currey proudly displays a bazooka, a .50-caliber machine gun, a .30-caliber machine gun, and his faithful M1 Garand. These are the weapons that he used to earn his Medal of Honor.

I tried to figure out how to get these guys out. The highest rank we had was a buck sergeant/assistant squad leader. We were all teenagers, the oldest one was maybe twenty-one years old, and I was the one with all the training. I knew what I was doing, since I had been in training the year before.

They had left their halftrack, and there was a whole case of anti-tank grenades and the launcher. I had to get close to the tank, but there was enough vegetation for me to get close. On the way up, I took out a few German soldiers. I got into position close enough, and although an antitank grenade will not take out a tank, they make a hell of a noise and a big burst of flame and smoke. It looked like an artillery shell hit it. I do not know how they did not see me. I started bombarding them with antitank grenades. They were right close together, and they abandoned them. I got credit for three tanks plus the fourth one from before. One of the men I saved was wounded. I said to the buck sergeant, "Look, when I start firing and covering you, I am going to sweep, each one of you one at a time," I said.

"I got a wounded guy."

"Well, can two of you help him?" Which they agreed they could do.

I got that light machine gun going, and as I started to fire to cover them, each of the men managed to get back, but as they got back to us they kept going, and they left the wounded guy there.

All day we were firing. There was a factory, and the first floor was all windows, and the five of us fired a few rounds through the windows to make it appear that we had more of us there. When the tanks fired on us, we were gone. It was two stories tall, so they thought we had a pretty good-sized outfit. As it got dark, the other injured tank destroyer man, who had been hit pretty bad with an artillery shell piece, laid there all day until we got him out of there. We had two wounded guys, five of us, and we had to reconnoiter. We found a jeep with two mounts on it for the wounded men, and one of our guys who could drive a standard transmission started to drive it.

I took control of the situation and had Shinn drive while the other men held the stretchers. I rode shotgun on the spare tire.

We went past that burning tank, and we were on the highway from Malmedy to Francorchamps. It was a dark night, and we had the small lights on the jeep. We were going, but we did not have the slightest idea of where we were in the middle of Belgium. We hit another regiment, a roadblock, and we were coming from the German side. We were challenged because they were worried about Germans infiltrating, but finally they let us in and took our weapons, our jeep, and our wounded. They did not believe our story. We went around telling our story, and no one believed us until we talked to someone who had some brains. The next day they moved us back to our regiment.

◆ ◆ ◆

AS EARLY AS DECEMBER 21, German logistical difficulties were becoming apparent when both the 2nd and 2nd SS Panzer Divisions

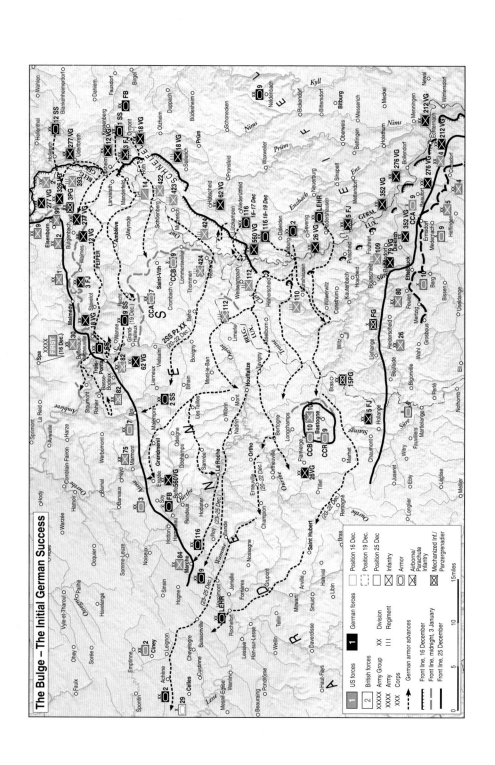

The Bulge – The Initial German Success

Legend

1	US forces	
2	British forces	
XXXX	Army Group	
XXX	Army	
XX	Corps	

1	German forces	
XXX	Army	
XX	Division	
III	Regiment	

German armor advances

Front line, 16 December
Front line, midnight, 3 January
Front line, 25 December

Position 16 Dec.
Position 19 Dec.
Position 25 Dec.

Infantry
Armor
Airborne/Parachute Infantry
Mechanized Inf/Infantry
Panzergrenadier

0 5 10 15 miles

The former headquarters of General McAuliffe is now a museum run by soldiers serving in the Belgian armed forces. *Latchodrom Productions*

sat idle for lack of fuel. An additional problem was German intransigence. This was the real antithesis of the U.S. Army soldiers, who had proved their ingenuity for improvising in the face of great adversity on many occasions. The Panzer Lehr and 26th Volksgrenadier Divisions had proved too weak to entirely subjugate the opposition. While fighting raged around Bastogne, the last German offensive moves continued to the west. The 116th Panzer Division had been repulsed at Hotton on December 21, but the 2nd SS Panzer Division continued to advance on Manhay, and the 2nd Panzer Division was thrusting toward Dinant.

Down in Bastogne, the city was well and truly under siege. On December 21, Gen. Heinrich Freiherr von Lüttwitz, the German commander, offered surrender terms to Gen. Anthony McAuliffe, the senior officer of the American units surrounded at Bastogne. McAuliffe's famous one-word reply: "Nuts!" It was actually Maj. Alvin Jones who took the terms to General McAuliffe and Lt. Col. Ned D. Moore who was acting chief of staff. The paper called for the surrender of the Bastogne garrison and threatened its complete destruction. It appealed to the "well-known American humanity" to save the people of Bastogne from further suffering. The Americans were to have two hours in which to consider. The two German officers, who brought the surrender terms to McAuliffe, would have to be released by the GIs at Bastogne at 1400, but another hour would pass before the Germans would resume their attack.

Colonel Harper, commanding the 327th, went with Jones to Division Headquarters. The two German officers were left with Captain Adams. Members of the staff were grouped around General McAuliffe when Harper and Jones arrived. McAuliffe asked someone what the paper contained and was told that it requested a surrender.

He laughed and said, "Aw, nuts!" It really seemed funny to him at the time. He figured he was giving the Germans "one hell of a beating" and that all of his men knew it. The demand was out of line with the existing situation.

But McAuliffe realized that some kind of reply had to be made, so he sat down to think it over. Pencil in hand, he sat there pondering for a few minutes and then remarked, "Well, I don't know what to tell them." He asked the staff what they thought, and Colonel Kinnard, his G-3, replied, "That first remark of yours would be hard to beat."

General McAuliffe didn't understand immediately what Kinnard was referring to. Kinnard reminded him, "You said 'Nuts!'" That drew applause all around. All members of the staff agreed with much enthusiasm, and because of their approval, McAuliffe decided to send that message back to the Germans.

Then he called Colonel Harper in and asked him how he would reply to the message. Harper thought for a minute but before he could compose anything, General McAuliffe gave him the paper on which he had written his one-word reply and asked, "Will you see that it's delivered?"

"I will deliver it myself," answered Harper. "It will be a lot of fun." McAuliffe told him not to go into the German lines.

Colonel Harper returned to the command post of Company F. The two Germans were standing in the wood blindfolded and under guard. Harper said, "I have the American commander's reply."

The German captain asked, "Is it written or verbal?"

"It is written," said Harper.

And then he said to the German major, "I will stick it in your hand."

The German captain translated the message. The major then asked, "Is the reply negative or affirmative? If it is the latter I will negotiate further."

All of this time the Germans had been acting in patronizing manner. Colonel Harper was beginning to lose his temper. He said, "The reply is decidedly not affirmative." Then he added, "If you continue this foolish attack your losses will be tremendous." The major nodded his head.

ANTHONY MCAULIFFE

Brigadier General Anthony McAuliffe (July 2, 1898–August 11, 1975) was divisional artillery commander of the 101st Airborne Division, and during the siege of Bastogne, he served as acting division commander for the first crucial week. At Bastogne, the 101st and 10th Armored Divisions were surrounded by seven German divisions. McAuliffe's place in world history was assured on December 22, 1944, when he replied "Nuts!" to a formal German surrender ultimatum. Men who

served with McAuliffe claim that he never used profanity when speaking, therefore any rumors that his initial verbal response to the German ultimatum was in stronger language remain completely unsubstantiated. Deeply respected by his men and widely regarded by fellow officers, Anthony McAuliffe was an intelligent, articulate, and courageous leader who rightfully deserves a prominent place in the history of World War II.

Private Paul Romanick, Battery B, 103rd Antiaircraft Artillery Battalion, 1st Infantry Division,
First Army, wipes and cleans a 40mm antiaircraft gun in snow-covered Sourbrodt, Belgium,
December 31, 1944. The gun's six swastikas represent each German plane it has brought down.
Bill Augustine/Lightroom Photos /U.S. Army/TopFoto/ Jon Mitchell/Redux

Harper put the two officers in the jeep and took them back to the
main road where the German privates were waiting with the white flag.

He then removed the blindfold and said to them, speaking through
the German captain, "If you don't understand what 'Nuts' means, in
plain English it is the same as 'Go to hell.' And I will tell you something
else—if you continue to attack we will kill every goddamn German that
tries to break into this city."

The German major and captain saluted very stiffly. The captain said,
"We will kill many Americans. This is war." It was then 1350.

"On your way, Bud," said Colonel Harper, "and good luck to you."

CHAPTER SEVEN

OUR WORST ENEMY

22 DECEMBER 1944

THE "HITLER" WEATHER THAT HAD hampered the Allies and deprived them of air support began to clear on December 22, and German troops, jammed on poor roads and short of fuel, were mercilessly harried from the air. General Patton inspected the III Corps dispositions and divisions on December 20, concluded that the corps concentration was proceeding satisfactorily, and the following day gave the order for attack at 0600 on the 22nd. Love or hate Patton, no one can deny that what he did with the Third Army was amazing. He managed to turn the whole army around and send them north in two days. Logistically, this was remarkable. The corps scheme of maneuver, issued to the divisions in the early afternoon, was simple. The III Corps would advance north in the direction of St. Vith. The 80th Infantry Division, on the right, would maintain contact during its advance with the left wing of the XII Corps. The 26th Division would form the center. The 4th Armored Division would advance on the left toward Bastogne.

When December 22 dawned, the XVIII Airborne Corps was still busy maneuvering to create a solid barrier along its forty-five-mile front against the Germans heading for the Meuse. Things were not going particularly well. The St. Vith salient had been dealt heavy blows, and the lines there were crumbling. The enemy had pushed along the Ourthe River Valley as far as Hotton and was gathering to the west of that river. General Hobbs, whose 30th Division was holding the corps' north flank, felt that his sector now was secure, although he knew that enemy reinforcements had crossed the Amblève. But he was concerned lest the Germans bring off a successful eccentric attack north of Trois-Ponts,

The town of St. Vith in the German-speaking area of Belgium was captured temporarily on December 24, 1944. The town suffered terrible devastation at the hands of German artillery and Allied bombers.

which would separate the 30th Division from the 82nd Airborne. On the morning of the 22nd, he told Gen. Matthew B. Ridgway about his concerns in a telephone conversation, but Ridgway gave him Gavin's assurance that the paratroopers would hold, that nothing would get through to the west. To the corps commander, the priority project in this sector remained that of eliminating the La Gleize–Stoumont pocket as rapidly and as thoroughly as possible, freeing the 30th Division and its attached armor for urgent work elsewhere.

After a quiet night along most of the 30th Division lines, the day came with intense cold, falling snow, and heavy overcast. Veteran troops by this time had learned that beautifully clear weather at the foxhole line often meant bad flying weather back at the airbases, but they knew, too, that close tactical support necessitated a decent modicum of clear weather. At 0806, the 30th Division air officer learned that his targets had been approved and that a fighter-bomber group would be on hand, "weather permitting." At almost the same moment, General Hobbs got the word that he could expect no help from the air. The resumption of the attack to deflate the pocket would depend on ground troops and guns—most of all guns. The artillery, however, was finding it difficult to get into good firing positions, and the American troops were so near the target towns as to require the nicest type of precision ranging. Prospects for the attackers seemed as discouraging as the weather.

The plan of December 22nd included the continuation of the drive to take La Gleize and Stoumont, plus an attack to mop up the 1st SS Panzer Division relief detachment, which had dug in north of the Amblève between Stavelot and Ster. Finally, a rifle company was sent from Stavelot to hit the Germans in the rear. Thereafter, the Americans were able to converge on the ridge, but as the day ended, pockets of the enemy still remained in the woods. During the day, other enemy troops had crossed the Amblève and for a time isolated one of Lovelady's road-blocks north of Trois-Ponts. But at no time on the 22nd did organized units of the relieving force of the 1st SS Panzer Division succeed in breaking through to Peiper in La Gleize.

John R. Schaffner: Very early, in the dark, the next morning (December 22), the Germans attacked again, and we [Battery B, Survey Team, 106th Infantry Division] were subjected to small arms and mortar fire off and on all day. At one point, mortar rounds were landing real close to my hole, and I was feeling very exposed with no helmet to crawl into. I could hear the mortar fragments and bullets smacking into the ground around my foxhole. Most of the mortar rounds were falling farther in toward the buildings. I saw one hit the roof of Captain Brown's command post. It

Infantrymen of the 4th Armored Division of Patton's Third Army firing at the enemy with their M1 Garands east of Bastogne shortly after the siege ended.

must have been during this time that Major Parker was wounded by a fragment. I'm not sure about that; I didn't witness it. There was a GI in a foxhole next to mine who would not fire his weapon. When I called to him to fire, he just looked at me. I didn't know him and don't know his fate either; I could not understand why he was not willing to help himself (and the rest of us). I have read since that this is not an unusual occurrence. There are always a certain number who will not squeeze that trigger, even when their lives are threatened.

Late in the afternoon, several tanks were heard approaching our position. Thankfully, they were ours. They rolled out in the open and fired their big guns into the German positions, and I thought, no problem now. With all this help, the day is saved. It got quiet again. And then the tanks left. Looked like we would be hung out to dry, but it did stop the enemy attack for a while. Thanks, tankers. Too bad you couldn't stay for dinner.

After dark I was moved in closer to the command post and dug another hole along with a GI named Randy Pierson. One of our guys made a run from hole to hole tossing everybody something to eat. I caught a box of "wet-or-dry" cereal and ate it dry. The two of us spent the night in the hole. One of us would sleep an hour and the other keep watch, and then we would alternate. This was the only kind of rest that anybody got. We had dug our hole reasonably deep and then further fortified it with some fence rails that we crisscrossed in front of it. I was sure that we would be attacked that night. I had thirty rounds of carbine ammunition remaining and a knife that I placed on the ground where I could reach it. I prayed that it would not be necessary. It got very cold that night, and the enemy did not attack. Another very long night. At the time, the weather was our worst enemy, but then in the morning things changed and weather took second place.

L. B. Clark: The plan for the 22nd of December was for Combat Command A to attack north on the Arlon–Bastogne highway on Combat Command B's right with Combat Command Reserve following Combat Command A. Early in the morning, the column halted to bridge an enormous crater blown in the road, which had been reported

Some 101st Airborne soldiers manning a .50-caliber machine gun in a freezing foxhole on the perimeter of Bastogne. Surviving Screaming Eagle veterans maintain to this day that "We didn't need Patton."

by us [37th Tank Battalion, 4th Armored Division] the day before. In the afternoon, the 51st Armored Infantry attacked Martelange. Major Parker and Captain Franks went into the center of town with the point. The enemy force in the town was small, but progress was halted because the bridge over the Sure River had been previously blown. The battalion displaced to the vicinity of Schadeck to be available for reinforcing fire to the 66th in Combat Command A.

In order to protect Combat Command A's right flank, Combat Command Reserve was ordered to attack and seize Bigonville, which was expected to be lightly held.

William W. Fee: Again, we [55th Armored Infantry Battalion, 11th Armored Division] were on our way early. It was fun to watch the tracks behind us swing around a bend or a corner, one after the other, as we sailed along. We passed German 88mm guns and American tanks and halftracks that had been knocked out. From time to time we passed Major Sandler, who was watching how things were going. We went as far as Rambouillet, 50 km southwest of Paris.

The field was wet, and for a while we considered sleeping in the track. But that would have imposed on Charlie Crouch, who had his hands full gassing up the track and looking after it. The boys tried to get fires going, but it took a lot of gasoline before the wood was dry enough to burn. Our platoon sergeant, John Cangley, would sneak up behind guys standing close to a fire, throw gasoline on it, and yell, "Whee! Feelin' the breeze!" He almost set "Sack" Vornoli and George Fisher on fire. The rain had us feeling low, and Cangley's pranks gave the observers something to laugh at. The victims did not find it funny.

As Jim Pike and I were in the chow line, Lieutenant Fagan called for our 3rd Platoon to eat first, to strike our tents, and to go on guard duty because German parachutists had been dropped nearby. We assembled in the dark. Telly, Jackson, Rienstra, Pike, and I were assigned to set up an MG at a road junction. The night was uneventful for us—but not for one of our squad leaders, we were told. He halted a Free French [Resistance] man on a bike, tried out some French, and looked down to see a pistol aimed at him across the handlebars. The biker asked, "Boche?" [German?], and our man pointed to his helmet as a way of answering. There was a lot of joking about who had actually halted whom.

John Kline: During the night, the road alongside the barracks was strafed and bombed. We [M Company, 423rd Regiment, 106th Division] could not see the target, but in the moonlight we could see that the plane was a British Spitfire. The English usually flew night missions; the Americans flew during the day. The weather was clearing and cold. There were many planes in the sky, so we knew we would probably be moved during the night to avoid the possibility of being strafed.

Albert Tarbell: At our company command post [Company H, 504th Parachute Infantry Regiment, 82nd Airborne Division] after the battle of Monceau, which was a farmhouse, we had two civilians who were supposedly living there and also a priest. We had our company switch-board and our radio contact with battalion set up, Sergeant Brett and I.

Those were very busy and trying times, our positions being very flexible. We did not really know what was going on. We had been in constant contact with the Germans right along, either in large groups or stragglers.

I did get a chance to talk to the priest and told him I was happy to see him there with Christmas just a few days away, hinting that he might be able to say mass for us. He told me that he would not be able to say mass because he needed an altar. He said he had to be in a church to do so. It struck me as odd because we have had mass said in all kinds of situations by our chaplains. Mass was said on top of food cartons, on top of jeep hoods. You name it, and it had been done. Just then I received word from the battalion switchboard that German paratroopers were to be dropped behind us. I was ordered to pass along the information to the platoon leaders.

I mentioned the incident about the priest in the orderly room, but in the course of the evening, nothing more was said or done. I mentioned it to my first sergeant and company commander that I was suspicious of the two civilians and the priest. Later on I found out that they were actually Germans who infiltrated the area.

◆ ◆ ◆

THE FIRST WEEK OF THE BATTLE was all but over, and the great counteroffensive by the German army was showing signs of grinding to a halt. On the night of December 22, 1944, the 387th Bomber Group received its orders to commence attack the following morning. This was good news because for the past week, at night, the group's airbase near St. Quentin, France, had been subjected to several German air raids, a strafing attack, and some reports of enemy paratroopers dropping in the area, but it was not over yet. Not by a long shot. Various teams of soldiers assuming the names of their commanding officers were finding themselves in the thick of it.

Most of the fighting on the 22nd centered around two battalions of armored field artillery: Colonel Patton's 58th Armored Field Artillery

Battalion, which had emplaced near Tillet after the Longvilly battle to support the 101st Airborne; and Colonel Browne's 420th, now operating as a combined arms team on a four-thousand-yard perimeter in the neighborhood of Senonchamps. Tillet is about six miles west of Senonchamps. Much of the intervening countryside was in the hands of roving patrols from Panzer Lehr, one of which had erected a strong roadblock midway between the two villages.

On the night of the 21st, the Germans encircled Tillet, where Patton, hard-pressed, radioed the VIII Corps for help. Middleton relayed this SOS to Bastogne, but Browne, himself under attack by the 26th Volksgrenadier Division Recon Battalion, was forced to say that the 58th would have to make its own way back to Senonchamps. Patton and his gunners never reached Team Browne, which had had its hands full. Browne's force not only had to defend a section of the Bastogne perimeter and bar the Senonchamps entry, but the soldiers also had to serve the eighteen 105mm howitzers, which, from battery positions east and south of Senonchamps, provided around-the-clock fire support for friendly infantry five to eight miles distant. Close-in defense was provided by a platoon of thirty stragglers who had been rounded up by an airborne officer and deployed three hundred yards south of the gun positions. (This platoon held for two days until all were killed or captured.) Browne's main weapons against the German tanks and self-propelled guns were not his howitzers but the seventeen Sherman tanks brought up by Team Pyle and Team Van Kleef the day before. These were disposed with nine tanks facing a series of woodlots west of the battery positions, four firing south, and the remaining four being placed on the road to Villeroux.

At daybreak, the first task was to clear the enemy from the woods, which lay uncomfortably near the firing batteries. Pyle's scratch force of riflemen entered the woods but found only a few Germans. Off to the northwest came the sound of firing from the area occupied by a battalion of the 327th Glider Infantry, so Browne reported to Colonel Roberts that his team would join this fight as soon as the woods were clear. Before the sortie could be organized, a detachment from Kampfgruppe Kunkel struck out from Villeroux against the American

The 3rd Armored Division's 83rd Reconnaissance Squadron reached the German border at Rötgen on September 13. The troops fought in the vicinity of Aachen until December 20, when the division advanced into the Ardennes, whereupon they played an integral part in liberating the northern sector.

flank. Direct tank fire chased the enemy away, but this was only the opener. During the afternoon, the enemy made three separate assaults from the woods that earlier had been reported cleared, and again the tanks made short work of the Germans (Van Kleef reported eighteen enemy tanks destroyed during the day).

As the afternoon wore on, fog and snow clouded the scene, and the tank gunners began to lose their targets. The American howitzer battery provided a static and, by this time, a well-defined target for enemy counter-battery fire. At twilight, Colonel Browne radioed CCB that his heterogeneous team was taking "terrible casualties." Earlier he had asked for more troops, and McAuliffe had sent Company C of the 327th and Team Watts (about a hundred men, under Maj. Eugene A. Watts) from Team SNAFU (one team that was not named after its commander). At dark, the howitzer positions had a fairly substantial screen

A GI looks studiously at the frozen solid body of a dead German soldier. The freezing weather conditions on the Bulge preserved the bodies and, as a result, made identification easier.

of infantry around them, although the enemy guns continued to pound away through the night.

The airdrop planned for the 22nd never reached Bastogne—bad flying weather continued as in the days past. All that the Third Army air liaison staff could do was to send a message that "the 101st Airborne's situation is known and appreciated." Artillery ammunition was running very low. The large number of wounded congregated inside Bastogne presented a special problem: there were too few medics and not enough surgical equipment, and blankets had to be gathered up from frontline troops to wrap the men suffering from wounds and shock. Nonetheless, morale was high. Late in the afternoon, word was circulated to all the regiments that the 4th Armored and the 7th Armored (so vague was information inside the perimeter) were on their way to Bastogne; to the men on the line this was heartening news. The biggest morale booster for the besieged troops of Bastogne came with McAuliffe's famous rebuff of the German ultimatum.

CHAPTER EIGHT

SIEGE, RELIEF, AND STRIFE

23 DECEMBER 1944

AROUND BASTOGNE AND ALL ALONG the battlefront, a milky sun cracked thin shards of light through the freezing haze on that bitterly cold morning of the 23rd. Finally, the skies were clearing, and an azure blue sky was greeting the day. This was going to be a special day for the besieged inhabitants of Bastogne. Eyes filled with quiet expectation gazed hopefully skyward as the day began. Then amid the sounds of explosions and flying bullets, the throaty rumble of C-47 engines could be heard in the distance. The clear skies enabled the resupply of Bastogne by air, which by December 23 had run critically low on ammunition and rations. Over 850 tons of supplies were delivered to the Bastogne defenders, with the loss of nineteen C-47s.

Two C-47s from IX TCC Pathfinder Group came in shortly after 0935 and dropped ten men each in the area where Colonel Harper's 2nd Battalion, 327th Glider Infantry was deployed. The Pathfinder team dropped inside the perimeter and set up the apparatus to guide the C-47s over a drop zone between Senonchamps and Bastogne. The first of the carriers dropped its six parapacks at 1150, and in little more than four hours, 241 planes had been assigned to Bastogne. Each plane carried some 1,200 pounds of supplies. They were going to help alleviate some of the terrible suffering that was being endured by both military personnel and civilians in Bastogne.

Troops all along the frontlines saw the formations coming and considered it "the most heartening spectacle of the entire siege." Though the initial parachute resupply missions gave the defenders of Bastogne a vital shot of hope, the need for resupply was still considered a dire emergency by all. Not all the ammunition sent was that requested. Heavy ammunition, more readily carried in gliders, was running low. Most of the supplies that were dropped by parachute were loaded in parapacks (attached to the underside of the aircraft), but the parapacking equipment was still in England. Only the groups of the 50th Wing were now on the continent. The resilient commanders of Bastogne were certain that as long as the artillery ammunition lasted, Bastogne would hold.

A German attack mounted by the 26th Volksgrenadier Division and the attached regiment left behind by Panzer Lehr began on the 23rd. The 5th German Parachute Division, now badly outfought and with gaping holes in its ranks, was of little help at Bastogne. Actually, this division was scattered on a front of eighteen miles, reaching from Neufchâteau clear back to the Sauer crossings. Indeed, during the day, the 26th Volksgrenadier Division had to take over the portion of the 5th Parachute line between Clochimont and Hompré because the American forces from the south threatened to pierce this very thinly occupied segment. Extensive preparatory fires by German artillery and Werfers opened the show while the infantry crept in as close as possible to the American foxhole line. By this time, the new-fallen snow had put every dark object in full relief; the German grenadiers now donned white snow capes, and the Panzers were painted white. (The Americans compensated by requisitioning Belgian bed linen to be used as impromptu ponchos and helmet covers. They also managed to procure whitewash for their armored vehicles.) The assault would be led by a tank platoon—normally four or five Panzers—followed by fifty to one hundred infantrymen. If this first wave failed, a second or third—seldom larger than the initial wave—would be thrown in. It is clear, however, that the German commander and his troops were cautious about employing massed tactics at this stage of the game.

The 39th Volksgrenadier Regiment was assembled to the west and northwest opposite Team Browne and the 3rd Battalion of the 327th. The activity of the American fighter-bombers now dominating the skies made it necessary for the Germans to wait for nightfall before going on the offensive. Through the afternoon, the fighters shelled Marvie. As night came on, the barrage increased in intensity, sweeping along the

Low-flying C-47 transport planes roar overhead carrying supplies to the beleaguered American forces battling the Germans at Bastogne, Belgium, during the enemy breakthrough on January 6, 1945. In the distance, smoke rises from wrecked German equipment, while in the foreground, American tanks move up to support the infantry in the fighting. *Associated Press*

battalion front and onto its northern flank—beyond Marvie—where Team O'Hara stood with its tanks.

At 1845, the 901st (with at least two tank companies in support) commenced a coordinated attack delivered by platoons and companies against the front manned by the 2nd Battalion and Team O'Hara. On the Bastogne–Arlon road, a group of tanks started north toward the right flank of the 2nd Battalion. The Germans seem to have had the village of Marvie as their main objective because by midnight, the fight had died down all along the line except at Marvie, where it burst out with fresh virulence. It is estimated that at least one rifle battalion and some fifteen tanks were thrown against Company E (now reinforced by an understrength company of airborne engineers) and Team O'Hara.

Three German tanks made their way into the south edge of Marvie, but O'Hara's tanks and assault guns stopped them by gunning down the Panzers silhouetted in the glare of burning buildings, enabling the Americans to hold on in the north half of the village. The threat of a breach here impelled McAuliffe to send the remaining half of Team Cherry to Marvie. Because this switch stripped Bastogne of its

The pathfinder unit of the 101st Airborne Division, dropped by parachute, sets up radar equipment near Bastogne, Belgium, December 23, 1944. Their job is to guide planes with medical supplies and ammunition to the division. *National Archives*

last counterattack force, Cherry's detachment, which had gone west to assist Team Browne, was recalled to Bastogne. An hour before dawn on the 24th, the battle ended, and quiet once again descended on the little village of Marvie. O'Hara's troops had accounted for eight Panzers in this fight, but the village was still clutched by both antagonists.

The events of the past hours had shown that the force under McAuliffe's command was overextended. The artillery west of Bastogne was particularly exposed, and the 327th Glider Infantry had already been forced to shorten its lines. Then, too, the segments of the perimeter defense were not as well coordinated as they might have been. The tankers of CCB complained that they had no idea of the airborne positions, and quite probably the regiments of the 101st were hazy as to the location of the small tank and tank destroyer detachments on their flanks.

Elsewhere in the Ardennes on December 23, Lieutenant Colonel Cantey of Company G secured permission to use a rifle company that heretofore had been in division reserve. It was brought up through Parfondruy and placed in defensive positions approximately one-half mile west of the town. The rest of that day was spent preparing plans for an attack to eliminate the hostile infantry that had infiltrated west of the Amblève River.

Meanwhile, Lieutenant Colonel Peiper, the German commander in La Gleize, fought a delaying action both west and east of that village. The 119th Infantry's attack from the west advanced in two columns, one guiding on the main Stoumont–La Gleize road, and the other column guiding on the secondary road that wound up to La Gleize from the La Gleize Station. The 2nd Battalion was left in Stoumont in defensive positions. The column moving astride the main highway into La Gleize was held up most of the day by the roadblock in the woods between the two towns, which Company G had originally put in, on December 21, and which the Germans had strengthened and now had covered with both tanks and infantry.

The attack of the 1st Battalion up the secondary road from La Gleize Station bogged down, chiefly because of tank fire from the high ground on the outskirts of La Gleize. This avenue of approach was so subject to the enemy's observation that tanks could not be effectively used, and infantry advance was very difficult. Probably the most effective pressure on the enemy was the constant artillery fire that was emplaced on La Gleize and anything that moved in or out of the town. Enemy casualties from this fire were heavy. By the end of December 23, the American line was roughly one kilometer west of La Gleize. The advance on La Gleize from the east that day was a failure as far as the tank attack was concerned. The two M-4 tanks that had been destroyed on December 22 completely blocked the only avenue of approach that the tankers found feasible. The 117th Infantry, however, was successful in reaching some farm buildings approximately five hundred yards southeast of La Gleize. This put the soldiers in a favorable position for enveloping the town from the south. Furthermore, Malmedy suffered terrible collateral damage as it endured a bombardment from Allied bombers, who mistook it for St. Vith. Clear skies were not always a blessing.

On December 23, the survivors of the defense of St. Vith, under command of Lt. Col. Thomas J. Riggs, and the 424th Infantry retired behind the lines of the 82nd Airborne Division.

It was December 23rd, and while the Battle of the Bulge raged along its eighty-seven-mile front, General Eisenhower confirmed the death sentence of Private Eddie Slovik, Company G, 109th Infantry Regiment, 28th Infantry Division, the only U.S. serviceman to be executed for desertion in World War II. One month later, Eisenhower ordered Slovik to be executed by a firing squad made up of members of the 109th Infantry Regiment. In later years, Slovik's wife petitioned the U.S. government for posthumous clemency for her husband. It was never granted, and she died a few years ago.

Donald Nichols: I believe it was on the night of the 23rd that the Germans launched another attack on our position [Company C, 21st Tank Battalion, 10th Armored Division], coming down the road we were guarding. This was a night attack. The first I knew of it was the MG fire, and a farmhouse was set afire to provide light. Our tank was rocked with a close explosion. We were ordered to fall back out of the lighted area. We backed up about fifty or sixty yards; however, things had quieted down.

W. D. Crittenberger: Thank God for the [December 23] airdrop. They dropped it near where we [420th Field Artillery Battalion, 10th Armored Division] were, and the 101st gave us all their 105mm ammunition. The red parachutes were artillery ammo, and the green parachutes were gasoline. The 101st was able to distribute the supplies to everyone once we gathered up all that we needed.

Myles Covey: We [B Battery, 14th Field Artillery, 2nd Armored Division] had a one-hundred-mile trip from just over the border in Germany. We were given three hours to get ready to go. There was total blackout, no communication, radio silence. At ten or eleven at night we left. They had no maps for us; we had to get down to the Bulge as soon as possible. The roads were icy with snow all over them, but we only lost three vehicles during the journey. We got down in the Celles, Belgium, area at six in the morning. They had a kitchen set up, and they fed us. We got gas and extra ammunition. We were unassigned and unattached,

The 424th Regiment, which was south of the other two regiments of the 106th Division that were captured, was able to withdraw and join with the 112th Regiment of the 28th Infantry Division. They formed a regimental combat team and were successful in helping counter the German attack. They actually drove the Germans back through the same area where the 106th had been in position in mid-December 1944.

and we took our orders directly from Eisenhower. I slept in the middle of three feet of snow, and the temperature was below zero most of the time during the Bulge.

Zeke Prust: Oh, that was the most beautiful sight in the world, when those clouds opened up [on December 23] and we [Service Company, 54th Armored Infantry Battalion, 10th Armored Division] saw all that materiel coming down. We knew some of it was landing with the Germans, but other than that it was an awesome sight. I was in Bastogne, and I was asked to do something as far as retrieval. We, our crew actually went into one of the homes, where the horses were, and there were big troughs made of concrete, and we laid in those troughs until the shelling was light. Then we got out and back to our area. It was our place that we called home.

We were so fortunate to be in a tank. When a tank was running, the transmission gave off heat, and there were so many who got frostbite. We were next to that transmission, and I tell you it kept us warm.

John R. Schaffner: It seems that the Germans had come closer each time our perimeter [Battery B, Survey Team, 106th Infantry Division] got smaller, and they were ready to end it. The fog would roll in and out, giving us limited visibility. I would fire at anything I saw moving around in range of my hole. This weather was tough on us, but I think it was to our advantage from a defensive point of view. I'm sure our enemy was not able to determine exactly what he had to overcome to take the crossroads. Whenever he came into view, we would drive him back into the fog. Our ammunition was running out. I had one clip of carbine rounds and could find no more. Word had come around that when the ammo ran out and the Germans came, it would be every man for himself to escape if you could, otherwise a surrender was prudent. We were apparently surrounded, but the Germans were taking the easiest route, the hard-surface roads. That left the fields open.

Late afternoon, probably after 1600, the final assault came. Mortars, small arms, and fire from tanks. I was in the stone building, sitting on the floor with my back to the wall. Harold Kuizema was with me. This room must have been a kitchen at one time because I recall a wood-burning cook stove and a GI who I didn't know trying to heat something at it. Something big hit that wall and exploded it right over our heads into the room. It must have hit high, or it would have gotten the both of us. As it was, it filled the room with debris and dust. That was all the motivation we needed to leave there. To wait for another one never crossed my mind.

We (Harold and me) went to the front door. They were coming, and we were going. It was that simple. Some of our people were going to the cellar. I didn't like that idea. So, once outside, I crawled to the road and the ditch. There were some cattle milling about on the road, and much smoke, so I got up and ran through the cattle to the ditch on the far side and once again dropped down to avoid the German fire.

On this side of the road was a snow-covered field, very open, but it was "away" from the attack, so that's the direction that I took. Not far into the field Harold went down. As I got to him I saw two GIs approaching from the other direction. It was apparent that Harold was not going any farther on his own, so between the three of us we moved him the remaining distance to the shelter of the woods and into the company of a patrol of infantrymen from the 82nd Airborne Division.

When we reached the shelter of the woods and I looked back at the crossroads, the whole sky seemed to be lighted by the flames from the burning building and vehicles. Our wounded man was evacuated, and I received permission to tag along with these 82nd Airborne Division GIs, which I did until late sometime the next day (the 24th) when I was able to locate some 106th Division people. There were some vehicles from the 589th with this group that were not with us at Parker's Crossroads, and one was loaded with duffel bags—mine was with them. Another miracle: clean underwear and socks.

◆ ◆ ◆

SHORTLY AFTER THIS, THE REMNANTS of the battalion were assembled in the vicinity of Eronheid, were moved to Hoyemont on the 25th and Dolembreux on the 26th, and were told they would be reorganized. After drawing equipment, in preparation for the reorganization, the battalion was moved to Xhos on the 27th and was notified that it would be disbanded. On January 1, 1945, the majority of the personnel remaining were transferred to the 591st Field Artillery Battalion and the 592nd Field Artillery Battalion.

General Gavin wrote a letter concerning the stand at Baraque de Fraiture:

> I was in the town of Fraiture [one mile northeast of Baraque de Fraiture] the afternoon you made your great stand at the crossroads.
>
> I had sent a Company from the 325th under Captain Woodruff to the crossroads to help hold it, so I started over

in that direction myself. The fire was so intense, however, that there was no way of getting there without crawling through the woods, and it was still some distance away.

I decided that I had better get more help, so I sent to the extreme left flank of the division for the 2nd Battalion of the 504th, where it had the 1st SS Regiment of the First Panzer Division bottled. In doing so, we uncovered the Germans and during the night of Christmas Eve they slipped through the 505th Parachute Infantry.

Nevertheless, I got the 2nd Battalion of the 504th to backup the crossroads, come what may.

That stand your defenders made at the crossroads was one of the greatest actions of the war.

It gave us at least a twenty-four-hour respite, so I thank you and all the brave soldiers who were under your command for that.

With best Regards, signed James M. Gavin
Lieutenant General, USA (Ret)

William W. Fee: The weather was colder than it had been. Before we [55th Armored Infantry Battalion, 11th Armored Division] started out, we crowded around a fire. It needed wood, but nobody would go get it. Soon we were on our way. About 1000 we went through part of Paris, but not the city center. For hours we rumbled down broad brick streets lined by spacious old houses. Ed Bergh and some others had a humorous incident with an old Frenchman, trying to find a toilet. Jack Morrison's track conveniently broke down in Paris, so he got to see his brother and picked up a fur-lined flying jacket.

Out in the country again, we had a break about 1500 and stood on the side of a hill, watching a farmer working across from us. Two hours later, we drove through Château-Thierry. Kids were playing on broad sidewalks with stucco houses in the background. We skirted Reims about 1900. We were told later that Ercil Pennick and Sergeant Ramsay, who stayed behind (in Reims, apparently), almost were strafed and that the Germans strafed and bombed a truck company.

About 2200 we passed a white railing that looked like the entrance to a camp [Camp Sissonne, 40 km north of Reims and 20 km east of Laon]. We pulled up to a barbed-wire fence, beyond which was a structure that was called a "flak [antiaircraft] tower." It looked like a windmill without arms. We dismounted and stood there shivering in the bitter cold, then struggled into a stucco or plaster barracks and found a room on the second floor. A pistol-packing paratrooper "caretaker" told us that the place had been strafed the night before, but it was good to be in a bed [double-decker] and under a roof.

Phil Burge: The weather cleared very mysteriously on December 23rd. I can still see those C-47s flying over, dropping supplies. If that had not happened, I would not be here today. That was a miraculous sight. It was an act of God.

Ralph K. Manley: I remember the air drops that happened on the 23rd. Part of them, of course, dropped in the German areas, and the Germans got re-supplies in some cases.

I was in a foxhole; actually, it was a defensive position. Normally, we [501st Parachute Infantry, 101st Airborne Division] were very lightly equipped, with rapid-firing weapons, folding-stock carbines, that type of thing, rocket launchers, or bazookas, as we might call them, antitank mines, things like that—on the defensive there, as opposed to being on the attacking part. And of course, not knowing fully the situation, we blocked all the roads so no more could come into the city of Bastogne with our outlying positions there. Some of the people, of course, who were in the city of Bastogne hadn't gotten any farther than the city itself, so it was a time of really not knowing or being familiar with what was really happening except that the enemy was attacking and you wanted to stop them, and that part we did.

We had no idea how strong the Germans were, but as a paratrooper unit, we were always surrounded and what have you, so that part didn't bother us. We were not armed with tanks or vehicles, or antitank guns or anything of that nature, fast-firing type of units. We had our rifles, our hand grenades, our antitank mines, and things of that nature, and

our explosives, composition C–twenty-five pounds of it, as a matter of
fact, with each demolitionist. So we could mold that around and actually throw it on the engine of a tank as it passed us and blow the engine
on the tank to get it out of commission.

We used "sticky bombs." It was a composition C explosive, a putty-
like thing. By molding a ball of that and putting a fuse and blasting cap
in it, then we could throw that on the back of a tank where the engine
was, and it would blow the engine of the tank and incapacitate it.

Robert S. Zimmer: We [1st Platoon, Company A, 22nd Tank Battalion,
11th Armored Division, Patton's Third Army] were driving through
Paris on December 23rd. The people were eight to ten deep on the
sidewalks and were swarming over the tanks with flowers, wine, eggs,
and kisses. We couldn't stop. An armored division is quite an impressive sight. I found out later that we were the only division in France at
that time, and it was thought that by driving through Paris instead of
around it, we would give the people of Paris a morale boost. It was quite
a sight! We still didn't know that the Germans had broken through,
but the French did, though. No wonder they gave us such a welcome.
At Sissone on Christmas Day, we got a rest from driving. We had to
break the tracks and replace the track connectors with extenders, which
added about four inches to the width of the track. Between each section
of track, we had to remove a one-inch bolt. It took all the strength of
one man to loosen the nut. Then, with a sledgehammer, we knocked
the connector off and hammered a new one on. It was an all-day job.
General Patton had promised everybody turkey for Christmas. We got
it . . . turkey and bread, period!

L. B. Clark: The 94th displaced to Perle, Luxembourg, the morning of
the 23rd to support this attack. The 177th Field Artillery Battalion (155
howitzers) was to reinforce our fire [37th Tank Battalion]. Bigonville
was a natural fortress situated on a hill that dominated the surrounding
country, and it was protected by steep slopes on all sides except for a
narrow, wooded saddle on the south. Due to the difficulties of moving
tanks on icy hills, the attack was launched late in the day by Combat

Some of the most difficult terrain to traverse was down on the Luxembourg/Belgium border. Due to the heavy snow, GIs were frequently forced to abandon their vehicles and go the distance on foot.

Command Reserve with two companies of the 37th Tank Battalion and two companies of the 53rd Armored Infantry under cover of preparatory fire from the 94th and 177th.

The attack bogged down as the tanks ran into a minefield, which disabled several tanks, including that of our observer, Lieutenant Guild. This was our last tank, but fortunately no crewmembers were hurt, and the tank was repairable. Contrary to expectations, Bigonville was heavily defended with what was estimated to be a battalion of the 5th Parachute Division dug-in in the woods and on the slopes of the hill and supported by some armor, including one Sherman tank and two assault guns, which were knocked out by the 37th. The enemy mortars were extremely heavy. Captain Temple, while acting as liaison officer and observing the battle, was wounded by their fire. That night the fight continued, the 94th firing supporting and interdictory missions on Bigonville and Arsdorf, where troublesome enemy artillery was thought to be located. Under cover of darkness, Mr. Wathen and his tank recovery crew dragged Lieutenant Guild's tank to the safety of a patch of woods, where they repaired it the next day.

John Kline: No reason was given for our [M Company, 423rd Regiment, 106th "Golden Lion" Division] delay. Someone said there had been a lot of prisoners taken. Maybe they were not sure what to do with us because of the large numbers. I am sure, from what I can see, we were clogging their transportation system.

Joseph "Joe" Ozimek: I remember it started to snow. This covered us [Battery C, 109th Field Artillery Battalion, 28th Infantry Division] from place to place. We slept in the snow. We would move a mile or two, set our three 105mm guns up, and fire a round or two, then move a few miles away. We got to Bastogne on December 22nd, and the 101st Airborne Division was there. The division's leaders asked us to set up our guns just outside of Bastogne. We got some hot coffee and K rations. Then we fired our guns until we had nothing more to fire. The next morning, the 23rd, at about 0630, the Germans started to shell us. There was not a truck or a 105mm gun without a hole in it. The only soldiers left after the artillery attack were a first lieutenant, twenty-one men from the 101st Airborne Division, and the remains of our battery—ninety-one men in total. So we burned the trucks and the guns and marched in the snow in a single file. It snowed so hard you couldn't see the second man in front of you. We walked knee-deep in the snow. We could hear the Germans talking and running their tanks, but we couldn't see them . . . and they couldn't see us. A sergeant led us with a compass to Neufchâteau, about twenty miles. Nobody fell out on that trip. That night we got some warm food and coffee.

Thereafter, we had to dig a defensive line all around the city of Neufchâteau.

Frank Towers: The fighting was severe and continuous. We [Company M, 120th Regiment, 30th Infantry] actually had more casualties from

The M7 Priest mounted a 105mm howitzer. Each U.S. armored division had three battalions of M7s, giving them unparalleled mobile artillery support.

frostbite of the feet and hands than actual wounds from enemy action. This required an enormous number of replacements continually throughout these two months. The logistics of keeping us supplied with ammunition, food, and replacements was an ongoing nightmare for our service units.

In order to assist Colonel Peiper in the execution of the German plan, the soldiers of the 3rd Parachute Division were dropped well behind our lines, and they created havoc by cutting phone lines, turning road signs in the wrong directions, and even acting as MPs and directing traffic in the wrong direction! All of the men in this unit were dressed in U.S. uniforms and, by devious means, confiscated many U.S. vehicles, which thereby gave credence to their being genuine U.S. soldiers and authorized to be there. Little thought was given to challenging them "so far behind the frontlines." Most spoke excellent English, which many of them had learned while living in the United States prior to the war, and they even knew our passwords of the day, which had been captured during the breakthrough from the 106th Division.

In this area, on the Western outskirts of Malmedy, one of our men, Pfc. Francis S. Currey, engaged a group of German tanks, a halftrack, and two antitank guns with a BAR, a bazooka, antitank grenades, a .50-caliber machine gun mounted in a U.S. halftrack that had been knocked out and abandoned earlier, and a .30-caliber heavy machine gun. He single-handedly knocked out three German tanks—one of which had the markings, fake of course, of the U.S. star on the turret and on the sides of the tank—and two halftracks, killed several German soldiers, and in the midst of all of this, saved five of his comrades from certain death, or from being taken prisoner. For this, Francis Currey was awarded the Congressional Medal of Honor and the Belgian equivalent, the Belgian Military Order of Leopold II with Palm.

Meanwhile, the Germans had claimed the capture of Malmedy, and the headlines of the *Stars & Stripes* proclaimed this. Thus, our

Relations between U.S. Army personnel and civilians in Bastogne were very good indeed. The civilians even offered up their bed sheets for the GIs to use as winter camouflage.

This civilian in Bastogne is showing his deep appreciation for being given a Lucky Strike by a GI.

Air Corps partners, the "9th U.S. Luftwaffe," as we called them, came over with their heavy B-24 bombers on December 24 and opened their bomb-bay doors directly over Malmedy.

Malmedy had been liberated in October 1944 with little or no fighting, since the Germans were on the run at that time, heading for their defenses along the nearby border of Belgium and Germany. So, Malmedy had been spared of any appreciable damage, and when we moved into the town on December 18, it was a beautiful and picturesque resort town where everyone was merrily going about his or her business as usual.

This suddenly changed the whole picture. Malmedy was a total disaster, with the entire center of the city laid to waste. Many civilians were killed and wounded, but we were fortunate in losing only a very few men of our own. Our biggest loss was our Christmas dinner, which was being prepared that day. Spam and bread is what we got. Three of our company's kitchens located within the city of Malmedy were totally destroyed.

Of course our Air Corps "friends" apologized, and they still could not understand just what went wrong. As they were apologizing, the 9th Air Corps was on its way, to make sure of the knockout, and they bombed Malmedy again on Christmas Day! This in spite of the whole city having been covered with our normal phosphorescent panels, to indicate that the area was occupied by our own forces.

As I mentioned, the entire center of the city of Malmedy was a total wasteland, and the next day, the *Stars & Stripes* proudly proclaimed that Malmedy had been retaken by our troops, due to the strong support of the Air Corps in stopping the German advance.

At this particular time, I was a liaison officer from the division HQ, which was located in the Hotel des Bruyeres in Francorchamps, to the 120th Regimental HQ, which was located in City Hall in Malmedy. I drove between these two points frequently, day and night, so it was prudent to find the shortest route. This led me to an unimproved road up over a mountain to the northwest of Malmedy and through the settlement of Burnenville, situated on top of the mountain. This route saved me many miles of travel and hours of time.

◆ ◆ ◆

DECEMBER 23 PASSED RELATIVELY QUIETLY in the Malmedy–Stavelot sector. The Germans contented themselves with sporadic firing across the river. It appeared that they lacked the strength needed to resume the attack to relieve Peiper over in La Gleize. A request was submitted to the II SS Panzer Corps to send the 9th SS Panzer Division to Stavelot. This request was refused point blank.

Major action did flare up again at La Gleize and along the north bank of the Amblève on December 23, where a part of the 1st SS Panzer Division relief force still maintained a foothold. In this sector, six American rifle companies were assembled to clear out the woods and

THE STORY OF THE KING TIGER IN LA GLEIZE

In July 1945, the American army began to assist the Belgians in hauling away and disposing of the rusting tanks left in their villages and fields after the Battle of the Bulge. King Tiger 213 lay in the Wérimont farm field where it had been abandoned, still minus the front of its gun tube. As the Americans began to haul 213 away, the proprietress of a local inn persuaded them to leave it in the town square in exchange for a bottle of cognac! It stood near the town civic building for several years, and in 1951 the Belgian army moved it to a better display area. Over the years, it has been restored under the direction of Gérard Grégoire, curator of La Gleize's December 1944 Museum. The amputated gun barrel posed a problem until M. Grégoire discovered a complete Panther gun tube buried beneath a farmer's hedge (it had probably been overlooked by the scrap dealers after the war). M. Grégoire persuaded the farmer to sell the find for the bargain price of one thousand Belgian francs, and 213 received a new gun when workers welding the Panther barrel to what remained of the original Tiger barrel and added a relic muzzle brake from another Panther. Tiger 213 remains in La Gleize today, the showpiece of Kampfgruppe Peiper relics.

The crew of this King Tiger II with Porsche turret discovered, to their chagrin, that the small back streets of Stavelot were not particularly conducive to large vehicles. They released a few rounds at the church about a hundred yards away before being brought to a halt.

A German King Tiger II tank lies abandoned in a narrow street in the Belgian town of Stavelot, December 26, 1944. *Allan Jackson/ Keystone/Hulton Archive/Getty Images*

repair the incision made by the enemy on the road between Trois-Ponts and Stavelot. Regrouping in the heavy woods took nearly all day.

In La Gleize the story was mainly one of frustration and failure. Most of Peiper's troops were driven to the cellars of the town by the incessant shellfire that increased as the day wore on and U.S. forces brought forward observers closer to the target. In the afternoon, elements of the American rifle companies reached the edge of La Gleize, only to come under machine gun and 20mm fire from streets and houses. Allied planes were promised to hit the town square. They came as agreed but hit Malmedy instead of La Gleize, their bombs burying a number of civilians in one of the hotel buildings before the strike could be called off.

Peiper still had to be driven out of La Gleize; the 1st SS Panzer Division bridgehead force north of the Amblève still needed to be eliminated. Nevertheless, this fight in the bend of the Amblève had become anticlimactic, dwarfed by far more important operations elsewhere on the northern shoulder of the Ardennes salient. Throughout the early evening of December 23, telephone wires connecting the headquarters of the First Army, the XVIII Airborne Corps, and the 30th Division were extremely busy.

CHAPTER NINE

CHRISTMAS EVE ON THE BULGE

24 DECEMBER 1944

GENERAL PATTON RADIOED A MESSAGE to the besieged General McAuliffe in Bastogne on Christmas Eve 1944. In true Patton style, it was short and to the point. It said, "Christmas Eve present coming up. Hold on!"

It also appeared that the British were finally going to get into the fray. Recently appointed Field Marshal Montgomery, confident as always but cautious, had taken steps during the day to bring the 1st Division (British) across the Meuse and into position behind the First Army in the sector southeast of Liège. Other British troops were on the move to assist the 29th Armoured Brigade (British) if the enemy should hit the bridges at Givet or Namur. This was good news to the First Army commander and his staff, not to mention that some elation was abroad as the result of Allied air forces activity on this clear day. Around Celles, a joint operation between the 2nd U.S. Armored Division and the 29th British Armoured Brigade began dismantling the 2nd Panzer Division.

During the morning of the 24th, preparations were being made around Manhay to counter the threat posed by the II SS Panzer Corps. The 7th Armored troops would deploy on the high ground south of Manhay and extend their line across the highway and along the ridge leading east. The 7th Armored would withdraw to the low hills north of Manhay and Grandménil and retain a combat outpost in the valley at Manhay itself. The 3rd Armored task forces had been promised support in the form of the 289th Infantry, due to arrive on Christmas Eve. The main body of the 2nd SS Panzer Division was moving in the direction of Manhay on the night of December 24.

At 0300 hours on December 24, an enemy foot column led by SS Lieutenant Colonel Peiper moved out of La Gleize. A group of 171 American prisoners were left behind to fend for themselves in La Gleize. The escaping Germans numbered around 800. They crossed the Amblève River on a small highway bridge south of La Gleize. At 0500 hours, the first German tank was blown up, and inside of thirty minutes, the entire area formerly occupied by Lieutenant Colonel Peiper's command was a sea of fiercely burning vehicles. This was the job allocated to a small detachment he had left behind to organize and complete the destruction of all of his remaining equipment. When the U.S. forces arrived in La Gleize, they found that the "small detachment" Peiper had left behind had done a very poor job of destroying the German materiel. Many vehicles were found to be in perfect working condition. According to official figures, the more important German armor captured at La Gleize included the following:

7	Mark VI tanks — TIGER
15	Mark V tanks - PANTHER
6	Mark IV tanks
8	armored cars
70	halftracks
6	SP 150mm howitzers
6	75mm or 88mm antitank guns
2	75mm assault guns
6	120mm mortars
5	20mm antiaircraft guns

The capturing troops found large quantities of ammunition for all of this armor. Gasoline, however, was very low. The gas tanks of most of the vehicles were empty.

For many thousands on the Bulge, Christmas of 1944 will always remain synonymous with mourning, suffering, and destruction. On the whole frontline, operations were carried out with the same desperate eagerness as in previous days. Moreover, a German counter-attack in Bastogne now seriously threatened to engulf the defenders of the perimeter.

The gloomy side of the picture was all too readily apparent. The fall of St. Vith had opened the way for fresh forces and new pressure against the army center and right flank. The 82nd Airborne Division was exposed to entrapment in the Manhay sector, and in the course of the evening an order to withdraw would be issued. The situation as it appeared in the VII Corps on the army right wing could accurately be described as a cliffhanger. On the left wing, in the V Corps sector, the enemy appeared ready to resume strong offensive operations, and after their Christmas Eve supper, Hodges and Lt. Gen. Clarence Huebner sat down to plan the evacuation of the corps' heavy equipment in order to leave the roads free in the event that withdrawal to the north became compulsory.

To further exacerbate the situation, the Allies experienced the first-ever attack by sixteen German Me-262 jet bombers. They attacked railyards in an attempt to upset the ability of the Allies to resupply. Thankfully, Hitler did not have many of these jets, otherwise the outcome of this battle could have been very different.

In Bastogne, the commanders and staffs took official notice of the holiday. General McAuliffe's message to his troops on Christmas Eve is recorded in many accounts of the battle. He rose to the occasion with an inspired communiqué in which he told his men about the German demand for surrender and his answer to them. Here's his Christmas message in its entirety:

24 December 1944

What's so merry about all this, you ask? We're fighting—it's cold—we aren't home. All true, but what has the proud Eagle Division accomplished with its worthy comrades of the 10th Armored Division, the 705th Tank Destroyer Battalion and all the rest? Just this: we have stopped cold everything that has been thrown at us from the North, East, South and West. We have identifications from four German Panzer Divisions,

Supreme Commander of the Allied Expeditionary Forces Gen. Dwight D. Eisenhower shakes hands with Gen. George Patton while Gen. Omar Bradley looks on. There's sufficient evidence to suggest that Bradley wasn't a great admirer of Patton. Despite this, he worked as the military advisor on the film *Patton*.

two German Infantry Divisions and one German Parachute Division. These units, spearheading the last desperate German lunge, were headed straight west for key points when the Eagle Division was hurriedly ordered to stem the advance. How effectively this was done will be written in history; not alone in our Division's glorious history but in World history. The Germans actually did surround us, their radios blared our doom. Their Commander demanded our surrender in the following impudent arrogance.

> *December 22nd, 1944*
> *To the U.S.A Commander of the encircled town of Bastogne.*
> *The fortune of war is changing. This time the U.S.A. forces in and near Bastogne have been encircled by strong German armored units. More German armored units have crossed the river Ourthe near Ortheuville, have taken Marche, and reached*

St. Hubert by passing through Hombres Sibret-Tillet. Libramont is in German hands.

There is only one possibility to save the encircled U.S.A troops from total annihilation: that is the honorable surrender of the encircled town. In order to think it over a term of two hours will be granted beginning with the presentation of this note.

If this proposal should be rejected one German Artillery Corps and six heavy AA Battalions are ready to annihilate the U.S.A. troops in and near Bastogne. The order for firing will be given immediately after this two hours term.

All the serious civilian losses caused by this artillery fire would not correspond with the well-known American humanity.

The German Commander

The German Commander received the following reply:

22 December 1944
To the German Commander:
NUTS!
The American Commander

Allied troops are counterattacking in force. We continue to hold Bastogne. By holding Bastogne we assure the success of the Allied Armies. We know that our Division commander, [Major] General [Maxwell D.] Taylor, will say: Well Done!

We are giving our country and our loved ones at home a worthy Christmas present and being privileged to take part in this gallant feat of arms are truly making ourselves a Merry Christmas.

A. C. McAuliffe
McAULIFFE,
Commanding

There have been various accounts of him uttering a more profane expletive on receiving that famous ultimatum, but they are unlikely.

Major General Maxwell D. Taylor, shown here in 1945, commander of the 101st Airborne Division, missed the opening of the German counteroffensive in Belgium during the Battle of the Bulge due to travel to Washington, D.C. He subsequently flew the Atlantic and passed through enemy lines in a jeep to return to his men at Bastogne. *Keystone/Getty Images*

General A. C. McAuliffe was an articulate and intelligent man. Privately, though, on the phone that night to General Middleton, McAuliffe expressed his true feelings about Christmas when he said, "The finest Christmas present the 101st could get would be a relief tomorrow." Despite McAuliffe's words, the situation was drastically bleak, and the defenders of Bastogne knew it. They were running perilously short of food and ammunition. Frostbite and pneumonia casualties were thinning their ranks almost hourly. And there was a numerically superior enemy force surrounding them.

Despite all the prevailing adversity, General McAuliffe's greeting to his troops proved to be in every part prophetic, even though the quiet of Christmas Eve did not last for long. That night, the town was bombed twice. Except for those bombings, Christmas Eve passed without

unusual pressure from the enemy. The journal entries of virtually all the different regiments used the word *quiet* to describe the situation at the time.

Over in the woods called Bois Jacques, just above Bastogne, paratroopers of E Company, 506th Parachute Infantry Regiment, 101st Airborne, were back in their foxholes after having repelled an attack earlier in the day. On this freezing Christmas Eve, Capt. Dick Winters uttered the words "hang tough." Despite being surrounded and ill equipped, they held the line.

W. D. Crittenberger: [December 24, Christmas Eve] was the worst day. The Germans decided to have a coordinated attack for the first time. We [420th Field Artillery Battalion, 10th Armored Division] called for help, and help came. We were fighting them off, and the 101st luckily looked at the situation and reduced the size of the line. Their leaders told us to move back closer to Bastogne, which was good because my battalion commander was wounded, fatally, our headquarters was hit and burned, and we were lucky we were able to move out by order and not because we had to. We got mortared by the Germans, which meant two things: they knew where we were, and they were getting close enough to mortar us. We beat some more attacks that night.

Dorothy Barre: On Christmas Eve we [16th General Hospital] were strafed by a German plane. You did your own work, but you did not know what was going on. We did have casualties from that strafing: two of our men were killed. I was off duty when it happened, but I was in a clubhouse visiting with the other nurses who were not on duty. On Christmas, we did not do anything different because we had been strafed. Before that, we had set up

This unfortunate GI from the 101st Airborne Division is lying dead at the perimeter of the woods at Bois Jacques, approximately two miles from the besieged city of Bastogne where, according to Bill Guarnere, "The trees grow in straight lines."

a Christmas tree in the tents that we decorated with bandages, and we had a turkey dinner.

William Kerby: On Christmas Eve, we [20th Armored Infantry Battalion, 10th Armored Division] were told that the Germans had parachuted men wearing white uniforms in around Bastogne. I posted guards at each corner of the building. My post was facing the aid station about thirty-five or forty yards away. All of a sudden, the night sky was brighter than the Las Vegas strip from the magnesium flares that the German bomber pilots had dropped. A few seconds later, the first German bomber dropped his first bomb on the aid station, a direct hit. The second bomb landed in our backyard and wiped out all our empty foxholes, leaving only the latrine . . . thank God! The second German bomber dropped down to strafe us with machine gun fire. All the GIs started to shoot at the plane with machine guns, rifles, and carbines. The German plane dropped a bomb that was a direct hit on a building two doors from ours. That building just happened to be a distillery. The bottles flew all over, and some were found two weeks later in the snow-banks. I faced toward the aid station, and Renée Lemaire was helping some wounded GIs out of the building. She went back in the building and came out helping more wounded, yelling, "Help, help, water, water!" The flames from the fire were intensifying. She was safe and sound out of the building but decided to go back in and help. Renée Lemaire never returned. The woman was a heroine and a saint. I am an eyewitness to these above facts. In 1994, the fiftieth anniversary of Renée Lemaire's death, a ceremony was held in Bastogne, Belgium, and a memorial plaque in her honor was placed on the building that now stands where the aid station had been.

Myles Covey: We [B Battery, 14th Field Artillery, 2nd Armored Division] met the Germans three miles from the Meuse River, and all hell broke loose. The Germans had the 9th Panzer Division and the 2nd Panzer Division spearheading. On December 24 the most decisive battle took place. As a medic, you did what you had to do. I did not have to treat many wounded, since I was back with the artillery. We had three battalions of artillery in our division, and they would call us on the radio, and the artillery would fire shots at them. Most of the time, we were within eyesight of the German tanks. The tanks and the infantry had more casualties than the artillery did, since they were at the head of the spearhead.

With number of guns knocked out and captured, the British could account for 100 percent of the 2nd Panzer Division being wiped out.

Clair Bennett: I recall we [Company F, 90th Cavalry Reconnaissance Squadron, 10th Armored Division] moved into someplace north and west of Luxembourg City, and it was about ten to twenty-five kilometers away from the city. The Germans were expending everything they had at the time. They had rocket launchers on their tanks, and they fired these rockets at different elevations and "walked" clear across the field. That's quite a harrowing experience. They have a horrible sound, not only floating in the air, but also the explosion. It was quite a morale breaker. That night when I got out of my tank, it was so cold; all the air that came down to keep the engine cool came through the hatches. I had to slide down the tank to keep warm. But it was pretty noisy, with all the rockets being fired nearby.

Seymour Reitman: I dug a slit trench near Elsenborn, Germany. I finally got a sleeping bag and a blanket, and inside the trenches we [2nd Battalion, 395th Regiment, 99th Division] took cans with rocks and gasoline in them and lit them to keep us warm. When we came out of the hole to move out, all you could see was our eyes and teeth because of the soot.

Don Olson: We [Troop C, 90th Cavalry Reconnaissance Squadron, 10th Armored Division] were posted in a patch of trees in a forest in Luxembourg. That evening there were artillery duels between us and the Germans, and they were firing over us. Trying to knock each other out. Our radio operator, who had just gotten a letter from his wife saying she wanted a divorce, went crazy that night. We had to hold him down to keep him from making too much noise because we did not want the Germans to know where we were.

The German unit to penetrate the farthest west was the 2nd Panzer Division of the Fifth Panzer Army, coming within fewer than ten miles (sixteen kilometers) of the Meuse by December 24 before being ordered back to the siege of Bastogne.

Albert Tarbell: We [Company H, 504th Parachute Infantry Regiment, 82nd Airborne Division] were moving out to another area, a position southwest of Lierneux. This was the first clear day we had had since we had been on this mission. We watched P-38s strafing German tanks and infantry. It sure was quite a show, and another very busy day. As usual, we didn't know what was going on, except for the rumors that were floating down to us enlisted men. It seemed that just as we would get set up, we would receive orders to move out again. The company commander told us that due to the attack by General Patton's forces to the south, and another group pushing in from the west, we had to move back to another line of defense. In other words, we were making a strategic withdrawal to consolidate our defenses.

We started moving out at approximately 2000 hours and what a walk that was! We walked across fields, roads, and whatever. I ended up in front of the column quite a few times. Whenever we came to a fence that had to be cut, I would use a pair of TL29 pliers to cut the wire. As we were moving along, the engineers were blowing down the trees onto the road for blocking, anything to place obstacles in the path of the German tanks and infantry. We could hear armored behind us. Whether they were ours or the enemy's, we did not know. It was past midnight when we reached our destination (Bra). What a Christmas Eve it was!

Donald Nichols: The next order was to fire all weapons at 0600 at the wooded and illuminated area we [Company C, 21st Tank Battalion, 10th Armored Division] had backup from. My tank commander told me to traverse my turret slightly and level my gun. I was pointing at the road area to my right front. I did not see anything there. At 0600, we got the command to fire, which I did. Apparently there was a German Panther tank on that road. He fired at the same time I did. My round knocked his tank out, and his AT hit our tank as it was in recoil and gouged some steel out of tank, sheering sprocket bolts out of the right side front track area. Their round must have then ricocheted off, sending a lot of sparks, as an acetylene torch does. The rest of the crew bailed out, and I continued to fire my .30-cal. co-ax MG until empty. I crawled around the 105 gun, reloaded my .30 MG, retrieved another 105 round from the ammo pit in the floor, loaded it, went back to the gunner seat, fired it, and, MG empty, again repeated the same as above. At that time, the rest of the crew came back and wanted to know if I was OK. I said OK but I could use some help. They came back, and I continued firing, but very shortly after that the ceasefire command was given. Resupply of ammo or food was not available, since they were rationed items. Because of the damage to the tank, we were limited in our movements; we stayed in that position until Bastogne was relieved with only slight repositioning. We were told to move back to Bastogne. We moved a short distance off the line to the rear and spent the night on our tank.

Frank Towers: On the fateful day of December 24, as I was traversing this route and was about to descend the slope of the mountain down into Malmedy, I heard the drone of planes to my rear. I told my driver to stop right there. We looked back and saw this great flight of B-24 bombers. What a wonderful sight to behold! I said to my driver, "The

Germans are going to catch hell somewhere," and he agreed. Little did we know at that moment that their target was Malmedy! In a few moments, we were appalled when we could see the bomb-bays of the planes open, and the bombs began to tumble out. It was total horror as we watched the bombs drop all the way down to their target, the heart of the city of Malmedy. Clouds of smoke erupted from this point, then flames reaching hundreds of feet into the air over Malmedy. I had a small camera with me, and I took a few photos of the planes, dropping their bombs, and then of the city shrouded in smoke and flames.

It was later learned that three of our 3rd Battalion kitchens had been totally destroyed and about twenty-five of our men were missing in action, all presumably in and around the kitchen areas, and no trace of them was ever found.

There is some question as to just when this action occurred, since everything and everybody was in a state of chaos. Whether this action took place on December 24 or December 25 is questionable, but the fact remains that we *were* bombed on both days. All of the company's records were destroyed in these bombings, so all we have are the accounts written in the history books and the recollection of others many years after the event.

We cranked up our jeep, raced down the slope of the mountain, and crossed the bridge over the river on the north side of the city. That was as far as we could go, since there was debris from the bombing all over the streets, making them impassable. People were running around screaming for help and needing assistance. Knowing where all of our medical facilities were located in Malmedy, all that I could do was to direct them to the nearest medical facility, where they could get help. Upon reaching the regimental command post located in City Hall, I found that all of the phone lines were out, and radio communication with Division HQ was not possible, due to the distance and the interference of the mountain between the two headquarters.

I was delegated to race back to Division HQ and advise them of the disaster that had just occurred, and to summon assistance at once. Almost immediately, as many of the medical officers and staffs as were available were summoned and dispatched to go to Malmedy to render any assistance possible to our own troops first, then to render assistance to the civilian population as needed.

Needless to say, the 105th Engineer Battalion was dispatched also to render assistance in clearing the main routes through the city as quickly as possible.

It was remarkable to note that, although the entire heart of the city was destroyed, the St. Quirin Cathedral was virtually untouched. Talk about miracles!

However, we recovered from this disaster rather quickly, since most all of the necessary ground support was almost immediately available because we were in the midst of the First Army supply depots, which had been abandoned by that unit on December 16–18, 1944.

In another action, in the small village of Petit Coo, another of our 30th Division men, Tech. Sgt. Paul Bolden, earned the Congressional Medal of Honor. He charged a building housing thirty-five Germans, under the cover of one of his comrades, who was armed only with a rifle. The Germans had pinned down his company for some time with heavy automatic weapons and small arms fire. His covering comrade was killed by this intense fire, but undaunted, Bolden hurled fragmentation and white phosphorus grenades into the doorway and windows of the house. He received return fire and was hit by four bullets in this action, then, despite his wounds and weakened condition, he charged the house again and sprayed it with a submachine gun. He waited for the Germans to come out to surrender, but none came out. Thirty-five dead Germans were in the house. None escaped. Technical Sergeant Bolden was presented with his medal by President Harry S. Truman in Washington, D.C., in September 1945, after returning home with the Division. Many more actions like these recipients occurred but were never adequately documented, so those involved in these incidents were awarded sixty-five Distinguished Service Crosses and an untold number of Silver Stars.

◆ ◆ ◆

RENÉE LEMAIRE WAS A BELGIAN nurse. Together with Augusta Chiwy, a nurse who was born in the Congo, Renée served with great distinction at the aid station of the 20th Armored Infantry Battalion.

According to John "Jack" Prior, MD, of the 20th Armored Infantry Battalion, Renée tended to shrink away from the fresh, gory trauma; Augusta was always in the thick of the splinting, dressing, and hemorrhage control. Renée preferred to circulate among the litter patients, sponging, feeding them, and distributing the few medications they had (mainly sulfa pills and plasma). To the wounded and dying U.S. soldiers, the presence of these two girls really boosted morale.

Around Christmas Eve, the decaying medical situation was worsening even further, with no hope for the surgical candidates, and even the superficial wounds were beginning to develop GAS infection (*streptococcus pyogenes*). At around 2030, another bombing raid began. Witnesses said that the night was brighter than day owing to the magnesium flares the German bomber pilots dropped along with their deadly cargo. It's estimated that about twenty injured were killed in this bombing, along with Renée Lemaire.

Dr. John "Jack" Prior: At 2030 hours on Christmas Eve, I was in a building next to my hospital [20th Armored Infantry Battalion, 10th Armored Division] preparing to go next door and write a letter for a young lieutenant to his wife. The lieutenant was dying of a chest wound. As I was about to step out the door for the hospital, one of my men asked if I knew what day it was, pointing out that on Christmas Eve we should open a champagne bottle. As the two of us filled our cups, the room, which was well blackened out, became as bright as an arc welder's torch. Within a second or two, we heard the screeching sound of the first bomb we had ever heard. Every bomb as it descends seems to be pointed right at you. We hit the floor as a terrible explosion next door rocked our building.

I ran outside to discover that the three-story apartment building serving as my hospital was a flaming pile of debris about six feet high. The night was brighter than day from the magnesium flares the German bomber pilot had dropped. My men and I raced to the top of the debris and began flinging burning timber aside looking for the wounded, some of whom were shrieking for help. At this juncture, the German bomber, seeing the action, dropped down to strafe us with his machine guns. We slid under some vehicles, and he repeated this maneuver several times

Augusta Chiwy

Augusta Chiwy epitomizes all the strength and power of the human spirit in the face of great adversity. Though Stephen Ambrose may have made only a passing reference to Chiwy in his *Band of Brothers*, her story is one of incredible courage and tenacity in the face of monumental hardship. To rise to the challenge and overcome all adversity takes a special kind of character.

before leaving the area. Our team headquarters about a block away also received a direct hit and was soon in flames. A large number of men soon joined us and we located a cellar window (they were marked by white arrows on most European buildings). Some men volunteered to be lowered into the smoking cellar on a rope, and two or three injured were pulled out before the entire building fell into the cellar.

I estimated that about twenty were killed in this bombing along with Renée Lemaire. It seems that Renée had been in the kitchen as the bomb came down, and she either dashed into or was pushed into the cellar before the bomb hit. Ironically enough, all those in the kitchen were blown outdoors, since one wall was all glass. I gathered what patients I still had and transported them to the riding hall hospital of the airborne division.

As Battalion Surgeon, 20th Armored Infantry Battalion, I am recommending a commendation for Renée Lemaire on the following evidence:

This girl, a registered nurse in the country of Belgium, volunteered her services at the aid station, 20th Armored Infantry

Battalion in Bastogne, Belgium, 21 December 1944. At this time
the station was holding about 150 patients, since enemy forces
encircled the city and evacuation was impossible. Many of these
patients were seriously injured and in great need of immediate
nursing attention. This girl cheerfully accepted the herculean task
and worked without adequate rest or food until the night of her
untimely death on 24 December 1944. She changed dressings, fed
patients unable to feed themselves, gave out medications, bathed
and made the patients more comfortable, and was of great assistance in the administration of plasma and other professional
duties. Her very presence among those wounded men seemed to
be an inspiration to those whose morale had declined from prolonged suffering. On the night of December 24 the building in
which Renée Lemaire was working was scored with a direct hit by
an enemy bomber. She, together with those whom she was caring
for so diligently, was instantly killed.

It is on these grounds that I recommend the highest award
possible to one who, though not a member of the armed forces
of the United States, was of invaluable assistance to us.

Jack T. Prior
Captain, M.C.
Commanding

Renée Bernadette Emilie Lemaire
Place du Carre 30
Bastogne, Belgium

♦ ♦ ♦

AS MENTIONED, RENÉE LEMAIRE was not the only nurse in
Bastogne on that day. She was assisted by Augusta Chiwy, another
Belgian nurse who lived to tell the tale. After years of searching,
we finally found her in Brussels. Madame Chiwy is one of the most
interesting ladies we have ever had the good fortune to meet. She
saved literally hundreds of American lives and lived through the most
traumatic time in the history of Bastogne.

Augusta Chiwy: The snow was very deep that year and you could have cut the fog with a knife. I don't think that I've ever been as cold. The wounded just kept arriving and their number was growing by the hour. The worst problem was supplies. We had almost nothing except a bit of sulpha [sulfanilamide] powder but no anesthetic.

Augusta Chiwy, volunteer nurse with the 20th Armored Infantry Battalion. *Latchodrom Productions*

I didn't know Renée very well. She was quite a bit older than me, very popular with the soldiers. We worked very hard to try and help these soldiers but it was extremely difficult and freezing cold. I remember going to the building next door to drink a glass of champagne with Dr. [Jack] Prior, who had invited me to join him. It was late on Christmas Eve when the German bombers came. We heard a tremendous crash bang and I thought that we had been hit by a shell or something. The explosion knocked everyone to the ground and for a few minutes it was chaos. I couldn't see anything because of the dust, but with Dr. Prior's help I managed to get up and get outside. The sight that I saw there was terrible. The aid station had been hit and was just a pile of bricks. You couldn't recognize the building anymore.

Some soldiers came to help us clear away the debris and get to the wounded. The wounded on the first floor . . . the bad cases were all dead, and we couldn't find Renée. We found her eventually, though. She was in two pieces. The doctor and I wrapped her body in a parachute. She had wanted a parachute to make a wedding dress. After the aid station was destroyed I went to work at the barracks with the doctor. I saw him again when he returned to Bastogne in 1994. He was a very, very nice man. A gentleman. I think of him often.

◆ ◆ ◆

AUGUSTA SPOKE TO US in September 2009. Before that, she suffered from selective mutism for many years after the war ended. She had not spoken of her wartime experiences until 1994, when she finally broke her silence after a meeting with her former boss, Dr. Prior. Her gargantuan efforts were never recognized or acknowledged by the U.S. government, but she deserves our respect, our admiration, and our deep gratitude for the tremendous work that she did.

Ralph K. Manley: I remember on Christmas Eve I was on the second story of a building that was there at that time with field glasses trying to cover the roads and see what was coming, and the artillery and bombing. The building began to fall down, so I jumped out of the window and into the street of rubble below. I actually broke several toes in my foot, but that was so minor that you didn't bother with that until years later, when I had them repaired.

◆ ◆ ◆

MEANWHILE, MOST OF THE CAPTURED 106th Division POWs were allocated to various Stalags around Germany and one in Poland, but there were a few who were singled out in some cases because they simply looked Jewish. These poor, unfortunate men would be sent to a horrendous labor camp called Berga.

One of the men subjected to slave labor was John W. Reinfenrath, B Company, 423rd Regiment, 106th Infantry Division.

John W. Reinfenrath: Christmas Eve we were sitting in the railroad yards at Diez, Germany. It was about dusk when the sirens began to wail mournfully. We had been there for a couple of days and learned in that time to recognize the first warning of aircraft approaching. Then a new sound came, which had to indicate a raid because at almost the same time we were shaken out of our lethargy by explosions. Before we had time to think about it we heard the whistle of bombs as they fell and held our breath. This yard was a target.

With the blast of an explosion, it felt as though a giant had lifted our car about four feet and then let it drop. There was a momentary silence and then a scramble for our steel helmets. Conversation that moments before had included cursing, food, and sex turned to prayers. I have a vague memory of starting with an Act of Contrition, an Our Father, etc. They were said aloud, and all around me I heard praying.

Those by the door pounded and called vainly to be let out. Events showed that we were probably safer in the cars than outside looking for cover. We heard that the doors had been blown off one of the boxcars at the end of the train and eight Americans had run out, only to be killed by the next bomb. Our car was hit by flying debris, but no one was injured. We had a few loose boards in our car. It was a horrible experience to be locked in and bombed by our allies. When I looked out the little window, I could see a gaping hole in the slate roof of a nearby building that had not been there before.

William H. Tucker: During late morning of December 24, 1944, Capt. Archie McPheeters Jr. received the order to pull back from the Salm River, all the way to Basse-Bodeux. Word came down that despite protests from Generals M. B. Ridgway and J. M. Gavin, Field Marshal B. L. Montgomery had ordered a major pullback of the 82nd Airborne Division to "tidy up the lines." We [I Company, 3rd Battalion, 505th Parachute Infantry Regiment, 82nd Airborne] were furious! We held a secure, almost impregnable position, centered at Rochelinval along the Salm River, and had beaten off major elements of a German SS Panzer Division. All our three platoons held the high ground . . . the idea of giving up captured ground to "tidy up the battlefield" was never accepted by the ranks of the 82nd Airborne—it was outrageous! But orders are orders, and they are meant to be carried out. It was planned to move the main body of I Company, assisted by two trucks (for ammo and supplies) at about 2000 on Christmas Eve. Part of 2nd Platoon (about ten men) was to provide a rearguard at both the river line and the railroad until first light—the three 60mm mortar squads were ordered to be united into one sole operating group (as in Holland, and despite narrow roads and thick woods). I was to supervise all three mortar gunners, hoping that the radios would work in case a fight developed and that they would remain fully operational in this hilly and wooded terrain.

Weather was a determining factor on many levels during the Battle of the Bulge. Most roads in the Ardennes back in 1944 were little more than cart tracks made for farm vehicles. Congestion became a major problem for both sides at various stages of the battle.

With everything in place, I Company moved up the road in the direction of Basse-Bodeux in good order. With about eight miles to go, the troops crossed the open area through the snow and started over the backside of the first hill in the deep woods—when suddenly firing started up front and on both sides of the column. Captain Archie McPheeters Jr. left me with the mortars and moved ahead. I was called by radio and asked for mortar fire to hit three hundred yards ahead on each side of the road. The mortars did the job and pulverized Jochen Peiper's people ahead. Our company kept moving the column forward, while the three mortars kept firing at each stop, even though they were limited to forward firing in order to clear the trees. The column took some hits from the flank but luckily without too many casualties. The fight didn't last long. I Company knifed through what was left of the main elements of Kampfgruppe Peiper trying to get back to the Fatherland. In the process, "OKITE" [I Company's radio call sign] picked up several prisoners. Major Hal D. McCown (2nd Battalion Commander, 119th Infantry Regiment, 30th Infantry Division, captured near Stoumont December 21, 1944), being taken back with the Germans, took off in the fighting and later joined up with I Company. As the retreating column cleared the woods near Basse-Bodeux, it set up a line of strong points on the snowy hills around the village. The snow continued to fall steadily, and the troopers hoped they would see their rearguard again. That proved to be the case, but not without some losses and hardships, in falling snow, over the railroad bridge, and up the hill toward Rochelinval, amid desperate enemy troops.

Charles Haug: We saw about twenty sharp flashes in the hills about three or four miles directly in front of us. A few seconds later, we heard a bunch of shells screaming over our heads and crashing into the woods about a half mile behind us. We looked at each other, and big smiles broke out on our faces all at the same time. These shells were American—we could tell by the sound. Did this mean that the Americans had stopped the Germans and were attacking back again? Did it? Were we only a few miles from the American lines again? Were we? We slapped each other on the back, and our hopes of getting back again had been raised sky high.

General Dwight D. Eisenhower, Field Marshal Bernard Montgomery, and Gen. Omar Bradley standing together at National Airport, Washington, D.C. Eisenhower's decision to appoint Montgomery as commander of the First Army during the Battle of the Bulge was not a popular one.

As we stood there, we saw more and more flashes, and more and more of our shells whistled over our heads. Now we knew for sure that these were Americans coming in our direction. We couldn't wait to get to them. We jumped into the river and waded across the icy stream. Lucky for us, it wasn't deep. The water came to about our knees, and it ran into our shoes, but we didn't care. The Americans were coming! We were soon on the bank on the far side, and as we walked, the icy water squished in our shoes. We started going down the road on the far side of the river. We were headed for the hills where we had seen the flashes from our artillery guns.

We hadn't gone far when we came to a small house and barn along the side of the road. We could see a light in the house shining through a crack in the door, and we rushed up to it hoping that maybe we would run into some more GIs. One of our guys ran up to the house while the rest of us hid in the barn. He walked into the house, and all was quiet. Soon he came back to the barn and told us to come in. He said that there were three Belgian civilians in the house and that they would tell us what they knew about the movements around the area during the past day. As soon as we were all in there, they all started to talk at once. We couldn't understand much of what they were trying to tell us, but we understood enough so that we found out that the Germans had captured all of this ground and were dug in, in the woods and hills all around. They said that the Germans had been going by in trucks for two days straight now, and they had seen hundreds of American prisoners being taken to the German rear by German guards. They said that there had been heavy fighting going on between the Americans and Germans all during this past day a few miles away. They also told us that they didn't think we would have much of a chance getting over to the American lines because there were thousands of Germans all over the place.

With this information, we decided that we would have to figure out some pretty clever schemes if we were going to get back without getting captured. One of the Belgians asked us if we were hungry, and we all shook our heads. She went down in her basement and brought up two loaves of dark bread and a small tub of butter anyway. We sliced the bread, put big hunks of butter on it, and had a real feast. We ate until the bread was all gone. There were about ten of us in the house, and we figured our chances of getting back were mighty slim. The bread and butter had tasted so good that each of us pulled out our billfolds and emptied every cent we had on the table in the house. We told them that that was our pay for the food. In a few minutes, we were out of the house and on our way once again.

We had gone just a few rods down the road when we heard a jeep coming from behind us. We jumped into the ditch, but the jeep stopped when it got to us. The driver had spotted us in the moonlight. We were very much surprised to find that there were two GIs driving the jeep. We thought these roads were taken over by the Germans. We soon found out that these two GIs were in the same boat as we were. Their outfit had been retreating for the past week, as we had been doing. They didn't know where they were going, but they wanted to get back to the American lines. As we were standing there talking, an American armored car pulled up behind them with about five more GIs in it. They told us that if we wanted to climb on, the armored car would go first, and we would all try to break through to the American lines.

As we started to load on, another jeep pulled up and stopped. There was getting to be quite a gang of us. The armored car pulled up in front, I got in the first jeep with a bunch of guys, and Frankie and Quimby got in the last jeep. The armored car and our jeep started out, but the last jeep seemed to have some trouble, and it didn't get started with the rest of us. This was the last that Frankie, Quimby, and I were together. They never did catch up with us. This was the last I saw of Frankie until I went to visit him a year later in Pittsburgh, after we were out of the army. Frankie told me this story of their adventure from this time on:

Frankie said that when their jeep finally got started, they had lost sight of us, so they just headed down the road in the same direction they had seen us go. They hadn't gone far when they came to a fork in the road, and here they must have taken a different road than we had just taken. They traveled for about a half-mile when they ran smack into a German roadblock. Frankie said that Kraut machine guns opened up on them, and those who weren't hit made a dive for the ditch. There was no place for them to run, so they just lay there. It wasn't long until the Krauts started tossing hand grenades in on them. One of the grenades landed alongside of one of Quimby's legs and exploded. Quimby's leg was broken and ripped to pieces. Frankie said he tried to help him as best as he could. A few minutes later, a bunch of Krauts rushed them and captured the ones who were still living. Frankie hadn't been hit, so they made him and another guy come up on the road, and they made Frankie take off all of his clothes so they could search him. They gave him back his pants and shirt, but they had been thrown in the snow, and he was about frozen stiff. Next they saw Quimby lying in the ditch, so they dragged him up on the road too. Quimby's leg was giving him a great deal of pain, but the Krauts didn't seem to care. They just stood and looked at him, and finally one of the German officers walked up to him. He took his rifle and pointed it at Quimby's head.

The story of the guys in our jeep was a little different. When we pulled away from Frankie and Quimby near the farm place, we took the other road at the fork. We drove about a mile without running into a thing, then we came to another small town. There was no road around the town, so we knew that we had to go through it. The armored car in front of us speeded up to about forty miles an hour and made a mad dash into the town with us following. As we came to the first house, we saw a German halftrack standing alongside of it and a Kraut guard standing in front of the house. As we drove by, his head made a quick turn, and as soon as we were past, we saw him run into the house. We didn't see another soul until we got to the last house on the other end of the town. Here, the same thing happened, and we saw him run for the house too.

By now, it was about midnight, and we were going full speed ahead. We must have gone about a mile out of the town when all of a sudden, we came up over a small hill in the road, and there right in front of us were two long columns of German infantrymen coming on foot in our direction. One column was on each side of the road. Both the armored car and our jeep stopped as quickly as we could. The armored car was still in the lead, and it really caught it. The Germans opened up on it with a terrific amount of small arms fire. I don't believe any of the men got out of it alive. Our jeep driver threw the jeep in reverse, and we started to back down behind the small hill we had just come up. Just as we were going back over the crest of the hill, a machine gun burst hit our jeep, and the driver was killed. The rest of us made a jump for the ditch, and we ran across a small open area toward some woods. There were about eight of us running, and the Krauts spotted us. They opened up again, and three of our men were hit. They all made it to the woods though.

We made an awful lot of noise as we were trying to run back in the woods, so we all stopped still for a minute. We could hear the sound of many feet running up the road we just left, and we knew it was a bunch of the Krauts looking for us. We all lay down in the snow and covered ourselves with it so they wouldn't be able to see us from the road. All eight of us were as still as could be, and we could plainly hear the Krauts talking among themselves just a couple of hundred feet away. Twice, they called into the woods and told us in English to come out with our hands up, but we lay still. Finally, the whole bunch started to walk down the road again, and we made our way deeper and deeper into the woods.

When we figured we were in far enough, we stopped to see how bad our three guys had been hit. One of the guys was a lieutenant, and he had been shot through both of his legs. None of his bones had been broken, so two of us had to help him walk from then on. One of the guys had been hit in the neck, and it was bleeding very badly. His left arm was hanging limp, and his jacket was covered with blood. He told us he thought he could make it all right if we didn't go too fast. The third guy had been hit in the seat. He said he could make it all right if he didn't sit down anyplace.

Next we checked to see what guns we had left. We had two rifles. The rest of the guys had all lost their guns when we jumped from the jeep a few minutes before. I was the only one who had a compass, so we set our direction for due west again. We had to walk slowly, and we tried to help the three wounded guys as much as we could.

We must have walked for about an hour through the woods, and the going was rough. We could find no trails anywhere, and by this time, our three wounded guys were almost exhausted. The lieutenant's legs had turned stiff from the wounds, and two of our guys had to drag him between them in order to keep him with us. The kid who was shot in the neck kept falling down all the time, and he was getting awfully weak from loss of blood. Each time we would stop to rest, the blood would drip from his limp arm, and the snow became stained with blood.

About four o'clock in the morning, we finally came to another road. We looked down the road, and we spotted another small town about a half-mile away. We knew that we couldn't keep going like this much longer, so we decided to hit for the town. We decided that if there were Krauts in the town, we would give ourselves up. With this thought in mind, we headed slowly down the road for the town. The moon was still shining bright, and we knew that if there were anyone in the town, they would see us coming. We got to within a hundred yards of the first building, and we stopped to see if we could hear any noises from the town. Everything was still. We started slowly ahead again. Suddenly, right in front of us, a voice in the still night yelled, "HALT!" We froze in our tracks. We could not see anyone, anyplace. Then the same voice yelled, "Who the hell are you?" We hollered, "Americans!" Then the voice said, "One of you come forward to be recognized."

One of our guys walked up to this first house, and we saw a guy step from the shadow of the house. It was a GI. It was hard to believe our eyes, but it was true. We had reached the American lines. We all rushed up to him and started to ask him a hundred questions. He said he was with the 82nd Airborne Division and that they had just captured this town about three hours before. There were about a thousand paratroopers in the town, and they were getting ready to start attacking in the direction we had just come from. They were going to start their attack at daybreak.

As soon as we got into the town, the paratroopers loaded our three wounded guys in an ambulance and headed for an aid station with them. The five of us who were left were taken to a house where the officers of this outfit had their command post. The officers said that they wanted us to help them, if we could. They unfolded a bunch of maps on a table and asked us to point out all the places we had seen heavy forces of Germans during the last couple of days. They said they needed this information so that they would know where to concentrate their forces when they started their attack in a couple of hours. We put a bunch of marks on their maps, but I don't imagine they used them once they started. When we finished, they loaded us in a jeep and hauled us back to their kitchen crew. Here, we were fed the biggest meal you would ever want to lay your eyes on—and we really ate.

L. B. Clark: The following day, Christmas Eve, the attack was pushed on against a stubborn defense, and Bigonville fell. Mopping up went on into the night. Over four hundred prisoners were taken, and one hundred enemy dead were counted. In the divisional picture, the situation could not be called bright. Combat Command B [37th Tank Battalion] on the left flank had received a worsting in a counterattack at Chaumont; Combat Command A had obtained its bridgehead at Martelange but was progressing slowly against road blocks, abatis, and stubborn resistance; Combat Command Reserve had just taken Bigonville after forty-eight hours continuous assault in a bitter fight.

William W. Fee: I had to get up at 0600 to watch for gasoline coming in. Coming back, I was almost run over by the 41st Tank Battalion, which was pulling out. We [55th Armored Infantry Battalion] turned in our duffel bags and sewed blankets into our bedrolls. In the afternoon, I wrote letters, and Charlie Crouch played his guitar. In the evening (Christmas Eve), I went to church, but first I went down and retrieved my .45 pistol from Magelli, who had "borrowed" it. Some of our officers and noncoms were drunk, and I wanted to get the pistol back before somebody got shot. The service was in a sort of school. A young first lieutenant, chaplain of the 575th Antiaircraft Artillery Battalion, preached a sermon. The division chaplain, a lieutenant colonel, was there. Henry Pope and Walt Zoppi went to the service too. Zoppi had been baptized in England on December 10. Both men were killed three weeks later.

Dick Goodie: To keep from freezing to death, we [486th Armored Antiaircraft Battalion, 3rd Armored Division] slept right on the snow, using it for insulation. We fashioned our bedrolls with pieces of waterproof tarpaulins and baby-crib mattresses. We had confiscated the mattresses from bombed-out homes in Stolberg. My crew considered them a prized item. They were about an inch thick, efficient, and formed a small bedroll—handy since we had to carry seven on the halftrack. On each mattress, we placed our thin, hooded mummy-bag and a folded GI blanket and brought the other half of the tarpaulin over everything.

We wore our uniforms and combat jackets in the bedroll, pulled our wool-knit caps over our ears, lay flat on our backs with a boot tucked under each arm, and made it through the night. Some of us slept with a pistol on our chests.

Each man had to get up at least once during the night to pull his two-hour watch. Sometimes it would snow, and there would be small breathing holes in the snow where the men slept. In the morning, we would throw gasoline on tar-soaked shell cases and start a fire to thaw water in our canteens for coffee. During the day, we wore overshoes several sizes too large and stuffed hay into them for insulation. Frozen feet were epidemic, causing thousands of evacuations and subsequent amputations.

But the seven of us made it through OK, in large measure, due to our "insulated" overshoes and our bedrolls fashioned with baby-crib mattresses.

On Christmas Eve, for the first time in a week, we had a chance to sleep indoors, in the cellar of a deserted house. We spread our bedrolls on the concrete floor—not much better than frozen ground, but we were in a house, a real luxury. We brought in a bottle of confiscated Hennessey five-star cognac (which we kept cradled in straw in an ammo well) and a few cigars. Someone found a scrawny shrub on the front lawn of a deserted home. Now we even had a Christmas tree. But our hope to celebrate the Holy Night was short-lived. At eleven the captain came to the cellar and told us that Peiper was expected to break through south of the hamlet; we were to go there on outpost and radio Battalion Command if he appeared.

Merry Christmas!

We followed the captain's jeep through the deserted hamlet and came to a farm, where we set up behind a stone barn. Our field of fire, over a barbed-wire fence, was a long, narrow, undulating snowfield that shone a metallic, yellowish-blue under a full moon.

We waited for Peiper, staring down the snowfield, listening all night for the clanking of his Tigers. But Peiper was late. No one slept. One of our crew griped all night. In the freezing weather, he stood near the gun, stomping his feet and thrashing his arms—as well as his lips—to keep from turning blue.

He asked, "How the hell can we stop Peiper's Tigers anyway with a 37mm peashooter?" He had a point there, all right, but I knew it would be useless to mention that our mission was to radio for help if Peiper showed up.

I didn't blame him much. In over ten months of combat, he had proven to be an excellent soldier: He was fearless and could have qualified for the Dirty Dozen. He just got emotional about Christmas and upset at the captain for pulling us out of that cellar.

◆ ◆ ◆

BY DECEMBER 24, THE GERMAN advance was effectively stalling just short of the Meuse. Units of the British XXX Corps were holding the bridges at Dinant, Givet, and Namur, and U.S. units were about to take over. The Germans had far outrun their supply lines, and shortages of fuel and ammunition were becoming critical. Up to this point, the German losses had been relatively light, notably in armor, which was almost untouched with the exception of Peiper's losses. On the evening of December 24, Hitler exacerbated the situation by flatly rejecting Gen. Hasso von Manteuffel's recommendations to halt all offensive operations and withdraw back to the West Wall. Kampfgruppe Peiper's push west had effectively run its course in the small town of La Gleize just east of Stoumont, and with the 30th Division bearing down on him, he was abandoning his armor and making his way on foot back to Axis lines. For the besieged and embattled defenders of Bastogne, help was well on the way.

During the afternoon of December 24, the 2nd Battalion of the 119th Infantry was brought down from La Gleize as reinforcement. A very careful plan of attack was worked out and put into execution. But, when the troops moved in for the kill, they found, as they had at La Gleize, that the enemy had pulled out the previous night. Practically no prisoners were taken on either side during the three days of this battle in the woods. By nightfall of December 25, the 30th Division held an unbroken line north of the Amblève River from Stoumont Station to Stavelot. From Stavelot east to Malmedy, the division occupied the same positions that it had taken on December 18. Lieutenant Colonel Peiper's 1st SS Panzer Division had been stopped and driven back to the line where the attack had started.

CHAPTER TEN

CHRISTMAS DAY ON THE BULGE

25 DECEMBER 1944

TO A SIGNIFICANT NUMBER of the world's population, Christmas Day is a family occasion. It's a very emotional and highly charged time of year. Back in the winter of 1914, there had been an unofficial truce on the Western Front between the opposing British and German forces on Christmas Day. British and Germans had left their trenches and shaken hands in the middle of no man's land on that occasion. Fighting on Christmas Day of 1944, however, was intense.

By this time, with the element of surprise long gone, the Germans were simply trying to blast through the Allied lines. However, even with a considerable "bulge" straining the front, the U.S. and British continually refused to allow the Germans an advantage. Instead of considering a retreat, the Germans simply sent forward more and more artillery to try and expand the bulge as far as possible. Walther Model, the commander of Army Group B, was being openly optimistic if somewhat deluded; his order for Christmas Day called for a breakthrough to the river Meuse and the capture of Bastogne.

On the U.S. side, there was a pervasive somber feeling of nostalgia emanating through the ranks. They did not have long to wallow in their thoughts, though, because persistent German attacks continued throughout the day. Patton was still vivaciously pushing north, and any day now his forward troops would make contact with the besieged and battered GIs in Bastogne. Any way you look at it, this was no place to spend Christmas back in 1944.

W. D. Crittenberger: Before dawn [on December 25], the Germans had another coordinated attack toward the west side of town, which broke through the airborne lines. I was sleeping in a barn, and the housing in that area had the animals hooked on next to the house. There was a cement floor, so we put down fresh hay to sleep on. I woke up when I heard an attack coming, and I told Stan Resor, who was my executive officer, to call our batteries and turn them to fire direct fire on these incoming Germans. I ran out to see what was happening in the headquarters area just in time to see one of our perimeter defense posts burst in front of me, blowing over the machine gun Four men were running away, so I told them, "Come on, men, help me put this machine gun back up." They came back and put it up. German infantry was coming, and our howitzers were firing against their tanks. They only had four tanks, but we burned three of them, and the fourth one surrendered later, and that was when one of the mess sergeants said, "Hey, Major, come over." He made me Christmas dinner: two hotcakes and a half a cup of coffee, with the hotcakes made from donut flour.

Martin examining a foxhole in Bois Jacques. These foxholes were dug by 101st Airborne soldiers who were tenaciously defending the perimeter of Bastogne against repeated German 5th Army attacks. The message sent to them from General McAuliffe was simple and to the point: "Hang tough." Temperatures in Bois Jacques frequently dropped to minus 28 degrees Celsius. *Latchodrom Productions*

Zeke Prust: On Christmas Day, a whole group of us [Service Company, 54th Armored Infantry Battalion, 10th Armored Division] actually, even though I'm not Catholic, we all went to Catholic mass at midnight. All of us, we attended a mass that was being held. It was all 10th Armored at the church and some regular civilians who were still there. We ate C rations (it might have been K rations). We did not have anything special whatsoever. It was strictly what we carried out with us.

Albert Tarbell: Christmas Day we [Company H, 504th Parachute Infantry Regiment, 82nd Airborne Division] were set up on a defensive line. Our lines of communication were very long. We had lines to the battalion from our company, to the platoons, and to the O.P. [observation post]. We started getting hit by German patrols later on in the afternoon and throughout the day and evening. It was always difficult to maintain line communications whenever we received artillery fire. But we could revert to the radio as far as battalion. We were able to maintain good communications to the platoons, either by line or runner. H Company sent out patrols after the action and returned with prisoners. There were three of them, whom another trooper and myself took to battalion. As we arrived at the command post, Colonel Cook was outside and saw us come in with the prisoners. He ordered us over to him, and I thought he was going to kill them. They thought so too. He took out his .45-cal. and stuck it into the first SS guy's mouth, and they went down on their knees fast. They certainly did not look like supermen then! What a Christmas Day that was. No turkey, hardly any water for coffee. Later, we did get some water for coffee by melting snow.

Allen Atwell: After the Battle of Hürtgen Forest, I did not have any feeling in my feet from frostbite. I remember that I was carried into the facility on a litter. I did hear buzz-bombs sputtering overhead. I was ordered down to this room where there were men and women, and they had me sit on a table while they poked my toes to show how I did not have any feeling. I figured it was a seminar on frostbite.

Since there is no real treatment for frostbite, they just laid us out on a cot with our feet sticking out, and if they did not get better they amputated them.

I had been in the hospital for four or five weeks when the Bulge broke and they emptied the hospital out, and I was on my way to Bastogne as a rifleman. I had been a regimental MP guarding a finance office, and they offered me the chance to be a division MP, which I took.

I directed traffic and escorted German POWs back, and I would be put at an intersection, sometimes by myself. We were not informed what the big picture was. We heard about the Malmedy Massacre and also the Germans being dressed in American uniforms. We came up with different passwords to try and catch any impersonators.

Christmas was very sober—we knew it was Christmas, but there was no special recognition. It was just another day.

Robert T. Gravlin: On Christmas Day, we [Company B, 23rd Armored Engineer Battalion, 3rd Armored Division] pulled through Lierneux. There was a large church there, and mass was going on, so I went into the church and attended mass.

We cut the Marche–Bastogne road and set up roadblocks around Soy. We had two Sherman tanks on the side of buildings where the road deadended into another road, a "T" intersection. We set up our 57mm cannon facing down the road, and I dug in with my bazooka about fifty yards farther down the road.

The Germans were still attempting to infiltrate our lines dressed like American soldiers and driving 106th Division vehicles. We had just dug in when an American jeep with four men wearing American uniforms came up the road. I got up and yelled, "Halt!" They kept going, but a machine gun on the other side of the road started firing. The jeep stopped, and we went up to them with our guns pointed. The driver and the two in back showed us their dog tags, but they didn't speak. Next to the driver was a first lieutenant. He showed us identification, but he spoke in King's English. I asked him if he thought Detroit would win the World Series. He said no, but they would put up a bloody good fight. We pulled them out of the jeep because the World Series had been between the Cardinals and the Browns. It was discovered they were Germans in U.S. uniforms. We sent them back to our G-2 intelligence group.

A little later on we heard the steel treads of a German tank coming down the road. As it got closer, we could see it was one of Germany's largest tanks—a Tiger Royal. As it got close to the roadblock, our 57mm opened up on it. It was like shooting peas at it—those shells just bounced right off. It continued to rumble toward us. When it got alongside where I was dug in, I fired my bazooka at it. I hit the tank on its turret, and that shell didn't penetrate either—I think it just made them mad. The tank stopped and began to rotate its 88mm gun toward me. Fortunately, I had cut the wire of a barbed-wire fence behind me, so I left the area. The tank fired a couple shells in my direction and then moved forward.

As it approached the "T" intersection, our Sherman tanks with their 75mm guns opened up on the Tiger—their shells didn't fare much better than my bazooka or the 57mm shells. The 75s bounced off the tank. The Tiger opened up on our Shermans and knocked them both out. In fact, one of the 88s went in one side of a Sherman and out the other side. When the Tiger got up to the "T" intersection, it was too large to fit around the corner, and as it was trying to maneuver around, we called in our artillery from our 105mm self-propelled guns, and their shelling with white phosphorus set the German tank on fire. As the German tankers bailed out, we captured them.

The bitter cold weather stayed with us—cold and snow, so no air cover. As we moved down the roads or fields attacking the Germans, we would stay by the rear of a tank and get a little heat from the exhaust pipe. The only bad feature of that, however, was the Germans would zero in on the tanks with antitank artillery and machine guns. Our light tanks were equipped with a short-barrel 37mm and machine guns, so they were no match for armor. They were used against infantry and ground troops. The Shermans were a match for the German Mark Series tanks but not the Tigers. In one sector, we surrounded a large number of German troops. They were mainly Wehrmacht (draftees), but they had "SS" officers commanding them, so they didn't give up until they were almost demolished.

We lined up the prisoners and G-2'd them (G-2 means search them). We took everything out of their pockets and threw it on a pile. An SS officer with them told me I could not search him because I was not an officer. I took his officer's cap off and threw it on the ground.

Then I proceeded to search him. He needed a haircut—I saw scissors on the pile so I hacked him all up. A regular Wehrmacht soldier standing next to him began to laugh. With that, the SS officer looked at him, and he wiped the smile off his face and came to attention. If that officer could have had a chance to kill me, I would have been lying on the ground. Many times in battle, the SS officers would shoot their soldiers if they tried to retreat.

That evening, my buck sergeant, John Schnoor, and I visited his brother in one of our 105mm self-propelled artillery companies. They had moved in behind us. In the edge of a little town nearby, we saw a butcher shop. We went in and asked him if he had any steak (in our broken French). He said, "Oui, si fait" (yes, yes indeed). He went out of the back of the shop and soon appeared with some large, red steaks. We gave him some Belgian francs for them and took them back to our squad. Using the blowtorch and a large frying pan we had liberated in Germany, we fried the steaks—they really tasted good. It had been a long time since we had had fresh meat. Later on, when we moved out of the little town into battle again, we saw where he had gotten the steaks. There was a knocked-out German field artillery piece with two dead horses pretty well carved up lying in back of the butcher shop.

Phil Burge: For Christmas dinner, I had cheese and crackers. We [Company C, 55th Armored Engineer Battalion, 10th Armored Division] stayed in basements to keep warm, and since General Taylor was in Washington, D.C., for Christmas, I used his generator to keep warm during my time in Bastogne.

Dick Goodie: Peiper didn't show up, and Christmas Day dawned clear and cold with bitter winds that swept up the snowfield. We [486th Armored Antiaircraft Battalion, 3rd Armored Division] stayed behind the stone farm Christmas Day, close to the guns. Our gun loader said he smelled like a tomcat and would love to take a bath. We all must have smelled badly, but no one took a bath during the Bulge, not even a whore's bath in a helmet. Except for an occasional change of socks, we never removed our clothes in six weeks.

A machine gunner of the 26th Infantry Regiment, 1st Infantry Division, guards a recently captured crossroads in deep snow. This was part of the mopping-up operation at the end of the Battle of the Bulge.

For Christmas dinner, we cooked ten-in-one rations over our one-lung gas stove. These meals, intended to give ten men nourishment for one day, consisted of large cans of processed meats mixed with eggs and other ingredients, which we cut into steak-sized slices and fried.

We finally moved back through the hamlet. MPs were directing traffic. We didn't trust MPs, since many English-speaking Germans, driving American vehicles and wearing our uniforms, had infiltrated our lines and were switching road signs, directing traffic in wrong directions, and causing chaos. Those who were captured were shot as spies. General Bradley hadn't forgotten the Malmedy Massacre of eighty-six GIs.

Moving past snowfields, we came upon recent battle sites. There were many frozen bodies in the ditches and fields, partially buried in drifting snow. A Graves Registration Unit was stacking bodies in deuce-and-a-half-ton trucks as they would stack logs. Many had died before the medics could thaw plasma under the hoods of jeeps.

Frank Forcinella: Christmas Day was nice for us [2nd Regiment, 5th Infantry Division]. They shelled us on Christmas Eve, and it was quiet for the next twenty-four hours. And I did see a couple of guys praying; we all did that. We did not get our Christmas meal. They did not want to take a chance bringing it up. We did not get our Christmas meal until December 28th. Then we had a nice hot breakfast, and we had pancakes, and we had blueberry syrup with ham, and we could eat however much we wanted.

Charles Haug: It was now early morning of Christmas Day, and the paratroopers left the town and started their attack into the woods ahead. The five of us jumped in a truck that was going to the rear for supplies, and we set out to try and find the rest of our 28th Division.

We rode back about ten miles, and we came to a large town. There were a lot of MPs in the town, so we asked them if they knew where the 28th Infantry Division was reorganizing. They told us that we would have to go about another twenty miles to the rear to another large town, and we would find the 28th Division trying to get organized there. We hopped on another supply truck, and soon we were back with the 28th.

It took about a week for us to get organized again. Thousands of green replacements were hauled into our town and assigned to our outfit. We also had to get all new equipment because nearly all of our artillery pieces, machine guns, etc., had been captured by the Germans. As soon as we had everything we needed, we started to train with our new replacements. We knew that we would soon be called forward again to help counterattack in the Bulge.

Helen Rusz: The nurses [59th Evacuation Hospital] made the Christmas. I called out one of the GIs, not a patient, and told him, "I want you to go out to the woods and get a Christmas tree."

He said, "What?"

I said, "Come on now, Jim, go on over and see if you can find a fir tree or some kind of tree and stick in something and bring it into the ward because we are going to have a Christmas party."

We did not have anything, but what we did was that everybody got a Christmas present from home; I got a big box of cookies and a big box of candy. What we did to decorate the tree was we took off our dog tags and hung them on the tree; we took our jewelry off and hung it on the tree. We also took cotton balls and stuck them in mercurochrome, which made them red, and we stuck them on the tree. We had so much fun decorating the tree with all these crazy things, but you know it was Christmas! Then we sang Christmas carols and passed around the cookies and candies and stuff and had a good time.

Don Olson: We [Troop C, 90th Cavalry Reconnaissance Squadron, 10th Armored Division] moved out of that area, but that morning the infantry came across a field and saw a lot of boys go down from German artillery. We were replaced by 3rd Platoon.

We went by a river where the Germans were on the other side; we set up booby traps to see if the Germans arrived.

We did not get our Christmas meal until about 1600 hours.

William W. Fee: Magelli woke us early: "We're moving out!" We ate in a hurry and scrambled into the track. Wahoo and I sat high up on the two rear seats and froze as the frigid air rushed by. We passed refugees going the other way and tough-looking Free French. We went through many towns, and at every house and corner, little groups of people waved to us. Many of the houses had been bombed, and the people looked poor and ragged. I got great satisfaction out of thinking that we had come over to rescue them. In one town, a French woman ran out with a pie for Sergeant Ramsay's track, just ahead of us.

By noon we had traveled about seventy kilometers northeast and were at our destination: Mezieres, France, fifteen kilometers from the Belgian border. [In 1962 Mezieres had 13,328 residents. In 1966 it was combined with four other towns to form Charleville Mezieres, with a population of about 50,000. Battalion headquarters were at Guignicourt-sur-Vences, ten kilometers to the southwest.] We parked the truck halfway up a steep, wooded hill and started a fire in a little can of gasoline. Wahoo threw a lot of gas on the fire and almost ignited Telly. For lunch we had C rations, and as evening approached, we climbed the hill almost to the top and set up our two MGs along a road.

Christmas dinner was not ready until about 2000. I stood guard at Telly's MG while the rest of his crew ate. They were late getting back, but there was plenty of turkey and fruit cocktail left when I got to the kitchen, at the bottom of the hill. In fact, they couldn't get rid of it all. My hands froze, but it was a fine meal.

William H. Tucker: As a beautiful, white Christmas Day dawned, I Company [3d Battalion, 505th Parachute Infantry Regiment], now with its rearguard back from the Salm defense line, settled along the snowy hills around Basse-Bodeux. We all thought, *Our company might at least have a few days of peace and rest before it had to go back to retake the ground it never wanted to give up!*

John Kline: Christmas Day in Dockweiler Dreis, we were on the march by 0630. Marched all day and night, no water or food, except snow. No Christmas, except in our hearts.

John Hillard Dunn: We took a twenty-four-hour break at Dockweiler Dreis waiting to board boxcars, as some of the POWs did, or continue the trek.

We spent that day, December 25, 1944, alternately cheering, running, shaking, and praying. The cheers were for the Allied bombers, the first to lay their deadly eggs on enemy territory since the German breakthrough began nine days earlier. Planes crossed the skies at all altitudes that day between their bases in England and the fluid but solidifying battle lines along Germany's borders with Belgium and Luxembourg. The order was out: "Put up everything we've got, even an ironing board if it'll fly."

We ran, after seeing the sunshine for the first time in more than a week, as the bombs from the Flying Fortresses and B25s—perhaps from a few ironing boards too—began to explode in our midst.

We shook from a combination of fear, the subzero cold, and the impact from the five hundred and thousand-pounders landing so closely. As the bombs detonated around us on what looked like a German military concentration from above, it appeared our luck had finally expired.

We prayed for obvious reasons, and most of us lived to pray our way through similar nerve-racking suspense in the upcoming days, weeks, and months. We prayed the airmen would get back to England alive. We wished we were up there with them, en route back to airbases where there were warm beds and something to eat and drink.

Christmas dinner for the captured Golden Lion infantrymen—plus an air force noncom who was captured while visiting his brother, a dogface, up front—consisted of hard tack (no excess of fattening calories) and something sweet and red that was presumed to be jelly or, perhaps, jam.

"It must be jelly," Bob Fecht, a GI from Wisconsin, quipped from between his chattering teeth, "because jam don't shake like that." It wasn't turkey and dressing like they were having on Burlington's South Hill, but it was something to eat. My raisin supply was long gone.

As the sun glowed more brightly later that day, more bombs rained from our planes. As they exploded, several GIs in the Panzer camp near the Dockweiler Dreis railroad depot were hurt and killed. There were screams and cries . . . but most of us lucked out.

After the bombers disappeared, we talked about our earlier Christmases, ones highlighted by bicycles, ice skates, electric trains, and sleds. Commando LaTournes, in particular, remembered Christmas in Connecticut—"God's country"—with his electric trains. One guy from Arizona said he enjoyed Christmas too, but he had never received an electric train on his Indian reservation or seen snow. We talked about people: Betty Grable's pinup poster in a white bathing suit, Bivouac Jones and his wife, Benny Goodman (whose rhythm number, "Henderson Stomp," kept running through my mind), and the Nazis living it up in Berlin while, like Nero's Rome, much of Europe burned.

There was an occasional thrust at humor. "Ah," Commando LaTournes called out in a voice approximating newscaster Gabriel Heater, "Adolph Hitler's a sorry man tonight.

Christmas Day 1944 will always be remembered by the men who were at Dockweiler Dreis . . . the ones who got on the boxcars there and the others, including myself, who resumed on foot the next day.

Erwin Kressman, 6th Army, Heavy Panzer Brigade, wearing his Knight's Cross, the highest decoration in the German Army.
Latchodrom Productions

Erwin Kressman: We [Kressman was a Jagd Panzer driver of the Heavy Panzer Brigade 519] were aware that we were not making the progress we should have been. Although we still had some fuel and our supply lines weren't that long, there was an atmosphere of desperation about it all. We didn't know that the whole Sixth Army effort was faltering and had been for a few days. I just drove my Jagd Panzer and did my duty as expected. Conditions were very cold, but I had experienced much worse on the Russian front in the east. In comparison, this wasn't so bad. Constant strafing by Yabos [P-47 Thunderbolts] didn't help the situation, though. I fought mostly in Germany around Nideggen, where I'd been during the Battle of the Hürtgen Forest. A couple of months later, I was awarded a Knight's Cross and given a courage vacation by the army. I'd earned it.

◆ ◆ ◆

IN THE SMALL TOWN OF STAVELOT at around 2000 hours on Christmas Day, Guy Lebeau went to church with his father and brother to attend the Christmas mass celebrated by Chaplain Lecrenier. It was a small congregation whose numbers were supplemented by GIs who had joined the locals to celebrate the mass. The Germans were not really celebrating their *Weinachten* on that day, though, and were in the process of raining shells on Stavelot, several of which exploded close to the church. Among the inhabitants of the district who attended mass, there were the unlucky parents of Julien Gengoux, who had been murdered by the 1st SS Division exactly seven days previous. It may have been a desperately sad Christmas for those GIs, but it was not much better for the civilians. Many no longer had homes to go to, some had been victims of Allied bombing, and some had seen relatives needlessly butchered by Nazi fanatics.

During the Battle of the Bulge in the Ardennes, Edmond Klein, a farmer who lived in Houvegné-Francheville, assisted a lost group of U.S. soldiers who were in the process of being hunted down by the Nazis. They came to his isolated farmhouse seeking shelter. Edmond knew that they were not safe there and that there was a real chance of them being captured. At great personal risk to himself, he took the initiative to guide the GIs throughout the woods to American lines in Petit-Thier. Once back at his farm in Houvegné, he discovered a second group in the same circumstances and selflessly repeated his actions. General Eisenhower, the supreme chief of the Allied armies, congratulated and thanked him personally for his bravery.

Monique Thonnon lived near Stavelot in the small hamlet of Parfonderuy. SS soldiers from Kampfgruppe Peiper murdered some members of her family, and she was badly wounded and left for dead. Her body was placed on a pile of corpses that the SS intended to burn. Fortunately, they couldn't spare the fuel to burn the corpses, so they left them. Monique regards herself as someone who escaped death at the hands of the SS on two separate occasions. She still harbors a deep hatred of the Nazi perpetrators. *Latchodrom Productions*

Rene Royaux and his whole family were held as prisoners by the SS in the cellar of their farmhouse near Stavelot for over a week. Kampfgruppe Peiper's SS soldiers took what little food was available and subjected Rene and his family to a horrific ordeal. They were starved, savagely beaten, and constantly threatened with execution. Rene managed to escape into the nearby woods where he remained hidden until the SS had left. *Latchodrom Productions*

Arlette Mignon lived with her family in a small house on the road between Stavelot and Trois Ponts. SS soldiers from Kampfgruppe Peiper burst into the cellar where she was hiding with her parents and two sisters. They shot and killed her mother and two sisters. Arlette was shot in the thigh, and her father received a bullet wound in his hip. Her father later testified in court at the trial of some of these SS men in Liège. *Latchodrom Productions*

This is the only surviving photograph of Arlette Mignon's two sisters.
Latchodrom Productions

Not far away, Gaspar de Wanne and his brothers conducted dangerous missions behind the German lines and closely observed the enemy's movements. Later, they transmitted this vital information to Allied staff, who used it to help conduct their planned counteroffensive.

When Germans surrounded the town of Stavelot, Mrs. Cottin-Schutz lived on the Rue Neuve. Her husband was, at that time, a prisoner in a Stalag in Germany. One day, she noticed a dejected and demoralized GI walking in her direction. He was holding a white handkerchief and doubtlessly wanted to surrender. At immense personal risk to herself and her four young children, Mrs. Cottin-Schutz bundled the GI into her house and hid him there. While German soldiers were in the process of rampaging through the houses in Stavelot, they inadvertently discovered the GI. They shot him in the head and then, in a despicable act of retribution, they callously murdered Mrs. Cottin-Schutz and her children.

The Americans in Bastogne endured despite unrelenting German assaults. There were many accounts of frostbitten fingertips actually getting stuck on the triggers of M1 Garands and other weapons. Air drops of ammunition, food, and medical equipment had provided a lifeline a couple of days previously, but the situation remained critical. Out in Bois Jacques, Sgt. Robert Rader and Pvt. Don Hoobler, both from the same town in the Midwest, sat in their frigid foxholes. Rader said, "As the night wore on, we talked of our homes, our families, and how they were spending their Christmas Eve. Don felt sure all of them were in church praying for us." They probably were, and that was a good thing.

On Christmas Day Hitler demanded that the town of Bastogne should be captured immediately. The Germans unleashed several armored attacks against the Bastogne pocket. Once again, they were driven back, with heavy losses. Inside the town, some soldiers attended religious services. Others tended to the wounded or buried the dead, but most were outside, holding the perimeter.

Meanwhile, back in the United States, the American people were learning about Bastogne. In their book *Rendezvous with Destiny*, Leonard Rapport and Arthur Norwood record how during the battle, men and women would look at maps printed in newspapers that showed one spot holding out . . . for days it was the one encouraging sight that met their eyes each morning. Hitler was obviously aware of what was pictured in these newspapers, and on the strength of that he decided that the town should be taken. Despite his unstable mental and physical condition at the time, he was well aware of the propaganda value of Bastogne. Once again, Hitler was completely ignoring the suggestions of his generals and officers to allow them to retreat to the Siegfried Line, known to the Germans as the West Wall. In the north, most German attacks had completely lost momentum, and as the 30th Division got into full gear, they were beginning to fall back.

At dawn on Christmas Day, up north near Manhay, GIs from Company I of the 75th lingered at the edge of the tiny village of Grandménil. As the soldiers waited for the order to attack, the Germans began an intense artillery barrage of their positions. Company I was to attack the village with the support of Sherman tanks. As the attack went in, Sherman tanks advanced up the village streets first, firing their

Wearing sheets as camouflage, soldiers of the 1st Infantry Division press on down a narrow lane near Faymonville during the Allied counterattack. *Imperial War Museum*

Christmas in Bastogne: troops of the 101st Airborne at a Christmas service while still under siege. *U.S. Army*

cannons point-blank into the occupied houses of Grandménil. The riflemen followed. First, they threw hand grenades into the houses; immediately after the explosions, they sprayed the insides of the houses with rifle fire and then entered. The Germans fought desperately, forcing the Americans to take Grandménil one house at a time. At day's end, Company I had driven the Germans out of the village and had dug their foxholes in a defensive line along the edge of it.

Christmas night would be another cold, cloudy night with temperatures falling below twenty degrees. This was the coldest winter in forty years, and the men of the 75th spent most of it outside, with frozen feet. They could not use their sleeping bags that night—"Purple Heart Bags," they were called. If the Germans counterattacked during the night, the Americans could be bayoneted in their bags before they could free themselves and reach for their weapons. There they lay on the frozen earth, shivering themselves into a fitful sleep. The story was repeated throughout almost the entire Bulge. Many had not even seen snow before, and now they were fighting to survive the harshest possible conditions.

CHAPTER ELEVEN

BREAKTHROUGH

O N DECEMBER 26, FOUR medium tanks roared up the road from Assenois. Machine guns sprayed the snow around them, and dark enemy forms ran and fell as red tracers played among them. A concrete blockhouse ringed by pines loomed ahead of the onrushing tanks. First Lieutenant Charles Boggess Jr., Greenville, Illinois, commander of the lead tank, spotted the emplacement from the open hatch of his Sherman. Down in the turret, Corporal Milton traversed the sights of his 75mm on the blockhouse and kicked the trigger. The tank bounced from the recoil as the shell crashed into the concrete. The breech of the 75mm slammed shut as the loader slapped in another round. The driver of the Cobra King tank slammed on the throttle and squinted through his dirt-splattered periscope as the medium tank rolled up to the smoking blockhouse. Bow gunner Pvt. Harold Hafner kept the hot barrel of his machine gun trained on the woods.

Lieutenant Boggess raised his hand and halted his clattering mediums before shouting, "Come here, come on out!" to khaki-clad figures in foxholes. "This is the 4th Armored!" The lead element of the 4th Armored Division had reached Bastogne. Charles Boggess had driven the first vehicle from the 4th Armored into the lines of the 101st Airborne.

Lieutenant Colonel Creighton W. Abrams, 37th Tank Battalion commander, and Capt. William A. Dwight of his staff were close behind Lieutenant Boggess in the tank rush that pierced the last German defenses south of the beleaguered town. Tanks of the 37th, along with the 53rd Armored Infantry Battalion, were the point of the 4th's spearhead into Bastogne. Behind them rolled ambulances and supply trucks for 101st paratroopers and tankers of the 9th and 10th Armored Divisions who had been holding the besieged town. Twenty-five minutes later, Maj. Gen. Anthony G. McAuliffe (then Brig. Gen.), commanding the 101st Airborne Division, shook hands with Lt. Col. Abrams and Capt. Dwight to celebrate the relief of Bastogne.

Patton's Third Army had forced a precarious corridor through the German army to reach Bastogne. They may have relieved the town, but the fighting was far from over. It was at this juncture that Patton made a rather uncharacteristic statement, saying, "We can still lose this war." He was probably reflecting on the intensity of the fight still raging around him and his Third Army.

Ralph K. Manley: On the 26th of December, as I recall, the weather broke, and in came planes from the Allies to help us out. We were happy to see that.

General McAuliffe sent a Christmas note to the troops in Bastogne. Here we were, far away from home and were called on to defend our country and give it the best we could. In the meantime, the Germans had dropped leaflets for us, leaflets saying this was our pass to a warm bed, and if we wanted to see our sweethearts again, and so on, the type of leaflets that were tried to encourage us to give

On January 16, 1945, the U.S. First and Third Armies met at the devastated little town of Houffalize and finally closed the pincer on the German army, thus completing the encirclement. Although fighting continued for a few more weeks in the south, the Bulge had ceased to be.

up, and of course that was the perfect paper for us to use to relieve ourselves and what have you.

General McAuliffe sent the word "Nuts!" when asked to surrender; actually, it was much more than that, but that was the printable stuff. We kinda used some vulgar words at the time that we wouldn't use in the press or today. [After he sent that "Nuts!"], we were not about to give up, even though they encouraged us to (the Germans did). But it did block their advance on there, and that was the end of it for that part.

Many civilians were in their cellars, and a number of them had canned meat. This was before the days of freezers and that type of thing. They would cook meat and put it into jars and pour lard over it to preserve it. They shared this with us. When we were digging some of the foxholes around, some of our soldiers came across gardens that had some potatoes left and things like that, dark black potatoes that had been frozen. But it was something to eat, and one of us even killed a chicken that had about froze to death and ate the raw chicken in order to have something to eat. Of course we did not get a resupply of K rations, which were all we had in the paratroops. We didn't have the C or D rations . . . or the canned fruits from the local people who were scared to death. Many of the locals, of course, had gotten out, but others stayed there, and so they, too, were subjected to the bombing and shelling that we were.

Robert T. Gravlin: After another big tank battle the next day, toward dark, I climbed up on one of our Sherman tanks with the hatch open on top of the turret. I was checking to see if anyone was alive inside. Just as I got on top and looked in the open hatch, an 88mm from a German Tiger tank fired point blank at my head—the tank was just about ten yards from me behind a bush. The concussion from the 88 blast knocked me off the tank, even though the shell narrowly missed me. I moved pretty fast getting out of there. After those huge tank battles, the fighting settled down to slugging it out in the forest hills and valleys. It was still bitterly cold, and more snow fell. Our bombers and fighters still could not get airborne to help us.

These two photographs testify to the age of the German soldiers drafted into the army in 1944. Many of them ended up in volksgrenadier regiments, and some, such as the 12th SS Division *Hitler Jugend*, even made it into the SS, which by that time was using recruits from captured territories to make up the numbers.

The Germans were counterattacking, and we were dug in around a valley, which they were attempting to come through. We had dug holes by using dynamite and TNT to break the frozen crust. We had to stay awake because some of the infantry troops assigned to assist us had fallen asleep in their foxholes, and the Germans snuck in and slit their throats at night. That is one of the most miserable feelings when you are so tired but you dare not fall asleep. We hadn't slept for at least three days and nights. We could hear German tanks starting their motors in the distance, so we laid mines and concertina (concertina was barbed wire rolled in coils) in the valley where they would attack. Later that night they did attack. Their tanks hit the mines, and their infantry got tangled up in the barbed wire and were cut down by our machine guns zeroed in on the valley. As they came to our positions, our artillery fired star shells in the air, lighting up the whole area. Finally, the sky cleared up and our bombers came over, dropping us provisions and catching the German columns lined up bumper to bumper, or tank to tank, on the roads. From dawn until dark our heavy bombers from the Eighth Air Force, and our fighter-bombers assigned to us, bombed and strafed the German vehicles and troops. Cheers went up from all of us at the sight of our planes. Fires and dense smoke went up from the tanks, halftracks, gas trucks, etc. The Germans could not maneuver their tanks on the narrow roads with forests lining the road, so they had nowhere to go.

The next day, clouds moved in, so no air force, but they had knocked the heart out of the German drive. We then pursued the retreating Germans, with occasional rear guard action from them.

Allen Cramer: The ride was not too comfortable. Up front were the driver and the squad sergeant, and also our halftrack carried the platoon leader, Lieutenant La Monica. In the back were the twelve men of the squad, six on each side, facing in. We were squad number one of the 1st Platoon, Company A, 21st Armored Infantry Battalion [11th Armored Division]. I am not sure of this, but we were told that at the speed of about ten miles per hour that we traveled at, it would take approximately twenty-four hours for the entire division to pass a given point. We were told that a halftrack got about two miles to the gallon of gasoline, and the tanks used about two gallons to go one mile.

We did stop at night. We camped out, and it was good to get out of the vehicles and walk around a bit. As we progressed north, we were warned that we could encounter the enemy at any moment, so the camp had to set up guard posts all around our positions each night. We privates had to take turns at guarding in two-hour shifts. I well remember a few times being on guard duty, all alone in the middle of the night some hundreds of feet from the campsite. We did not really believe we were that close to the Germans, but since we could not be sure, it was two hours of peering out into the darkness and trying not to let the imagination take over from reality.

The next few days seemed to pass quickly, and we knew we were finally headed into combat, something we had been well-trained for, but something not many of us looked forward to.

Our food was decent, the cooks having kept up with the rifle squads. On Christmas Day, we were getting nearer to our destination but still far enough away that we could stop our travels and enjoy a full turkey dinner. It seemed so strange to be enjoying this wonderful holiday dinner in the cold outdoors of northern France in the winter.

Although we enlisted men did not know it at the time, the official history tells us that on December 26, our 11th "Thunderbolt" Armored Division was ordered forward to protect Bastogne's crucial lifeline, the Bastogne–Neufchâteau Road. It would be only a short while until our "baptism of fire."

Memory has a way of crowding traumatic events so that the exact chronological sequence is impossible for me to establish. I know what came first and what came last, but some of the incidents in between that I will try to describe may therefore be in random sequence.

With the first shell that landed in our area, spraying its deadly shrapnel, there were injuries in our company. I did not see this actually happen, but word soon spread that one of those injured was my very close friend, Dan Danielson. Dan was in another platoon of our company, and I had some trouble finding out how serious his wound was. I was assured by members of his squad that the injuries did not appear too serious and that he had been removed and was on his way to a field hospital. It would be several months until I saw Danny again when he returned to our company. I was overjoyed to see that he was OK and had fully recovered from his wound.

During the first hours of this first day in combat only one clear incident stands out. Shells from the German 88s were dropping in as we advanced on foot, and some of our soldiers were sustaining wounds. We were in a country scene with no buildings in sight. The terrain was flat, the weather clear but cold, and a few inches of snow was on the ground. At one point, after hearing a shell coming in very close, I felt a terrific bang on my lower leg. It was severe enough that I thought I must have been wounded by a piece of shrapnel. I looked down at my leg and did not see any break in my clothing, nor was any blood visible. Upon further inspection, I realized that I had probably been hit by a rock thrown up by the exploding German shells. The pain in my leg soon went away, and all that I suffered was a bruise. I went on with my squad and considered myself lucky. I tell this story because it will have more meaning later in this narrative.

On one of our days (I believe it was the last of my four days in the Battle of the Bulge), we were driving forward across a field and approaching a wooded area. The Germans saw us and were dropping artillery shells all around us as we drove forward. All of us sat crouched down as low as possible to get what protection the sides of the halftrack afforded. Suddenly, with the sounds of the exploding shells and the shrapnel hitting the sides of the vehicle, Lieutenant La Monica turned to the squad and yelled, "Dismount!"

At first no one moved. Each of us, sensing the others were not moving, remained sitting and thinking that it would be extremely dangerous to even lift our heads up a bit, never mind getting up and jumping out of the halftrack. The lieutenant shouted his command again, and since we were extremely well trained to obey such an order, we, almost in unison, got up and jumped over the side.

Again from our training, we knew the first thing to do in such a situation was to seek cover. There was not much to choose from in this still, open field, but I saw, a few yards up ahead, a shallow hole in the ground. It was just big enough to hold a person and had probably been created by a shell blast. It looked perfect, and I started to run toward it. But Private First Class Yost, whose first name eludes my memory, ran right by me and jumped into the hole, lying face down. Since that spot was gone, I ran a few yards to the left and went down to the ground, which was covered with a few inches of snow. I turned to look at Yost, and as I did so, a shell landed right in the hole with Yost. A huge explosion and smoke and debris rose from the site, and there was no human being left where Yost had been a moment before. I will never forget Yost and that moment.

William W. Fee: We [55th Armored Infantry Battalion, 11th Armored Division] just sat around all day, keeping our stuff in good shape. The next day, there was talk of strafing during the night, but if so I slept through it. The story was that someone in B Company fired a .50-caliber

These dejected-looking German POWs were captured by troops from the 30th "Old Hickory" Division, also known to the Germans as "Roosevelt's SS."

MG at "Bedcheck Charlie" [a German nuisance plane], who responded by strafing a small fire.

Albert Tarbell: We [Company H, 504th Parachute Infantry Regiment, 82nd Airborne Division] were still receiving Kraut patrol probing attacks on our company lines. There was a lot of activity at the outposts. Our company was to set up as an eight-man outpost in the right sector of our line. I received this message on the switchboard from Battalion, from Lieutenant Rivers. He talked to Sergeant Tague about the outpost. Sergeant Tague said the woods in that area were full of Krauts. Lieutenant Rivers told Sergeant Tague that there was a meeting at Battalion with Intelligence, and they concluded there were none now. Nevertheless, they set up the outpost around 1600 hours.

That night we received a call from one of the outposts that there was a German soldier walking toward our lines. He was crying and moaning. They let him walk on into our lines, and a couple of the troopers brought him into the CP. He had been shot on the side of the head. We could see where the bullet had entered into his front left side. He was incoherent—an SS trooper. An officer in the CP said he would be better off if he were dead. You could see his expression. He seemed to understand but was unable to talk. I offered to take him to the medics, to get him off our hands. When we arrived, we could see that they had their hands full. They didn't have much hope for him but said if he were alive in the morning, they would ship him out with the others to the hospital. I inquired the following day and was told by one of the medics he was still alive and off to the hospital.

John Kline: We [M Company, 423rd Regiment, 106th "Golden Lion" Division] stopped at a cluster of farm homes about eight miles north of Mayen. We are billeted in one of the barns. No food. I notice that here, in Europe, the farms are not laid out the same as they are back home. You can walk through the country for several miles before you see any farm buildings. In the States, there is a farm every half mile or so. In Germany, you always see several farm homes and barns clustered together, as if they were built that way for protection. Many of them have a common courtyard arranged around a square, with each family living in buildings on opposite sides of the square. Maybe a throwback from the old feudal system.

Zeke Prust: We [Service Company, 54th Armored Infantry Battalion, 10th Armored Division] had one man who went out to the latrine we had made, he went out and a shell hit him when he was out there and killed him. The 4th Armored coming through, it was an unbelievable sight. We just wanted to get out of there, and that's what we did. My entire company got up and left as they came in.

Dick Goodie: A day after Christmas, Peiper had run out of petrol, had lost all of his tanks, and was retreating back to Germany with eight hundred survivors. To the south, Bastogne was finally cleared after Gen. Anthony McAuliffe replied "Nuts!" to a surrender demand, and the fighting intensified. Up north, Baron Manteuffel's Fifth Panzer Army, after penetrating

Casualty estimates from the battle vary widely. American casualties are listed as being between 70,000 and 81,000; British as 1,400; and German casualties at between 60,000 and 104,000. More than 100,000 German soldiers were taken prisoner. In addition, 800 tanks were lost on each side, and 1,000 German aircraft were destroyed.

nearly fifty miles through the Allied lines, was stopped at Celles, four miles short of the Meuse River. The Battle of the Bulge was now checked in all areas.

Charles P. Boggess: Dawn of December 26, 1944, right after a cold Christmas, our unit [37th Tank Battalion, 4th Armored Division] was only three miles from Bastogne. I mounted my CO's personal tank for a very "special" mission. It had been decided that a special team, mainly consisting of C Company, 37th Tank Battalion under temporary command of its XO, Capt. William A. Dwight (S-3), would take a secondary road, leading from Clochimont through Assenois to Bastogne, in order to break the siege of that town and to contact the surrounded American defenders. This kind of surprise attack was to take place in enemy-held territory. Acting as point vehicle, I would lead with *Cobra King* followed by another seven tanks, halftracks, and some other extra vehicles. My personal crew consisted of Pvt. Hubert Smith (driver), Cpl. Milton Dickerman (gunner), Pvt. Harold Hafner (bow gunner), Pvt. James G. Murphy (loader), and myself as commander; we were all battle veterans. We moved full speed, firing straight ahead, with the other tanks firing left and right. We weren't supposed to stop on the way, either. As soon as we cleared the first little town, I called for artillery support (four artillery battalions were available) on Assenois, that is, ahead of the convoy—our column entered the place still under friendly fire, such was our speed and progress. After clearing Assenois, we ran into more enemy resistance, and mopping up was required with help of our halftrack-borne C Company, 53rd Armored Infantry Battalion. We then came across a large pillbox, which we at once destroyed. There certainly was a lot of confusion, since the

Germans hadn't expected us to break through via this secondary road; nevertheless enemy fire was considerable, and we lost four Shermans on the way.

As my tank cleared the following woods, we came upon an open field with colored canopies (from previous supply drops). I reckoned we were now approaching friendly lines. Our column subsequently slowed down, on the lookout for friendlies, and we seemed to recognize a number of foxholes with helmeted figures. Taking no chances, I called out to them, shouting to come out to us, indicating we were part of the 4th Armored Division. After several calls, an officer emerged with a smile and said, "I'm Lieutenant Webster, 326th Airborne Engineers, glad to see you guys!" It was 1650, December 26, the 4th Armored Division, had broken through enemy lines and reached its objective— the siege of Bastogne was over . . . although the fighting wasn't.

◆ ◆ ◆

MANTEUFFEL'S FIFTH ARMY HAD ALMOST reached the village of Celles in the west, close to the river Meuse. Their repeated attempts to break out of the pocket created there continually ended in frustration. Consequently, like Kampfgruppe Peiper, they were forced to abandon many vehicles and armor. The skies were now ruled by American and British fighter-bombers, who relentlessly strafed both advancing and retreating German columns. The 4th Armored had covered 120 miles from Saarbrücken to Bastogne in just seven days. Here lay the true strength of the U.S. Army: its capacity to move huge numbers of men and armor at a moment's notice to wherever they were needed. This mobility was the antithesis of the German army, which was rapidly losing any remaining impetus. The 6th Armored Division was closing in on Luxembourg, and the Third Army requested the release of the 11th Armored, the 87th Infantry, and the 17th Airborne, who were being held in reserve at SHAEF headquarters near Reims. A full-scale counterattack by the Allies was now underway, but the fighting was far from over.

CHAPTER TWELVE

IT ISN'T OVER YET

27 DECEMBER 1944

I NCLEMENT WEATHER CONDITIONS PERSISTED throughout December, and apart from suffering casualties incurred by
enemy action, U.S. Army medics were inundated with GIs going
down with weather-related conditions.

INFORMATION FROM 64th MEDICAL GROUP RECORDS:
27/12/44. Extreme cold during period caused heavy number
trench foot and frostbite cases. Evacuation slow because of icy
conditions.

On December 27, Gen. George S. Patton, as articulate and direct as
ever, offered a thank you to God in his prayer at the Pescatore Chapel:

Sir, this is Patton again, and I beg to report complete progress. Sir,
it seems to me that you have been much better informed about
the situation than I was, because it was that awful weather which
I cursed so much which made it possible for the German army to
commit suicide. That, Sir, was a brilliant military move, and I bow
humbly to a supreme military genius.

Having achieved the goal of penetrating the German salient and
relieving some of the surrounded forces, Patton was eager to continue
his counteroffensive. Eisenhower had reconstituted his own reserve
with the 87th Infantry and the 11th Armored. He released these to
Bradley's 12th Army Group on December 27, and Bradley immediately
assigned them to Patton, on the condition that he employ them on his

left (the west, which was the direction from which they would approach his command, but the move was also intended to prevent Patton from deciding to employ them in an attack to the east, across the Rhine).

Despite not being warmly welcomed by some sections of his subordinates in the north, General Montgomery was demonstrating his considerable skill as a commander. His approach was quite different from Patton's, emphasizing thorough preparation and risk minimization. The units of his initial command, the 21st Army Group, consisting of the British First and Canadian Second Armies, were located well north of the Ardennes, with the U.S. First and Ninth Armies (part of Bradley's 12th Army Group) between them and the German offensive. At the same time, Montgomery's forces were a primary objective of the German plan, which foresaw cutting the Allies in half, capturing the port of Antwerp, cutting the 21st Army Group off from its supplies, and ultimately surrounding and destroying that force. As the actual attack developed, Montgomery, whose approach stressed unity of command, asked for command of all Allied forces north of the salient, including the U.S. First and Ninth Armies.

After the SHAEF command conference on December 19, Eisenhower had given command of the forces south of the salient to Bradley and those north of the salient to Montgomery. It must be noted that American commanders did not receive this decision positively, but as an afterthought, they understood the need to simplify and clarify command relationships and accepted the decision. Montgomery believed quite rightly that there was little to prevent the Germans from "bouncing the Meuse and advancing on Brussels." He promptly moved four

Medical personnel inspect the feet of fellow GIs for the presence of "trench foot," a condition rife in the cold, damp conditions of the Battle of the Bulge.

U.S. Army medics were particularly hard-pressed during the Battle of the Bulge. In addition to the obvious battle wounds as the battle progressed, they had to treat an increasing number of weather-related maladies, such as hypothermia, trench foot, and severe frostbite.

divisions to block the approaches to Antwerp and dispatched British reconnaissance troops to examine and report on the state of defenses at the Meuse River bridges.

The German Panzer forces had actually aimed at crossing the Meuse between Givet and Liège. Montgomery had reacted promptly to this danger, and British forces were now engaging German counterparts at the farthest westerly penetrations on the Bulge. Montgomery sent word to Eisenhower at SHAEF on December 27 that his counterattack would be ready on January 3. However, the 116th *Windhund* (Greyhound) Division had been almost in sight of the river Meuse. It had advanced as far as Hotton and caused some serious problems there.

By the morning of December 27, however, the whole Marche–Hotton front had quieted (all German units in that area had been ordered to Bastogne). In the enemy lines, the crippled and demoralized 116th

Panzer licked its wounds and dug defensive works while on the left of its position, the XLVII Panzer Corps retired to a shortened position in order to free men and tanks for the new fight brewing at Bastogne. The 84th Infantry Division sent out patrols and captured 592 German prisoners.

Kampfgruppe Peiper's unit may have been scattered in the woods between La Gleize and St. Vith and scrambling back to German lines in an every-man-for-himself manner, but the German army was not finished yet. Just south of there, Allied fighter-bombers had been strafing the 2nd SS Panzer in and around Manhay, and General Ridgway had decided to use the fresh 3rd Battalion of the 517th Parachute Infantry, which had just come down from helping the 30th Division in the La Gleize operation, for a night assault at Manhay. This attack, made an hour or so after midnight and preceded by an eight-battalion artillery concentration fired for twenty minutes, gained quick success. By 0400 on December 27, the paratroopers had cleared the village, and by dawn, airborne engineers had cleared the fallen trees from the road back to Werbomont. A platoon of medium tanks moved in to cover the approaches to the village.

The loss of Manhay ended the 2d SS Panzer battle in this sector, and the German corps and division commanders agreed that there seemed little chance of starting the attack rolling again. On the morning of the 27th, Gen. Josef "Sepp" Dietrich ordered the 2nd SS Panzer out of the line and replaced it with the 9th SS Panzer Division. The 2nd SS Panzer would move west to join the 560th Volksgrenadier Division and the newly arrived 12th SS Panzer Division in a new Sixth Panzer Army attack directed at the Hotton–Soy–Erezée line. Around this time, Hitler issued direct orders to von Manteuffel to bring his forces back to Bastogne and capture that town at all costs. Bastogne had become a symbol of Allied resistance to the German onslaughts. Hitler had seen newspaper reports, and even in his fragile state, he knew only too well the propaganda value of this particular siege.

The march west by the 12th SS Panzer Division had taken much longer than reckoned, for the slow-moving 9th SS Panzer had jammed the roads in front of the 12th SS Panzer, there had been a series of fuel failures, Allied air attacks had cut most of the march to night movement, and, just as the division was nearing the Aisne River, orders had been given for the rear columns to go to Bastogne. All that the 12th SS Panzer could employ on December 27, the date set by the army commander for the new attack, was the 25th Panzergrenadier Regiment, most of which was already in the line facing the 3rd Armored. The 2nd SS Panzer contribution, therefore, was limited.

On the southern shoulder down in Luxembourg, the U.S. 35th Infantry Division reported that it had advanced 6.6 km, along a division front 10 km wide. The division had much more trouble with the terrain and the weather than with the Germans, who were dug in on a series of hills about five thousand yards behind the river Sure. The broken terrain was very difficult to traverse, and there was about six inches of snow on the ground. The 35th trucked through the positions of the 4th Armored Division, crossed the tanker's bridge at Tintange, and then drove German outposts of the 5th Parachute Division from the village

GIs hitch a ride on a King Tiger, formerly of the German army's 506th heavy tank battalion. After it was captured by American troops, Company B, 129th Ordnance Battalion got the Tiger II running again. *U.S. Army*

of Surré. To the west, troops from the 35th were advancing northward but were stopped by fire from a German pillbox at Livarchamps. The 320th Glider Battalion also crossed the Sure. Soldiers from one company had the discomfort of having to wade the icy river on foot before they took Boulaide and Baschleiden without casualties. They faced the 15th Panzergrenadier Division before they continued their advance north.

Meanwhile, William F. Fee was in a different sector of the Bulge with the 11th Armored Division.

William W. Fee: [On Wednesday, December 27] my feet were so cold that I warmed them by a fire in a can of gasoline, having taken off my galoshes, shoes, and socks. Down below, where Charlie and Parris slept on the canvas cover for the halftrack, they had a fire burning all day, and

A dedicated Nazi, Josef "Sepp" Dietrich became a member of the Schutzstaffel (SS) in 1928 and was selected by Adolf Hitler to become one of his personal bodyguards. In late 1944, Hitler gave him command of the Sixth SS Panzer Army. At the end of the war, Dietrich fled west and surrendered to the U.S. Army on May 8, 1945. He was found guilty of killing prisoners of war in Belgium and was sentenced to twenty-five years of imprisonment. Dietrich served only ten years. He died of a heart attack at Ludwigsburg on April 21, 1966.

we kept warm by it. We cleaned the .50-caliber MG, stretched the belts of MG ammo to loosen the cartridges a little, and bore-sighted the bazooka [a portable tube from which an antitank rocket was fired].

About 1700, Pike and I were alerted by Sgt. Harvey "Red" Brancefield to be ready to go "on outpost." We ate our chow and sat on our bedrolls by the fire. We were assigned to Staff Sgt. Duey Morgan's squad and rode in his track. We passed B Company, where we were almost fired on by an overzealous sentry who said we didn't give the password correctly. Lieutenant Murphy and Sgt. Bill Basso were in charge of the platoon's three roadblocks, and Ackley drove them around in a peep [jeep]. Private Hyman Schulman had had some high school French and was interpreter. Pike and I manned a .30-caliber heavy [water-cooled] MG. He sat at the gun, and I flagged down vehicles with my .45. We were told to shoot anybody with a 9th Armored Division patch because Germans were wearing them.

During our first tour of guard, the door of a house opened, and a French woman invited us in for tea. I knew only a few words of French and tried to explain that we could not leave our post. Between tours, Schulman, Pike, and I went in. Lieutenant Murphy, Basso, Silverstein, Ackley, and Brancefield came in too and had coffee. With Schulman interpreting, we had a good time and stayed late.

We slept in a barn. I had only about fifteen minutes' sleep before I had to go on guard again. It was very cold, and I kept walking to keep warm. Then a third tour, just before dawn.

◆ ◆ ◆

FOR THE POWS AT THAT stage in the Battle of the Bulge, it was a very different experience.

John Hillard Dunn: At Koblenz, on or about December 27, 1944, we were ushered into a large building near a river, either the Rhine or the Moselle, as protection from the bitter cold. The structure, one of three standing side by side that were each as large as the Burlington auditorium, had windows but was not heated. But it was warm compared with being in a ditch, and we were thankful to be in it.

The next day, a tremendous bombing raid lasting from midmorning to late afternoon plastered the city.

I was never so scared, before or since. The big building we were in actually lifted and then settled back on its foundation each time the bombs fell near us. I huddled under my blanket for protection from the flying glass. Several times I was absolutely certain I was doomed. Ed Brewer felt the same way. There are, I can attest, no atheists in the foxholes or amid thunderous bombing attacks.

When we exited the building the next afternoon, we saw that the identical structures on either side of us not occupied by GIs had suffered massive, direct hits. So had a warehouse across the street, which, one of our guards said, had first been considered as the place for us to be billeted. The smashed-flat warehouse had been ruled out, we were told, because it was already windowless from previous air raid damage.

As we marched out of Koblenz, much of the city was in shambles, and flames shot from gaping holes in the streets. German civilians shouted obscenities at us and shook their fists . . . but they were too preoccupied with their own misery to do us harm.

The final stretch of our march was to Stalag 12A at Limburg more than a hundred miles along the up, down, and winding roads from Schönberg.

John Kline: We [M Company, 423rd Regiment, 106th "Golden Lion" Division] arrived [in Koblenz] in the afternoon. We were fed soup and bread served from a portable kitchen. Koblenz is a big city. It had taken a lot of punishment from bombings. We were walking in groups of about five hundred. I was on the left side of our column, next to the street curb. There was a uniformed German photographer taking pictures of our group as we walked by. I noticed he used a Leica camera. A civil-

ian, dressed in a business suit, walked over to the curb near me. He made a loud remark and then hit me alongside the head with a briefcase. The guards made him get back. They told us that the civilians were very upset because of the recent bombings. Maybe the civilian had lost some of his family. Later, I thought this might have been a staged protest for propaganda purposes. Why would there be an army photographer there with a businessman, alone, with a column of POWs marching by?

We were billeted in one of three large, brick barracks (which I remember being just on the south edge of Koblenz). They were three stories

This GI from the 101st is "hanging tough" as ordered and checking the .30-caliber machine gun on his battered Willys jeep before going into action near Bastogne.

in height. Somebody said they were part of a former officer training center. We were forced to take all of the beds out of the three-story building and store them in a large building across the street. When we were in Dockweiler Dreis, we had been issued two old, gray, German army blankets. We slept on the floor using the blankets. It was at least out of the weather.

♦ ♦ ♦

ONE OF THE MOST IMPORTANT ASPECTS of any battle is the morale of the combatants. It is not always about numbers and means. General George S. Patton Jr. understood the importance of keeping up morale. He said, "Moral courage is the most valuable and usually the most absent characteristic in men." He talked the talk and walked the walk, as they say, and it's well documented that on occasion, he was capable of saying the wrong thing. A rude, arrogant, xenophobic, and frequently controversial man, he did not only understand how to fight a battle, he understood the mindset of his men. James L. Cooley once said that no one could motivate and inspire a GI like General Patton. Nevertheless, that was not a ubiquitous opinion because not all GIs liked his style of leadership. In some quarters, he was detested. The famous slapping incident of a battle-fatigued GI in Sicily had incurred the scorn of the Western press and caused outrage in the higher echelons of the military, but he remained undeterred. Like most leaders who feel, rightly or wrongly, that they have a higher purpose in life, Patton strode confidently toward what he considered to be his destiny.

Many have heard the story and seen the movie portrayal of General Patton's prayer for better weather in order to more efficiently kill the Germans in the winter of 1944. However, few know of his Christmas greeting that was issued along with that particular prayer. Contrary to popular belief, the prayer was not commissioned during the Battle of the Bulge. It was on December 14 that General Patton had the famous exchange with Chaplain O'Neill to write a prayer for good weather and to give a copy to each member of the Third Army. The Chaplain mentioned that it was not customary practice for men of the cloth to pray for clear weather in order to kill fellow men.

Patton's response was direct: "Chaplain, are you teaching me theology or are you the chaplain of the Third Army? I want a good prayer, damn it."

After working out the logistics, each member of the Third Army (approximately 250,000 at the time) was issued a small card on December 22, 1944. By this time, the Battle of the Bulge was well under way.

On one side of the card was the famous prayer:

Almighty and most merciful Father, we humbly beseech Thee, of Thy great goodness, to restrain these immoderate rains with which we have had to contend. Grant us fair weather for battle. Graciously hearken to us as soldiers who call upon Thee that, armed with Thy power, we may advance from victory to victory, and crush the oppression and wickedness of our enemies and establish Thy justice among men and nations.

When Patton originally ordered the cards made, some of the general's men convinced him to include a Christmas greeting for the troops. On the reverse side, the card had a personal message from the general:

To each officer and soldier in the Third United States Army, I wish a Merry Christmas. I have full confidence in your courage, devotion to duty, and skill in battle. May God's blessing rest upon each of you on this Christmas Day.

G. S. Patton, Jr.
Lieutenant General
Commanding, Third United States Army

The next day, the weather cleared and remained perfect for about six days while the Third Army pushed north to relieve the 101st Airborne at Bastogne. Upon reviewing the weather, Patton said of the chaplain, "Chaplain, you're the most popular man in this headquarters. That's a potent prayer you wrote there. You sure stand in good with the Lord and the soldiers." Chaplain O'Neill then received a Bronze Star medal.

An American roadblock is set up with a .30-caliber machine gun. The M1917 model was used in World War II, but the gun's weight (over one hundred pounds battle ready) meant that it was mostly relegated to static defense areas and in antiaircraft duty in the highly mobile conflict. The weapon fired the standard .30-06 round in fabric or metal link belts.

On Christmas Day, Patton wrote in his journal that the day "dawned clear and cold; lovely weather for killing Germans, although the thought seemed somewhat at variance with the spirit of the day." Patton went on to write how they managed to provide every soldier with turkey. Those in the front had turkey sandwiches while everyone else had hot turkey. Love him or loathe him, there was only one Gen. George S. Patton Jr.

Vilify or venerate, I think most opinions agree that he was the right man at the right time. Clearer thinkers among us would maybe hesitate at the prospect of following someone into battle who believed he'd enjoyed a previous life and would return again. Either way, he rose to the challenge, and he did his duty.

On December 27, 1944, the Third Army was in full control of evacuation and clearing of casualties in Bastogne. The surgical consultant of the Third Army was informed by the morning of December 27 that contact had been well established between elements of the 4th Armored Division and the troops holding Bastogne. A corridor was established, and medical supplies were being sent in. That night, at 1900, the medical inspector of III Corps entered Bastogne and contacted the 101st Airborne Division. The final details for complete evacuation of casualties were agreed upon at that time. A convoy of ambulances followed through the "corridor" of Assenois and returned with casualties from Bastogne to take them to field hospitals. Complete evacuation of all casualties from Bastogne was effected by 1200, December 28, the total number of casualties incurred amounting to 946.

The battle still raged to the north and south of the Bulge and around Bastogne, but by this time, the tide had definitely turned in favor of the Allies. The official estimate from the command of 12th Army Group states the following:

> Preoccupation with the key position of Bastogne dominated enemy strategy to such an extent that it cost him the advantage of the initiative. The German High Command evidently considered further extension to the west or north as both logistically and strategically unsound without possession of Bastogne, as that town overlooks the main roads and concentration areas of the spearheads. By the end of the month, the all-out effort in the north had become temporarily defensive; in the west there was a limited withdrawal, and the array of German forces around Bastogne clearly exposed the enemy's anxiety over that position. Until the Bastogne situation is resolved one way or the other no change in strategy can be expected.

CHAPTER THIRTEEN

THE END GAME

V ON MANTEUFFEL HAS BEEN QUOTED as saying that the initial objectives were unfeasible and that, according to him, the offensive was over as early as December 18. Von Rundstedt, on the other hand, claimed that by December 24 he knew that the Meuse could not be reached, even with a limited objective strategy. He very bravely informed Hitler of this fact and even suggested that the German army should go on the defensive. Hitler characteristically refused outright to comply with this suggestion. Former chief of staff and Panzer expert Heinz Guderian told Hitler on December 24 that the attack had failed. He went on to plead with Hitler to completely suspend the attack in the west and send what remained as reserves to the Eastern Front. This request was also ignored. Hitler no longer trusted his generals' advice and preferred to rely on his own questionable judgments. This meant that he was going to continue the fight in the west and even attempt to level the field by sending in more reserves. Consequently, the 9th, 3rd, and 15th Panzergrenadier Divisions were released to support the offensive in the west. On December 26, Hitler provided Gen. Erich Brandenberger with the 9th and 167th Volksgrenadier Divisions. Meanwhile, the Allies were conducting some of the most phenomenal troop movements of the whole Second World War. During the first week of the attack, the First Army in the north moved 248,000 troops and 48,711 vehicles into the Bulge.

Although it is impossible to measure the exact number of rifle battalions and tank battalions committed by the Germans during the initial breakthrough attack, it is probable that the overall ratio of German infantry to American was approximately three to one, with a ratio of six to one at points of concentration. By January 2, 1945, the Germans had thrown eight armored divisions, twenty infantry divisions, and two mechanized brigades into the Battle of the Bulge. During the battle, the Americans committed eight armored, sixteen infantry, and two airborne divisions. The strength of the German infantry divisions across the board probably averaged little more than 10,000 men. The normal German rifle regiment numbered 1,868, as contrasted with the American infantry regiment of 3,207 officers and men.

The majority of the German Panzer divisions had the same manpower configuration as the two U.S. square armored divisions (the 2nd and 3rd), that is, a little more than 14,000. The six remaining U.S. armored divisions had around 10,500 officers and men in their ranks. The armored weight of the opposing divisions, however, strongly favored the Americans, for the German Panzer division brought an average of 90 to 100 medium tanks into the field, whereas the American triangular division was equipped with 186, and the two square divisions had 232 medium tanks in their organization tables. Hitler personally attempted to compensate for this disparity by ordering the attachment of separate army tank battalions of 40 to 50 Panthers or Tigers to the regular Panzer divisions.

Panther against Sherman. It's often speculated what precisely the ratio of Panthers to Shermans was. Some notable historians say seven Shermans to one Panther; others put the figure much higher. Regardless of the numbers, it's a fact that U.S. tank crews learned quickly in battle and developed tactics to help deal with the heavier German tanks. It was this inventiveness and flexibility in battle that continually flummoxed the Germans, who were at best intransigent. Companies of Shermans would employ fairly

General Erich Brandenberger commanded the German Seventh Army, which attacked through Luxembourg. Despite having an impressive combat record, Brandenberger was regarded as a "staff" by Gen. Walther Model.

elaborate flanking maneuvers to get in shots at the weak armor on the sides of the Panthers. U.S. tank crews also added armor to the fronts of their Shermans in an effort to negate the Panther's frontal armor advantage. Tank crews began welding double one-inch plates to the fronts of the M4A1(76)W to give additional armor protection. These modifications became typical in the later stages of the war, especially on 3rd Armored Division M4A1(76)Ws. The uneven plate on the cast-hull M4A1 made this job difficult; braces had to be welded in order for the plates to be secured at the edges. Moreover, the Sherman was a multifaceted vehicle that could move swiftly and be adapted for various purposes.

The Panther design reflected the German manufacturing industry's level of craftsmanship that favored optimal design over mass production considerations. The Panther was a clear example of the engineering adage that "perfection is the enemy of excellence." The extravagance of the Panther's design inevitably meant that it would fight outnumbered, and it often did during the Battle of the Bulge. Although it's difficult to gauge the exact number of German tanks used during the battle, it's widely acknowledged that there were around 1,800 Panzers in the Ardennes, of which some 250 were Tigers, and the balance was divided equally between the Mark IV and the Panther.

Günter Peukert was an experienced 88 gunner with the 272nd Volksgrenadier Division. His regiment took three hundred prisoners from the U.S. 78th Division at the Battle of Kesternich, which coincided with the Battle of the Bulge. *Latchodrom Productions*

Incidentally, none of the above-mentioned tanks are present in the film *The Battle of the Bulge* or the other film that makes a reference to the battle, *Patton*. For some inexplicable reason, both films used U.S. ex-Korean War tanks painted in various colors to represent the opposing armies. When it came to armor, the American self-propelled 90mm tank destroyer and the 88mm German equivalent were highly respected,

A dead German soldier, killed during the German counteroffensive in the Belgium-Luxembourg salient, is left behind on a street corner in Stavelot, Belgium, on January 2, 1945, as the Battle of the Bulge moves on. *U.S. Army Signal Corps*

for they had the power to penetrate whatever armor they faced, they could square off along the winding Ardennes roads and defiles, and they were both hard to destroy. Most World War II analysts come down on the side of the 88mm for accuracy of fire, but they were both formidable weapons. Both the German army and the Allies used 75mm towed antitank weapons, and not surprisingly, both forfeited these towed weapons and other towed artillery in large numbers during the battle. In the mud and snow, and under direct fire and infantry assault, the task of attaching gun to truck or tractor was difficult and hazardous. Furthermore, in heavy and close combat, the tow vehicle often was shot up or immobilized while the gun, dug in, remained intact. It should also be pointed out that the 105 Howitzer in the right hands could be a devastating weapon too. It's often said that at Parker's Crossroads, those U.S. 105mm guns were fired as accurately as sniper rifles. Ultimately, it was the mobile, tactically agile, self-propelled, armored field artillery and tank destroyers that had the greatest influence on the course of the battle in the Ardennes.

After the relief of Bastogne, Allied air superiority became even more apparent, but even they had limited success, and the overall effect of sustained air attack on the German army is often exaggerated. Air attacks against the choke points that developed along the main and subsidiary German supply roads may have seriously impeded both tactical and logistic movement, but it did not stop them—far from it, in fact. The 9th Bombardment Division dropped 136 tons of high explosive on St. Vith, which stood in the open with a wealth of bypass routes around it on relatively level ground, but it did not stop German traffic. Even when the RAF dropped 1,140 tons in a carpet-bombing attack at St. Vith, which reduced the town to rubble, the road center was out of commission for only a day. The damaging effect of the Allied air attacks against rail lines, bridges, and marshaling yards at and west of the Rhine is quite clear in the history of the Ardennes campaign, but the time sequence between specific rail failures and the resulting impact on German frontline operations is difficult to trace. From December 2 to January 2, the Eighth Air Force, 9th Bombardment Division, and Royal Air Force Bomber Command made daily attacks against selected railway bridges and marshaling yards using an average of 1,800 tons of bombs per day.

Despite Allied domination of the air over the Ardennes battlefield, the German armies never were really isolated, except in a very few occasions, such as Kampfgruppe Peiper in the north at La Gleize. He fell victim to an overly ambitious thrust, the terrain, and superior opposition rather than air attack. The terrain, with its sequence of river barriers and multitude of winding, steep gradients may have favored air attack as opposed to troop and vehicle movements, but this did not really impede the German army to any great extent until the very late stages of the battle during the retreat. Although the Allied air forces failed to isolate the Ardennes battlefield, they did succeed in dealing the Luftwaffe a mortal blow, thus making the task of their comrades on the ground much easier. General Adolf Galland, commander of the Luftwaffe fighter arm, wrote the Luftwaffe epitaph in this manner: "The Luftwaffe received its death blow at the Ardennes offensive."

Bastogne had been relieved on December 26, and supplies were flowing into that city as the wounded were being moved out.

Belgian girls and American soldiers of an armored division share a peaceful moment while washing clothes in a stream, January 1945, somewhere along the northern flank of the German bulge, in the Ardennes region of Belgium. *Associated Press*

Nevertheless, the fighting was far from over. Hitler was committing even more reserves to the fray. Despite the protestations and advice of his generals, he remained oblivious to reason, even when it was pointed out in no uncertain terms that the German army in the west was drastically short of weapons and ammunition. The German High Command claimed that before the U.S. counterattack on January 3, 1945, there was no shortage of artillery ammunition in the field. This statement merely serves to reflect the remote and isolated view of the high headquarters, for despite the one hundred ammunition trains of the special Fuehrer

Reserve, the troops in the Ardennes operation did suffer from a shortage of ammunition. This shortage was reported as early as December 21 by the divisions attacking at Bastogne. Thereafter, as the American front solidified, the Germans consumed ammunition at a rate of 1,200 tons per day. The lack of ammunition should be charged to transport failure rather than to paucity of artillery shells at the Rhine dumps. The Panzer Lehr Division, for example, was the first to report that it had run out of fuel, and then on December 28 it reported a shortage of ammunition because of the "lack of transport."

The American troops, by contrast, never suffered any notable failure of ammunition at the guns. The Third Army, for example, was able to move an average of 4,500 tons of ammunition per day during the last half of December.

A popular myth about the Battle of the Bulge concentrates on the lack of liquid fuel as the main cause of the German army's failure to reach its objectives. It should be noted that although fuel shortage was a contributing factor in the eventual failure of the Ardennes offensive from the German perspective, it was not the only reason. Despite the decline in the production of liquid fuel during 1944, Hitler was able to amass a reserve for the Ardennes offensive and allocate over four million gallons for this purpose. Using the German measure of one "consumption unit" as the amount of fuel required to move all the vehicles in a formation a distance of sixty-three miles, it may be reckoned that of the five consumption units requested by Model, only one and one-half to two were at corps dumps on December 16; yet there may have been as much as nine or ten consumption units available at railheads near the Rhine River.

The course of the campaign showed at least three errors in

La Gleize, Belgium. An ambulance, carrying wounded from the front to the rear for hospitalization, passes a knocked-out German Mark VI Tiger II (Royal) tank that is being repaired so that it can be sent back to the United States. The front is only two miles away.

German planning. Distribution often failed to move with the same speed as the armored advance. The bad terrain and weather encountered in the Ardennes reduced the mileage gained from a tankful of fuel by one-half. And, finally, the expectation that the spearheads would move, in part, on captured gasoline was mistakenly optimistic, The supply of liquid fuel failed to keep pace with the tactical demand. Fuel was scarce, so consumption was a serious problem. For instance, a Tiger II consumed 500 liters per 100 km (2 gallons per mile). The Tiger carried 860 liters (227 gallons)

Model was one of the few field marshals who dared to openly oppose Adolf Hitler on the *Wacht am Rhein* plan; he wanted to use all reserves to wipe out the Americans at Aachen. Despite his protests, Hitler could not be dissuaded, and Model was forced to concede. Nevertheless, he did play an integral part in the Battle of the Bulge. On the morning of April 21, 1945, he committed suicide by shooting himself in the head.

of fuel in 7 tanks, giving it a maximum range of 110 to 120 km (68 to 75 miles) on the road and 80 km (50 miles) cross country.

There are two phases in the history of German liquid fuel supply during the Ardennes campaign—the one before and the one after December 23, when the Allies took to the air over the battle zone. During the first phase, the movement of fuel was impeded by bad roads and traffic congestion. Vehicles failed or ran out of fuel and were often abandoned by the roadside. The attempts to introduce horse-drawn supply or artillery columns into the stream of motorized traffic during the first days of the offensive greatly slowed the distribution system. As early as December 20, the 12th SS Panzer Division, scheduled as one of the leading formations in the Sixth Panzer Army advance, was brought to a halt because there was no fuel except for a few gallons for the mechanized reconnaissance battalion. On December 21, the 2nd SS Panzer Division was ordered to relieve the 560th Volksgrenadier Division in the battle at Fraiture but was unable to move for thirty-six hours due to lack of fuel. In the Fifth Panzer Army, there were reports as early as December 19 of a "badly strained" fuel situation. Three days

By December 22 in Bastogne, artillery ammunition was restricted to ten rounds per gun per day. On December 23, C-47s flew over the city and accomplished the most accurate airdrop of World War II, providing the besieged U.S. Army troops with much-needed supplies.

later, Fifth Army commander von Manteuffel was informed that the advance of his armor was "gravely endangered" because of the failure of fuel supply. During this phase, there seems to have been considerable disorderly pirating from the forward fuel dumps. Eventually, German commanders learned to send a reconnaissance detail to the fuel dumps before they committed their supply trains in a fuel-consuming trip to what might be a dry supply point.

The supply phase after December 23 is characterized by Allied fighter-bombers pounding roads and supply points while snowdrifts stopped the movement of traffic through the Eifel. Shortages of fuel in the Sixth Panzer Army assumed calamitous proportions in the period between December 23 and 25. The Fifth Panzer Army was in dire straits by December 24, in part because of the arrival of armored and mechanized formations that had come into the army area without reserve fuel. Even when bad flying weather blunted the edge of the Allied air attack, the sporadic stoppage of supply movement at the ground level continued. By the end of December, three of the five divisions were practically immobile. We can conclude, therefore, that the main contributing factor in the defeat of the German army in the Ardennes was lack of transport rather than lack of fuel.

There are many reasons given for the failure of the Ardennes offensive from the German perspective, but we believe the five main factors to be as follows:

1. The failure by the Sixth Army in the northern sector to break initial American defenses. Those GIs proved to be more tenacious than anticipated; complete and rapid rupture of these defensive positions was consequently not achieved.

2. Lack of cohesion among the Kampfgruppes in the north led to an eventual breakdown in communication that exacerbated an already precarious situation. Moreover, tactical support and logistic transport had not kept pace with the advance of the combat formations.

3. Underestimation of the rugged terrain in the northern and southern sectors severely restricted close operational control and fluidity of movement. The mass of maneuver required free use of the road network in the salient, and this had been denied the attacker, most notably at Bastogne and St. Vith, but at other points along the Bulge as well.

4. The strength of resistance by U.S. divisions on the northern and southern flanks had caused the opposing forces to become gridlocked, therefore, they could not keep pace with the advances being made by von Manteuffel's Fifth Army in the center.

5. The German forces largely underestimated the tactical reaction of the American forces. Their commitment of reserves was far more rapid than anticipated. The eventual disparity of the opposing forces in the field regarding men and materiel combined with Adolph Hitler's wish to run the battle from Berlin rather than advocate the "command control" system that had initially worked so well for the German army.

Members of a field artillery unit of the 30th U.S. Division are seen moving along the front line in the Ardennes region near Stavelot, Belgium, January 14, 1945. *Associated Press*

The German army knew the terrain in the Ardennes well enough, but despite this, good old Teutonic intransigence held sway again. Maybe Patton was right to situate his Third Army in the Alsace region. The much-contested Alsace area of France had long been a thorn in the side of the Germans. During the abortive Operation *Nordwind*, the last German offensive on the Western Front, three German divisions attempted to encircle and annihilate the 100th Infantry Division. This operation only lasted three days. On January 4, the German High Command formally called off the effort. As General Simon, the attacking corps commander, caustically observed, the assault had shown only that the German soldier still knew how to fight and how to die, but little else. Patton's prophetic quote was now coming to pass. He had stated quite emphatically, "No bastard ever won a war by dying for his country. He won it by making the other poor dumb bastard die for his."

At the end of December down on the Bulge, there was still a lot of fighting going on. The battle was far from over, but the initial impetus of the German army had more or less dissipated as it contended with increasingly fervent attacks from fresh Allied reserves.

Ralph K. Manley: I remember the attack on Foy. That was one where it was so difficult—around Dead Man's Corner, places like that, where you can see, even today, some of the signs. [We brought] some of the

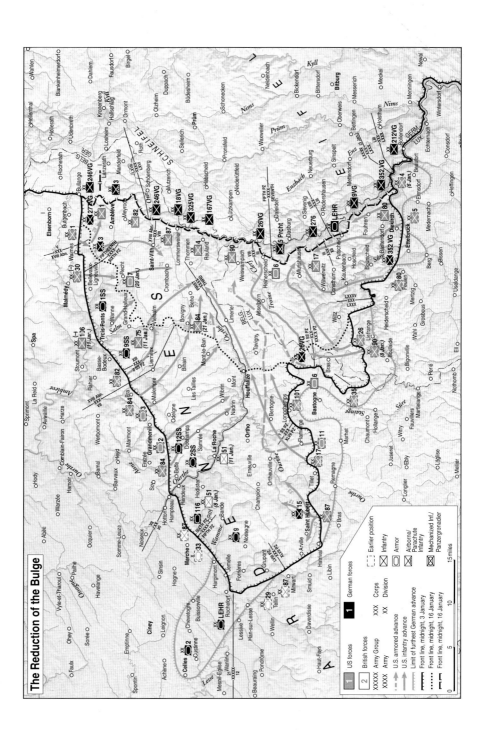

The Reduction of the Bulge

US forces

British forces

German forces

▢ 1	Army Group XXXX
▢ 2	Army XXX
	Corps XXX
	Division XX

Earlier position

⬚ Infantry
◯ Armor
⬗ Airborne/ Parachute Infantry
⬘ Mechanized Inf./ Panzergrenadier

➤ U.S. armored advance
➤ U.S. infantry advance
➤ Limit of furthest German advance
···· Front line, midnight, 3 January
▬ Front line, midnight, 16 January
┗ Front line, midnight, 16 January

0   5   10   15 miles

signs—we shouldn't have, but we did—back to our unit [501st Parachute Infantry, 101st Airborne Division] to show where we had been during this tremendous time. The Germans were everyplace, it seemed, but somehow or another we managed despite the cold and despite the threat of our feet being frozen from the wet snow on our boots. We'd take off our boots in the foxhole and rub our toes because otherwise gangrene would set in, and you would have frostbite on your toes, which greatly bothered many because they couldn't walk anymore.

We tried to get two men to a foxhole so one could get five or ten minutes sleep, and two men could keep each other warmer than one man by himself. You could take off your boots and rub your toes and maybe take your wet socks and put them under your arms or in the crotch of your legs to dry from the heat of your body so that you could put them back on and protect your feet. I did not get frostbite on my feet because of taking off my boots and rubbing. Also, with two men in the foxhole, one would be firing and the other could be working on his feet until he was needed. It was fighting the weather just as much as fighting the enemy, because they were not always attacking, nor did we attack. We were holding at that time, and that's not usual for a paratroop unit. We were an attack unit, light weapons, that type of thing. We had no artillery to fight back. We had our bazookas, our hand grenades, and our rifles to stop the Germans, and that part we did. As a matter of fact, we had a large truck in the center of Bastogne that had a bunch of mines on it, and the demolition squad was there unloading those mines, but it took a direct hit and wiped all of them away off the map. Even to this day you can see twelve men on a marker there in the cemetery at Bastogne.

Major General Matthew B. Ridgway (XVIII Airborne Corps) and Major General James M. Gavin (82nd Airborne Division) meet in the Belgian Ardennes, January 1945.

It was getting close to the 16th or 17th of January when we sensed victory was in the air, when we

Infantrymen of the 3rd U.S. Armored "Spearhead" Division march to the front lines in the Ardennes region of Belgium, January 13, 1945. *Associated Press*

knew it. It seemed about a month from when it started to when it turned against the Germans. Of course, after that you could take prisoners by the hundreds from the Germans because they knew it was the end of it. So from that moment on we were not defending positions so much as taking prisoners from the Germans. We knew the war was over then because at that time whole units would surrender to you, and you were not equipped to handle them. We as paratroopers were not used to handling that many. We would corral them in a barnyard or something of that nature to hold them until the ground troops got there and could take over that position.

I recall seeing Patton's troops. His troops would say they fought by his guts and our blood because he did have the guts to move ahead. He was great for that; he was the one who challenged every ounce of energy that the troops had, and he did it by pushing forward his tanks and his units.

Robert T. Gravlin: We [Company B, 23rd Armored Engineer Battalion, 3rd Armored Division] joined up with the Third Army toward the end of January and pulled back for a rest and re-equipment in the town of Durbuy, a kind of a resort town in peace time. Here we stayed in a big hotel with no heat or plumbing. We dug latrines behind the hotel and used a blowtorch turned on a radiator for heat. But it was a welcome relief to get out of the bitter cold and have a roof over our heads. Those of us who were Catholic went to mass in a little stone church. The mass was said by a Belgian priest who spoke a little English. The Battle of the Bulge was undoubtedly one of the worst battles of the war. I came out of it pretty good—I had a finger and toes frostbitten, and my nose was so stuffed up I had to breath out of my mouth. I ate sulfa tablets like candy to keep my fever down. In Durbuy, I was able to see an army doctor, and he treated my sinuses and said I was on the verge of pneumonia and gave me some kind of medicine. Of course, at that time we didn't have any of the wonder drugs—sulfa was about the most powerful, and your system became immune to it. So it was pretty much survival of the fittest.

While at this rest camp, we had steel plates welded on the front and sides of some of our Sherman tanks. On others, they put reinforced concrete in an attempt to repel the German 88s. After a short stay in the rest camp, our equipment was repaired, and a few brand-new Pershing tanks were shipped in to us. The Pershing was a heavier tank with a 90mm gun with 4,200-feet-per-second muzzle velocity. It was a match for the German heavy tanks. We were given the directive to move back into Germany around Stolberg and go on the attack again.

During the time we were in Belgium and the Battle of the Bulge, the Germans strengthened their defenses and moved up more and heavier artillery and mortars. They also blew up the Schwamanuel Dam and flooded the plains around Düren to keep the plains muddy so we couldn't move our tanks through the area.

Our commanders made a decision to take our own road with us. We would build a corduroy road and go over the mud. So for a week and a half, we cut down trees of about a foot in diameter. We cut them in lengths of about nine feet and wired about five or six together to make a flat section. We then attached sections to each side of our tanks, half-tracks, personnel carriers, etc. We were taking our road along with us.

Albert Tarbell: We [Company H, 504th Parachute Infantry Regiment, 82nd Airborne Division] were still receiving a lot of action from the SS

Members of Company I, 3rd Battalion, 16th Infantry Regiment, 1st Division, First Army, travel by tank during their advance on Schopen, Belgium, January 21, 1945. © *Bill Augustine/Lightroom Photos/U.S. Army/TopFoto/Jon Mitchell/Redux*

in front of us. [On December 28, 1945,] the woods were loaded with SS troops. Our artillery and mortars were taking care of them. All during this time, the weather had been very cold with plenty of snow, and food was scarce. The men's feet were usually wet and cold most of the time. We could not change our clothes, therefore we had to just let the clothes dry on us. The cold weather was just as tough on us as the fighting. Sometimes you would think, if you were wounded, at least you would be where it was warm and clean, and you would have a good meal, and above all some good sleep and rest, maybe. We continued to lose more men, and half of the time we did not even know their names. They were just fellows we had seen as replacements back in France a couple of weeks earlier who had changed and aged.

William W. Fee: Slept most of the day [on December 28, 1945]. At night, we [55th Armored Infantry Battalion] went back to the roadblock and visited in the house when we were not on guard. I listened as Schulman

A group of German prisoners, guarded by three Yanks, start their long journey from the battlefield after being captured by the Second Armored Division of the First Army near Malempré, about fifteen miles southwest of Stavelot in Belgium, January 20, 1945. *Associated Press*

spoke with the family: mother, daughter, and grandfather. The mother, middle-aged, pale, and thin, did all the work, such as tending the fire in the stove and chopping wood for it with a scimitar-like axe. She said that her husband had been in a German prison camp and had been killed when the Americans bombed it. Schulman and I had brought her soap, which she had said she needed, matches, and D rations [dark chocolate bars]. She was very grateful, saying that they did not have enough to eat because they were not farmers. She had looked forward to the Americans' coming but then was disappointed when they shot up the town and had no food for them.

The grandfather, an old man with whiskers, had been a prisoner in the previous world war. He admired my .45, pointed it, and said, "Boche." He asked about our religion and our jobs at home. He was surprised that these were the same work that Frenchmen did. He asked, "Capitalists?" because he thought that there had to be some among us.

When he went to light his pipe and started searching in the fire for a hot coal, Schulman handed him a strike-anywhere match. The old man thanked him, took out his pocket knife, and split the match in two, to get two uses from it. Then he pocketed the slivers, found a hot coal, and held it in his calloused fingers to light the pipe.I wished very much that I could communicate with the grandfather and asked Schulman to inquire whether the old man could understand Latin, the only language I had studied in high school. "No" was the answer. Was I perhaps a priest?

The daughter then offered to teach me some French. She was thirteen or fourteen, plump but not bad-looking. When we came in, she was sitting up in the double bed in the corner, dressed for sleep in a heavy flannel nightgown, and she stayed there the whole time. It probably was the best way to keep warm.

During the lesson, an officer came in. [Seeing Schulman engaged in conversation with the mother and me with the daughter, he grinned lasciviously and said, "I see what you guys are up to!"] He more or less demanded coffee, and none of us liked the way he was acting. [The mother said to Schulman, "He's not a nice man."] I was angry about this and soon left.

We didn't sleep in the barn because the farmer didn't want us there, saying we had trampled his unthreshed wheat. Frank Prioux, a French-

Members of the 44th Armored Infantry, supported by tanks of the 6th Armored Division, move in to attack German troops surrounding Bastogne, Belgium, on December 31, 1944.

speaking Cajun driver from Louisiana, found us a second-floor room in another farmhouse, over the barn. There was a considerable cow odor in the hall outside our room. Sometime later on, a GI came in with a big Nazi flag with a swastika on it. He said he'd gotten it from a fellow who'd found two on the Siegfried Line and sent the other one home. It occurred to me that the Siegfried Line would have nice pill-boxes to sleep in. And so I turned in for the last time in the only "home" I had in Europe. The next day we had early chow, cleaned up the house, and threw our trash out by the barn. (There was plenty of it.) Then we mounted up and drove away—destination: Germany. The Bulge experience was over.

◆ ◆ ◆

JOHN HILLARD DUNN SPENT the remaining months of the war fighting for survival in various German POW camps. Eventually, he was liberated and lived to tell the story. He wrote the following of his liberation day.

John Hillard Dunn: 04/13/45
   Helmstedt, Germany
   Liberation, 1000—Friday the thirteenth:

An American artillery captain just walked into the infirmary with a large box of cigarettes and D-ration bars (chocolate, hard as a brick) and K rations. Boy, he looks good. He says he is happy to see us. If he only knew how happy we are to see him. I couldn't help it, I had to cry. The captain said the Americans were moving about sixty miles a day, and he cannot keep his guns set up or keep up with the tank and infantry units.

1700—We are taken to a general hospital in the city to wait for ambulances. I am so weak that I cannot walk without help. They take us to the second floor of the large hospital. Then gave us a shower and delousing. It is so nice not to be scratching every minute of the day. Those lice used to run races up and down my back. The German doctors looked us over as if to diagnose our problems. Most all of us are diarrhea cases.

The beds are nice and clean. It looks like the road home now! I hope so. It has been a long, terrible, humiliating four months.

George doesn't give up when it comes to scrounging for food. He came into the hospital with some gin and bread that was given to him by a tank driver. He seems to be a little stronger than me, and he doesn't have the severe cramps that I have. He is able to walk. I could not stand the gin. I think George only had a little sip of it. Our stomachs must be about the size of a golf ball.

American infantrymen march on a snow-covered road southeast of Born, Belgium, on January 22, 1945. *Associated Press*

Later in the evening, some boys from a tank repair battalion brought us white bread, butter, and eggs. That was the best meal we have had for a long time, even though the bread was stale. Who in the army likes scrambled eggs? We do! This has been a great LIBERATION DAY!

◆ ◆ ◆

THE FOLLOWING IS A WITNESS statement made by a GI (2nd Lt. John J. Modrak Jr., Company C, 33rd Armored Regiment, 3rd Armored Division) concerning the activities of German soldiers during the Battle of the Bulge.

John J. Modrak Jr.: 4317 U.S. Army Hospital Plant
APO 887, U.S. Army
February 22, 1945

The incident took place at approximately 1300 hours, January 8, 1945, about five miles from the German town of Mayen in the Malmedy—St. Vith Sector. Prior to this time, I had received instructions from my commanding officer to take a platoon of five light tanks to a certain objective. Before reaching this objective, I was to contact G

Company, 33rd Armored Regiment, and get information regarding the situation in the area beyond the sector held by them. The commanding officer of G Company informed me that the section through which we were to pass was harassed by light arms fire, and he did not think it advisable for us to continue further. However, I had my orders from my commanding officer to proceed, so the five tanks containing my men and myself continued moving in the direction of the objective, with me riding in the lead tank.

After following a road for quite some distance, we reached a road branching off to the left in the direction of the town of Fraiture, which we were to follow. My tank turned into this road first and had proceeded only a short distance when it struck a land mine. There was a terrific blast, and for the next few minutes I was not conscious of my actions. The next thing I knew, I was outside the tank and had dragged my driver, T/5 Joseph Garcyka, with me. In the blast, Garcyka's right foot had been blown off above the ankle and was hanging by threads of skin. My assistant driver, Pfc. Willard Forsythe, and gunner, T/4 Abe Simmons, had managed to escape from the tank.

Meanwhile, the enemy opened up with light arms fire, and it became necessary for us to move to the protection of our disabled tank. I fired my pistol until I received a wound in my left hand, at which time I took up an M-1 and started firing it. By this time, the second tank in the platoon had entered the road and had come to a stop. Private Baker, the gunner in the second tank, jumped out and ran over to give us assistance. In a short time, all of us had become more or less seriously wounded. The first and second fingers on my right hand had been shot away, and the third was badly mangled. There were also deep gashes in my right leg that I presumed were caused from shell fragments. T/5 Garcyka was bleeding badly from his amputated foot, so I removed my belt and made a tourniquet to stop the flow of blood.

About this time, German soldiers, some in field gray and others in black uniforms, started coming out of the woods and running and shouting across a field toward us. I saw our situation was hopeless, so I ordered the second tank to turn around and leave without us. The second tank had no sooner reached the road junction than it was

A U.S. Army half-track crosses a temporary bridge over the Ourthe in the war-torn Belgian city of Houffalize, January 1945. *Associated Press*

knocked out by heavy shell fire or a bazooka gun. Shortly thereafter, the Germans were upon us, and we were taken prisoner. My men were badly wounded, so I begged the Germans to see that they were given medical treatment and taken to a hospital.

Instead, one of the Germans in a black uniform walked over and shot Garcyka, Simmons, and Baker as they lay helpless on the ground. One of the other German soldiers walked over to me and asked if I was an officer. I said that I was and demanded that my men be given the treatment accorded prisoners of war. Instead, the Germans started looting our persons. From me, they removed my wristwatch, pistol, compass, and a compass case containing a large amount in German money. Besides taking our money and valuables, the Germans removed part of our clothing, exposing us to the snow and bitter cold.

Around 1600 hours, Pfc. Willard Forsythe and myself were carried across the field into the woods where the Germans had their CP. Here, they laid us on the ground. Again, I asked that we be given medical treatment and be carried to a hospital. Finally, one of the German

An army jeep moves down a cleared street in Bastogne on January 8, 1945, after the men of General Patton's army have relieved the besieged city from the pressure of German attack. Debris is still heaped high on the sidewalks, and numerous buildings are shattered beyond repair, courtesy of German bombs. *Associated Press/Charles Haacker*

medics put a light dressing over my wounds but did nothing to relieve the suffering of Forsythe.

During the next few hours, it started snowing again. I noticed in the woods that the Germans had several tanks. One of the Germans in a black uniform and with the rank of corporal seemed to be in complete charge. All the enlisted men would obey his every order instantly like puppets on a string. I am sure that it was this corporal who shot Garcyka, Simmons, and Baker out in the field. Later, Sgt. Joseph E. Clark, commander in charge of my second tank, was brought to the CP, but in a little while he was carried further back, and I do not know his ultimate fate.

Meanwhile a German officer came over and for a few moments looked us over casually, but he did nothing to prevent his men from further stealing of money, valuables, and clothing from our persons.

In a short time, the officer left, and I never saw him again. While we were at the CP, they removed my wallet, containing a good-sized sum of French francs, photographs of my wife and baby, and my arctic shoes and had started taking my combat shoes but for some reason did not take them. Among other things, I saw them remove a field jacket from Forsythe.

Along about this time, our own troops started laying down a heavy mortar fire in our immediate vicinity. I tried to crawl over to the protection of one of the German tanks but was ordered away. By now I was suffering so with my wounds that I neither cared whether I lived or died, so it did not concern me too much having to lie out in an exposed position. Forsythe all this time had been crying for medical attention. His condition was critical, and he kept talking about his wife and family. At times I believe he was somewhat delirious.

Around 2100 hours, the Germans' position in the woods appeared to be untenable, and they showed signs of preparing to move out. Again I asked one of the medics to take us to a hospital, but he replied that we were to stay where we were. Just before leaving, the German corporal I thought was the one who shot my other men walked over to Forsythe and shot him, and then he came over to me and shot me also, the bullet passing through my groin and coming out at an angle almost severing my private parts. After that I lost consciousness and knew nothing more until around noon the next day.

When I came to, I was lying in a pool of blood. I made several attempts to get to my feet but was too weak to make it. I finally started crawling out of the woods and across the field to the road. It wasn't long after this that I saw the most welcome sight in the world when one of our own tanks came down the road. They picked me up and carried me to a hospital. I learned later that on the previous day the other three tanks in my platoon had escaped to safety.

Albert Tarbell: January 3, 1945

We were being relieved from our position and going into a bivouac area. The area where we went was a pine grove and was sheltered from the wind. I slept in my "sleep sack," and I really had a nice sleep. The

American prisoners are led away from the front after being captured by Germans, December 1944. *The Granger Collection, NYC*

following morning when I awoke, I was so nice and warm. I was surprised at how comfortable I felt. I uncovered my head and then found out that during the night it had snowed. The light snow acted as insulation against the cold.

January 4, 1945

We received C rations in hot water and coffee that morning. Then we were back on the road again. I remember how nice the scenery was with the snow on the tree limbs. The weather was nice—cold, but we were on the march, and everyone was warm. I remember later on getting so tired from walking. Just when you think you can't go another step, you would get a ten-minute break and a smoke. It is amazing how rested you can get. We finally arrived at an area where we went off onto a trail going up a hill that was very steep. We left all our gear, except for our weapons, at the foot of the hill. We started climbing that hill, and we were really beat. We had made contact with the enemy. We were on top of a mountain or a high hill, and we were getting casualties there. Everyone was perspiring from the climbing and from the adrenalin rush. We found a CP area around some trees and put our casualties there. There was but one blanket among us, which we used to cover our wounded. I found a small tree that I could put my hands on and started to walk around it to keep from freezing during the night. After a while, three others joined me. A person can sleep and walk like that. We told the newer men not to fall asleep because they could freeze. That had to be one of the longest nights I ever spent.

January 5, 1945

When daylight finally came, we realized we were behind the enemy. We could tell which fellows fell asleep because they could barely walk. Their feet were frozen. Colonel Cook came walking by, and he was laughing and telling us how the prisoner walking behind him had surrendered to him while he was relieving himself. Shortly after that, someone pointed to the clearing below at a convoy going by on the road. Later, beyond that, in the field, we saw horse-drawn caissons (German). We put what firepower we had into the convoy and artillery into the caisson with the German soldiers on them.

January 6, 1945

This was another busy day. And, as usual, cold and miserable. Another day to wonder if this is your day to get it. Lieutenant Rivers' platoon came back from patrol with five POWs. My friend Phil Foley came in from the rear echelon. He had been on leave in Paris when the Bulge started. The guys were just catching up to us. We had a nice get together, and he was telling me about his furlough in Paris. He brought me a Christmas present: a nice pipe. He knew I lived to smoke a pipe when there was time to do so.

The company commander, Captain Koppel, and Sergeant Kogul ordered me to go to the battalion medics that evening. When we arrived, Captain Kitchen and Captain Sharpario were there, and they were glad to see me. There were four of us from H Company. First they gave us a hot meal, and then we had a nice hot shower. The doctors

This U.S. antiaircraft team on the northern shoulder still had a job to do. The Luftwaffe committed around 2,400 tactical aircraft to the Battle of the Bulge.

then inspected our feet for frostbite or anything that could lead to an infection. You see, all the while we're on line we could not take proper care of our body, while we were fighting and moving around in the severe cold weather. Doc Kitchen and Doc Sharpario said to me, "It's about time you got down here to see us." They then gave us a big blue pill to take with a hot cup of coffee. We had already received fresh clothing after our shower. We took the pill, which they called "blue heaven," and they issued us blankets and told us to get into the hay mow on the upper floor of the barn. Half of it was the aid station. We climbed up into the hay mow and bedded down in the hay. Just then, the artillery, which was stationed nearby, opened fire. I was wondering how I was ever going to get to sleep with all that noise.

Allen Cramer: Although we [Company A, 21st Armored Infantry Battalion, 11th Armored Division] had been in the combat zone for perhaps a couple of weeks, this was the fourth day of being under direct and, it seemed, almost constant fire from the German artillery. We had sustained a great many losses, and it seemed to me that at least half of our company was gone, either killed or wounded.

My memory is not clear as to what exactly preceded this episode, but sometime in the afternoon we began to advance from the relative safety of a wooded area out into the open area of a large field. There were more woods about a half-mile ahead of us, and it was our intention to get to that area and secure it. The weather was good, but it was cold. We moved forward, walking in several inches of snow that covered the field.

The sergeant, who was our squad leader, had his dozen men spread out with perhaps fifty feet or so between each of us. We were to watch him for hand signals. Although we could not see the Germans, they apparently could see us, and before we had advanced a few hundred feet, the shells from the German 88s began to fall in our area. I saw the sergeant put his arm up and then quickly bring it down toward the ground. This was the signal for us to "hit the ground." I saw the men of my squad fall to a prone position, and I did the same thing. This afforded us some protection from the deadly shrapnel that was flying around. The shells came in quick succession, making a frightening siren-like noise. As each shell fell to earth in our midst, a very loud explosion followed.

Within moments, I suffered a devastating blow to my upper left back area, just under the shoulder blade. I remember this moment with utter clarity; it felt as if someone had hit me with a full blow from a large sledgehammer. After the initial shock, I realized that I had no further pain, and I thought I had once again been struck by a rock as had happened to me on our first day under fire. I could not see any of my squad, or anyone else for that matter, and so I began to crawl forward. As I did so, I felt a warm, wet substance running down the left side of my body; the air was very cold, and the snow was not melting.

It seemed as though I was alone in this frozen field when suddenly a stranger, an American soldier with a growth of beard, came crawling around a bush. I did not recognize this man but asked if he would do me a favor, look at my back, and determine if I were truly wounded or had I merely been hit with another rock or perhaps a piece of frozen earth. He took one look and said something like, "Don't worry, you are going to be OK."

I could tell by his tone that he saw more than he wanted to tell me. I accepted his suggestion that he guide me back to the wooded area we had left earlier and see if we could hook up with some other Americans. I could still feel what I then realized was probably blood running down my side, but I had no pain whatsoever. I did not find out who this Good Samaritan was until a half-century later.

Suddenly, a jeep appeared and two soldiers jumped out, came up to the medic, and said they could only take two at a time. They asked him to pick out the two most seriously wounded. I was more than surprised when the medic pointed at me and said that I was the one they should take first. I was quickly put onto a stretcher and carried to the jeep.

I was strapped onto a carrier on one side of this open vehicle. Another wounded man was soon strapped onto the other side of the jeep, and we were driving between the trees and away from the battle-front. I was not allowed to take my rifle or my ammunition belt with me, and I had to just leave them back on the ground in the snow. This was a serious thing to an infantryman who never parted from his rifle. Even when I had had a chance to get into a sleeping bag, the rifle went with me. I felt so impotent without it.

I am not certain how long the jeep ride was, but my impression was that it was a relatively short ride. I was carried into a large room, perhaps even a tent that was being used to give what emergency treatment was required before the wounded were moved to a real hospital.

I do not remember any doctor coming over to examine me, but I am not sure that I was staying wide-awake all the time. Not only had I lost a lot of blood, but also I had not slept in a lying-down position for several nights.

There were, however, two incidents that happened here that stand our clearly in my memory. One was that a Catholic priest came to me, spoke softly, and asked me if I would like the last rites. This normally would have scared me, but I was in no pain, and since I was lying there in relative comfort, the thought of my dying did not enter my mind. When I told the priest that I was Jewish, he remained friendly but quickly changed the subject. He even offered me a cigarette that I declined. I didn't think of it at the time, but later on, when I realized I had a suspected lung wound, the priest's offer was a strange one.

The second incident was when a medical aid man came over to ask me if I had any weapons or ammunition with me. They were very strict on not allowing anything like that in this building. I explained to him that I had been requested to leave my rifle and ammunition belt back in the snow when the men from the jeep put me on the stretcher. As he was about to leave me, I suddenly remembered that I had two hand grenades, one in each of the side pockets in my jacket. As I relayed this information to the aid-man, I removed the grenades and put them on the floor. The aid-man got quite excited and called for help, saying something like, "Hey, this guy has live grenades here." No one wanted to even touch them, but eventually someone came and removed them. I thought what a difference there was between the medical personnel and the infantrymen who lived with this type of weapon night and day.

I have no idea how long I stayed at the field medical station; I must have been going in and out of some kind of deep sleep. I do not even remember being carried out to the ambulance. When I once again became aware of my surroundings, I realized I was still on a stretcher and securely placed on a rack in the back of the ambulance. I am not sure if I was the only wounded person or even if there was a medical person in the back with me, but I was somehow made aware that we were on our way to a real hospital. I must add that I was still without pain, just extremely tired, and I believe I slept most of the trip.

◆ ◆ ◆

THE BATTLE FOR THE TOWN of Thirimont, January 14, 1945, is one in the history of the Battle of the Bulge that is rarely remembered, except by the divisions who fought against one another. Thirimont was a small town between Malmedy and St. Vith, and the Germans had dug in there to try to hold back the Allied advance. Now a sergeant, Francis Currey (Company K, 120th Regiment, 30th Infantry Division) once again was called upon to lead the way against the Hermann Goering Paratrooper Division, along with parts of the Adolf Hitler Panzer Division. The regimental headquarters of the Germans was in a strategic place outside of Thirimont, and Currey decided that he wanted to take it.

Francis Currey: As I am going across this field, running like hell, right below my elbow there was Gould, another nineteen-year-old who was with me at Malmedy, and I said, "What the hell are you doing?"

Gould took one right through the skull, and he was dead before he hit the ground.

They opened up on us with a machine gun, and I got one nice, clean hole right near my elbow.

So, who comes behind us but Lucero. I flop down, and then Lucero gets behind me, and he lobs a grenade over me toward the regimental headquarters house, and we go right in behind the grenade. We were a hell of team, the three of us, even though Gould was killed.

I arrive at the regimental headquarters, and I am downstairs, and the Germans are upstairs. We were lobbing grenades at them, and they were lobbing grenades at us. We were shooting at one another and all that stuff. They barricaded themselves in the room above us, and we could not go up the stairs to attack them. It was a stalemate. Come dark, this executive officer was there with me, and I tell him, "You go."

Then he told me, "No, you go. That is an order, you go."

A GI from the 30th Division surveys the snowy landscape around Thirimont northeast of Malmedy. It was here that Pfc. Francis Currey almost earned a second Medal of Honor by taking out two Panzers single-handedly.

And I said, "What the hell do you mean, order?" which, for me to be saying that at the time to an executive officer was unheard of.

So, I said to myself, *I am going to set the goddamn place on fire.* It was a barn/house combination with hay next to it, and I would burn them out. It was in a key position on the hillside.

Frank Forcinella: January 16, 1945. As we [2nd Regiment, 5th Infantry Division] got our guns and boats ready, we were to cross the Sure River. The SS troops on the other side knew we were coming. Before I got into the boat I got hit, and when I got hit I felt nothing. It was bitter cold, I had a jacket on, a big coat,

Emil Gosse and his comrades hitch a ride on a Sherman in Luxembourg as the battle draws to a close. Fighting continued in Luxembourg until early February. *Latchodrom Productions*

but all of the sudden my stomach and everything felt warm, warm as hell. This was the blood that was all coming down, and this was the first feeling I had. The first aid man was treating the other guys, but he took care of me right away. He then asked me to take a guy with one leg back to the aid station behind where we were, and this was six in the morning. [The one-legged guy] and I struggled along, we rested, and we finally got up the hill after midnight. It took me eighteen hours to get up to the aid station. The operation to get the bullet out was at 0200. Today, you would go to sleep for an operation, but they gave me penicillin and numbed the pain. When the surgeon started operating on me, it felt as if they were pounding a spike into the area, but they got the bullet out. I rested up for two weeks and then got sent back out to the lines.

Emil Gosse: The 304th [Infantry Regiment, 76th "Liberty Bell" Division] pulled out of Boston [on November 24, 1944] on the U.S. Troop Ship *Brazil*, and we didn't know where we were going. We arrived in England at Southampton, and one month later we crossed the English Channel

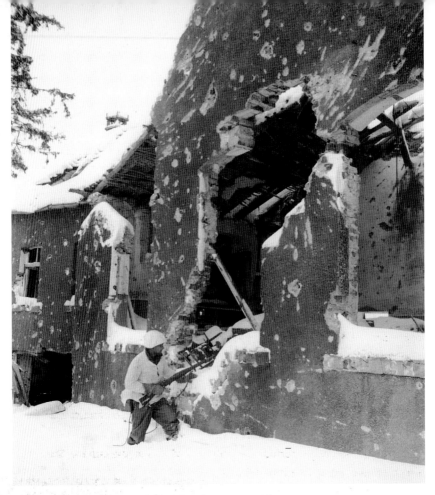

U.S. Army Pfc. D.C. Cox of Company M, 26th Infantry, 1st Division, searches for German snipers among the ruins in a Belgian town near Muringen, January 30, 1945. *Bill Augustine/Lightroom Photos /U.S. Army/TopFoto/Jon Mitchell/Redux*

to Le Havre and made our way up the Seine River to Roven, France. From Roven, we went to Beausaint in Belgium.

From Beausaint, we moved in convoy into Luxembourg, and the soldiers in the 1st Battalion went into the line at Dickweiler, where they experienced the first taste of enemy fire. I had only been in a freezing foxhole for a few days when I accidentally took my first prisoner. He was a young German guy who had been a barber before the war. I took him back to our HQ, and he cut everyone's hair. Did a good job too. We may have been cold and dirty and tired, but at least we had great haircuts. After intense fighting, our 1st Battalion crossed the Sauer River at Echternach and then went on into the Siegfried Line. Those Germans still had a lot of fight left in them.

POSTSCRIPT

THE VETERANS IN THIS BOOK lived through the largest land battle in United States Army history. My grandfather, John A. Collins Jr., just like many of these veterans did in order to join the army, lied and said he was eighteen when he was actually seventeen. He trained with the 10th Armored Division in Fort Benning, Georgia, and was sent overseas with the division in September 1944, landing in Cherbourg, France. After surviving the 10th's first major taste of combat in Metz, he, along with Clair Bennett, rested and refitted in Sierck, France, near the German border. After the division received word that the battle had broken out, he rode up with the 90th Cavalry Reconnaissance Squadron, Company F to Luxembourg.

During the Bulge period, he provided vital reconnaissance for the 10th and other divisions who fought in and around the Bastogne area. Due to the secrecy of the 10th Armored Division's mission, the lack of maps, and poor visibility, the cavalry did not know where exactly they were, since many towns looked similar, but they were able to find out what direction the Germans were attacking from. To pinpoint my grandfather's exact location is almost impossible, but traveling throughout the Ardennes, you get a sense of how difficult the terrain was in some areas. He survived the Bulge but was wounded in the Battle of the Crailsheim in

The German cemetery at Recogne. When German soldiers of World War II were killed in Belgium, Allied burial parties moved all of the corpses into two collecting cemeteries: Lommel (39,000) and Recogne-Bastogne (7,000). The latter included casualties incurred during the fight for Bastogne.
Latchodrom Productions

The Mardasson Memorial in Bastogne, Belgium, honors the dead and wounded American soldiers of the Battle of the Bulge and represents the gratitude of the Belgian people. *Shutterstock*

Germany in early April 1945 and continued to fight on until the war ended in May.

When he returned home, he rarely spoke of his experiences—except for his hatred of green beans, since they were the vegetable he always had in his rations. He also shared some of the funny stories. According to relatives, he had nightmares, but he rarely spoke of the horrors he saw during his time in Europe. The only souvenirs of his time in World War II are a Nazi banner, a piece of a Nazi officer's cap insignia, and a German Luger pistol.

I began my journey by trying to find out his story, but I soon began searching for stories of other veterans who saw both similar and different things during the battle. Several of the veterans never spoke about until I contacted them. I may not know the exact places my grandfather fought in during the Bulge, but anywhere I see a 10th Armored Division plaque, a tank turret, or a statue of Patton, I know that he was nearby. He passed away before I was born, so I never had the chance to interview him, but the veterans featured in this book helped fill in his story through their experiences. Even if he did not do anything extraordinary, his service was enough to make him my personal hero of the Bulge.

—Michael Collins

Wounded members of the 101st Airborne Division, heroes of Bastogne, unable to march, watch their buddies from the window of a Fifth Ave. building in New York during the city's V-E Day parade. *Seymour Wally/NY Daily News Archive via Getty Images*

Sources

Authors' interviews

◆ Robert Kennedy ◆ Allan P. Atwell ◆ Dorothy Barre ◆ Joseph Ozimek
◆ Albert Tarbell ◆ W. D. Crittenberger ◆ Clair Bennett ◆ Don Olson
◆ Helen Rusz ◆ Nelson Charron ◆ Seymour Reitman ◆ Ted Paluch
◆ William "Stu" Getz ◆ Ralph Ciani ◆ Harold "Stoney" Stullenberger
◆ William Hannigan ◆ Ralph K. Manley ◆ Wayne Wickert ◆ William
"Richard" Barrett ◆ Charles Hensel ◆ Zeke Prust ◆ Frank Forcinella
◆ Robert T. Miller ◆ Francis Currey ◆ Myles Covey ◆ Augusta Chiwy
◆ Hans Baumann ◆ Erwin Kressman

Authors' correspondence

John R. Schaffner

Personal memoirs and audiotapes

John Kline (http://ice.mm.com/user/jpk/battle.htm)
Frank Towers
James L. Cooley (Robert Cooley's transcription)
Donald Nichols
Phil Burge
William H. Tucker
Robert T. Gravlin
Allen Cramer

Internet sources

http://users.skynet.be/wielewaal/Chaumont.htm
www.3ad.com (3rd Armored Division History Foundation)
www.11tharmoreddivision.com (11th Armored Division Association)
www.bloodybucket.be (Groupe Belge de Reconstruction
    Historique Militaire)
www.indianamilitary.org (Indiana History Organization)

INDEX